ASSASSINATION

records the greatest tragic drama of our time. It is the moment-to-moment chronicle of immense human loss and courage, stress and nobility, grief and resilience.

It is a story that embraces the great and near-great and the obscure, the most pitifully warped and the most heroic. This work probes deeply for the answers to profoundly troubling questions. Complete, authoritative, intensely gripping, it is a book that every American must read.

ASSASSINATION

The Death of President John F. Kennedy

RELMAN MORIN

A SIGNET BOOK

PUBLISHED BY THE NEW AMERICAN LIBRARY

SIGNET TRADEMARK REG. U.S. PAT. OFF. AND FOREIGN COUNTRIES
REGISTERED TRADEMARK—MARCA REGISTRADA
HECHO EN CHICAGO, U.S.A.

SIGNET BOOKS are published by
The New American Library, Inc.,
1301 Avenue of the Americas, New York, New York 10019

FIRST PRINTING, MARCH, 1968

PRINTED IN THE UNITED STATES OF AMERICA

1

The five men working on the sixth floor of the Texas Book Depository Building hurried downstairs for lunch earlier than usual that day. They were excited. In a little more than a half hour, they expected to see the President of the United States, John F. Kennedy. His airplane already was approaching Dallas. After a welcome at the airport, he was to ride slowly through the city. Newspaper maps of the route to be taken by his motorcade showed that he would pass directly in front of the Book Building.

In the planning, this ended the parade. The Book Building, at the corner of Houston and Elm streets, was to be the last point where the cars would be moving slowly. Passing through crowds, the drivers held the motorcade speed to ten or fifteen miles an hour, giving the President the maximum exposure—which was one of the primary purposes of his trip to Texas—and affording thousands of Texans more than a fleeting glimpse of the beautiful woman beside him, Jacqueline Kennedy. Her husband often jokingly asserted that in their travels, at home and abroad, she was a bigger attraction than he.

Once past the Book Building, no sizable crowds were expected. The drivers were to increase speed, and in five minutes more, the cars would roll to a stop in front of the Trade Mart, where the President was to deliver a speech. He was due there at 12:30.

The date was November 22, 1963.

Most of the employes in the Book Building planned to eat lunch early and then stake out a place on the street, before the crowds grew too big, or in the windows of the building. The whole area was an ideal vantage point, for where Houston comes into Elm, there is a sharp left turn. To negotiate it, the drivers would have to slow to a snail's pace, giving the spectators an extra-long look at the Presi-

5

dent and his wife and the Texans in the motorcade, Governor John Connally and his wife, Lyndon Johnson and Lady Bird and Senator Ralph Yarborough in the next car, and the congressmen and VIP's behind them. People had been gathering at this strategic corner since midmorning.

And so at about 11:45, the five men broke off work. They were laying a plywood covering over the old floor. They piled into the two freight elevators on the sixth floor and slammed the gates. Laughing, they played their usual game, a race to the ground floor.

Passing the fifth floor, they saw a man they called "Lee." His full name was Lee Harvey Oswald, but they didn't know that.

In fact, Oswald's co-workers knew almost nothing about him. He had been employed in the Book Building since October 16, a little over a month. His job was filling the orders for books. He was quiet and respectful, prone to say "Sir" not only to his superiors but to all the men. He was not unfriendly, but he seemed to discourage the casual, easy relationships that usually form between men who work together. He neither invited nor exchanged confidences. He showed no interest in sports, politics, women, or any of the other staples of male conversation. When he spoke at all, it was to ask a question in connection with his work. He held himself apart, withdrawn, silent, enigmatic.

Like the others, Oswald generally ate lunch in what the men called the "domino room" on the ground floor. They played dominoes there and talked until the time came to go back to work. Oswald would sit alone at a table, reading—and apparently with total concentration—a discarded newspaper. He was frugal. He never bought his own newspaper and brought it to the "domino room."

On Friday, November 22, he was not seen there, neither before he started work in the morning nor at noon. But Oswald was so unobtrusive that his absence was not remarked.

Nor did anyone happen to notice that he stepped out of character that day. He initiated a conversation with a workman named James Jarman, otherwise known as "Junior." Around 10:00 A.M., Jarman would recall, Oswald was standing at a window on the ground floor, staring at the people already gathered in front of the Book Building. He turned to Jarman and asked, "What are those people doing there?"

6

Jarman replied, "The President is supposed to be coming past here pretty soon."

"Do you know which way he will be coming?"

"Yes," said Jarman. "He's supposed to come down Main, turn on Houston, and turn again into Elm."

"I see," Oswald said.

Considering that Lee Oswald was an avid newspaper reader, these were strange questions, indeed. It is scarcely credible that he did not know Kennedy was coming to Dallas and the route of the motorcade.

The Dallas *Morning News* and Dallas *Times-Herald* are thorough, well-edited newspapers. Days before the President reached Dallas, they had filled columns with news of the impending visit, the main story and numerous "sidebars," ancillary reports developed by ingenious editors. They had fully covered Kennedy's receptions in other Texas cities and interpreted the political significance, as they saw it, of his foray into the state. Discussion was not confined to the news and editorial pages; a sportswriter had found grist for his column by suggesting topics that Kennedy might safely discuss in Dallas. On the day of the President's arrival, the newspapers carried editorials about his visit, along with a certain message, bordered in black, like an oversized death notice. On several days, the newspapers printed maps showing the streets through which the procession would go, starting at the Dallas airport, passing through the city, and out to the Trade Mart. After such saturation coverage, only a man living in a tunnel deep beneath the Trinity River could have remained completely unaware of the when's, where's, and why's of the scheduled events of Friday, November 22.

Yet Oswald, with his questions to Jarman, indicated that it was all news to him. Probably, he intended to convey precisely this impression. He may have been deranged, but he had a certain psychotic cunning.

As the morning wore along, Oswald appeared at least once on the sixth floor of the Book Building. He may have been there more than once, but there was no reason why this should attract the attention of the men laying the plywood covering. In filling orders for books, he might have to go to any floor. One of the five men saw Oswald "kicking around" among the boxes and cartons piled high in one half of the room.

To install the flooring, the men had cleared the west end of the sixth floor, moving all the stock to the other half.

7

They left corridors through the jumble and along the windows looking down on Elm Street so that the men filling orders could get to the books they needed. The boxes were stacked so high that a person standing at a window in the east wall would have been completely hidden from view of anyone standing in the cleared half of the room. They also would conceal him from people looking out the windows on the upper floors of the Dal-Tex Building across the street.

And if this person planned to fire a rifle through the open window at an object moving along Elm Street, he had the perfect aerie.

Oswald alone knew that he had carried a rifle, disassembled and concealed in a brown paper bag, into the Book Building when he came to work that day. He probably went straight to the sixth floor and hid the weapon deep in the pyramid of boxes near the southeast window.

Charles Douglas Givens was one of the plywood-layers who went downstairs for lunch shortly before noon. He washed, drank a glass of water, and patted his pockets, feeling for a package of cigarettes. Then he remembered he had left them in his jacket upstairs. He rode the elevator back to the sixth floor. He found Oswald there, after having last seen him on the fifth floor. The sound of the elevator gates rumbling open, of course, would have alerted Oswald. Whatever he had been doing, and where, in the moment before he heard the elevator will never be known. But when Givens stepped into the room, Oswald was walking toward the elevator and away from the southeast corner.

In his hand, Oswald held a clipboard with three order slips attached, as though he was still working. The clipboard would be found later amid the pile of boxes and cartons. Later, too, some reading aids, known as Roller Readers, would be found in the southeast corner, some 40 feet from the place where they were supposed to be stacked. They were smaller than the boxes of books and easy to carry.

Givens fished the cigarettes from his jacket, turned to Oswald, and said, "Boy, are you coming downstairs? It's near lunch time."

"No, sir," Oswald said. However, he asked Givens to close the elevator gates when he reached the ground floor, giving the impression that he intended to descend in the elevator soon.

That was around 11:55.

Some 15 minutes later, another of the floor-layers appeared unexpectedly on the sixth floor. Bonnie Rae Williams was looking for "the guys." He wanted company while he ate lunch and watched the President's motorcade, which should be coming in a few minutes. To Williams, the room seemed deserted. He sat down, leaned back against the boxes, and disposed of a chicken sandwich and a soft drink. Then, hearing voices beneath him, he went down to the fifth floor to await the parade with the other men.

Where was Lee Oswald while Williams was eating lunch? In all probability, he was sitting like a graven image in the southeast corner window, having reassembled his rifle. No doubt, when he heard Williams' footsteps, he slipped it back among the boxes. He had had all the time he needed between the appearances of Givens and Williams to complete his preparations. Had Williams heard Oswald or otherwise discovered him, he would have found nothing untoward about it. Oswald usually kept to himself, and now he was sitting alone, with the window open, waiting to see the President of the United States.

Oswald was not one of "the guys." He was anything but good company. Yet Williams, through some quirk of fate, might have decided to remain with him in the southeast window until the procession passed.

If circumstances had altered the little tableau on the sixth floor by only a hairline, in only that small degree. . . .

12:29 P.M.

Police motorcycles turned into Houston Street from Main. Behind them, a gleaming blue limousine approached the Texas Book Depository Building.

2

In November, 1963, as John F. Kennedy entered the fourth quarter of his term in office, he was just beginning

9

to come into his own. He was like a miler starting the fourth and final lap of the race, still fresh, well positioned, and with every reason to believe he would win. He was looking forward with immense zest to the Presidential wars of 1964. He enjoyed going "out there," speaking directly to the people, sniffing the atmosphere away from Washington. He drew strength from the crowds that lined the routes of his motorcades and thronged into halls where he spoke. This time he expected to be returned to office with an undeniable mandate, not the minority margin of 1960. No doubt, two elections in Massachusetts often came to mind. In his first campaign for the Senate, in 1952, he had won after a cliff-hanger. Then, six years later, he saw a landslide develop and was reelected with 73.2 percent of the vote. Why shouldn't his Massachusetts political history repeat itself on a national scale? And this was to be a stabbing thought, one of the most painful for his friends. "Jack was looking forward so eagerly to a real victory next year," a woman in the White House would say. "And now he's been robbed of that—."

In September, Kennedy had traveled through the Northwest. The size of the crowds that greeted him, their reactions to his speeches, and the reports of the Democratic captains along his route all combined to enhance his feeling of optimism. The outlook was bright.

His popularity, although lower than the high-water mark, nonetheless stood at a high level. At one time in the first three years, public opinion polls rated it at 79 percent. When the same surveys showed a substantial decline, Kennedy was not disturbed. "If I were still 79 percent after a very intense Congressional session," he said, "I would feel that I had not met my responsibilities."

Evidently, he felt that he had met his responsibilities. For in spite of crises abroad and frustrations at home, the atmosphere in the White House in the autumn of 1963 retained much of the euphoric bounce of Kennedy's first days there.

No President, not even the two Roosevelts, shouldered the awesome burdens of the office with more eagerness and self-assurance than John F. Kennedy. Harry Truman said he felt the weight of the solar system when he suddenly realized he was President of the United States. Dwight D. Eisenhower came to office reluctantly, yielding to his stiff-backed sense of duty after repeatedly refusing to consider running in 1948. By contrast, John Kennedy said, "Sure, it's a big job, but I don't know anybody who can do it better than I can. I'm going to be in it for four years. It isn't going to be so bad. You've got time to think"—and then the inevitable Kennedy touch—"and besides, the pay is good." Another time, he said, "I don't shrink from this responsibility. I welcome it."

He had concerned himself with the problems immediately, two months before they actually were his.

On the third day after his election in 1960, he boarded the family airplane, "Caroline," to fly from Hyannis Port to Palm Beach. Shortly after takeoff, Kennedy had come to the forward section of the plane and sat down at a table habitually occupied by reporters who had covered his campaigns in the primaries and then in the Presidential election. That day, I suppose each of us thought he simply wanted to gas, as he often had done on flights between speech-stops. He would sit there, sometimes in his undershirt, talking about crowds, assessing the status of the campaign, evaluating opponents, or simply venting a lively but usually controlled Irish temper.

All that was past now. He was the President-elect, and he had two months to draft a legislative program and consider appointments.

As the "Caroline" veered southward and crossed Long Island Sound, which was the color of malachite in an uncommonly brilliant sun, Kennedy eased into a seat at the table and began talking about South Vietnam. He said a morning news broadcast had reported an attempted *coup d'état* in Saigon against Ngo Dinh Diem, the president of that country. I had been in Vietnam several times and had interviewed Diem at length. The talks usually lasted four hours. Kennedy knew this, although I don't recall having told him. (He continually startled editors and writers with the extent of his knowledge of them and of media operations. Laura Bergquist reports that he even knew about the progress of the romances among Washington correspondents.*) Now he asked some questions about Diem and the intricate problems of South Vietnam. An absence of two months, in the swift running course of events in Vietnam, was and is more than long enough to outdate the value of anyone's knowledge of the situation there, and so I was not very helpful to him. He said, "As soon as I heard

* Laura Bergquist and Stanley Tretick, *A Very Special President* (New York: McGraw-Hill Book Company, 1965), p. 6.

about this thing in Saigon, I got on the phone to Allen Dulles." Dulles was then the head of the CIA. "He says Diem's all right and things seem to be under control. But I have an uneasy feeling . . . maybe we should be doing more for that country. . . ." His voice trailed away.

I confess that I was impressed. Here was a man who had become the President-elect only about 48 hours earlier, and already he was concerning himself with a problem of foreign policy.

Then he changed the subject. "Lyndon's invited me to his ranch to hunt deer," he said. "They tell me they hunt 'em in jeeps." His expression indicated that he did not find the prospect appetizing.

In the montage of memories of the flight from Hyannis Port, another vignette remains.

Kennedy returned to a chair in the center section of the airplane and sat looking out the window, apparently lost in thought. Meanwhile, Caroline Kennedy's nurse was having a problem. She had opened a plastic container of what looked like custard and was trying to interest the little girl with it. Caroline was being obdurate. She crinkled up her nose and pirouetted away. Suddenly, she danced toward her father, clambered up on his lap, demanding his attention. She dug into the container and held the spoon close to his mouth. He took a bite. Caroline then nestled back against him and quietly finished her morning snack. For the moment, the man who was soon to be President of the United States was simply the prisoner of a precocious child.

Kennedy went unaccompanied to the first meeting with Eisenhower to discuss the transition between Administrations. He passed through the streets of Washington so inconspicuously that few persons would have noticed. The quiet gesture pleased the old soldier, and although they were worlds apart in so many ways, a rapport developed between them at once. It was to remain until the end, respect ripening into affection, a rare phenomenon between a President and his successor.

Kennedy's image of grace and gaiety, wit, style, and intellectual elegance took shape rapidly in his first days in the White House. Words changed. "Discussion" now became "a dialogue." A problem no longer was "complicated"; it was "sophisticated." Even one of the several Federal budgets came to be called "sophisticated." Politicians regard humor as a two-edged sword, and rightly. There were people who had voted against Adlai Stevenson, mistaking his wit for frivolousness. But under Kennedy, humor in government became not only permissible but fashionable. A State Department officer hung a framed reminder on the wall of his office, "Modern nations must make war the way porcupines make love—very cautiously." Robert S. McNamara, the Secretary of Defense, became "The Thinking Machine," although this would have applied equally well to the rhetoricians-in-residence, Theodore Sorensen and Arthur Schlesinger Jr. In one of his daily briefings, Pierre Salinger, the Press Secretary, announced that Kennedy had appointed a Republican to the Federal bench. A reporter asked, "How many Republican judges does that make now?" Salinger replied, "I don't know, but the figure must be astronomical." Then, since this was scarcely a joking matter, he quickly added, "Seriously, the President's record in this respect, etc., etc." Along with such pedestrian announcements, Salinger, deadpan and chomping on a cigar, would answer questions about Caroline's pets—Macaroni, the pony, and Zsa Zsa, the beer-drinking rabbit. In memory, and perhaps in fact, it seems that laughter leavened the grinding toil of government during those years as never before in Washington.

Laughter and a yeasty quality, the fermenting of ideas and buoyancy—these Kennedy characteristics stamped his Administration and marked his own image.

Like every successful politician, Kennedy worked at image-making. His instinct for it was shrewd and sure. As a medium for studying gestures and expressions, television is far superior to the mirror that old-time politicians had to depend on. Kennedy watched the reruns of his televised news conferences. One night during his campaign, he was about to go on live TV in Connecticut with his three sisters. He supervised every detail of the set like the most meticulous of movie directors. He was to sit at a table with the handsome Kennedy women on both sides of him. Before he sat down, he rearranged their places several times. And just before the cameras came on, he spoke sharply to Eunice Shriver, like a father to a little girl. "Eunice," he said, "sit up straight. You're slumping." Since the sisters are so attractive, Kennedy had them with him whenever possible when he made speeches. In Illinois, he said, "My sister Eunice lives here. I have another in California and another in New York. We have them stashed out in all the key states that we hope to carry."

13

In the White House, Kennedy made himself accessible to editors, publishers, and the taipans of the communications media. To one of these, who considers himself "an adviser to Presidents," Kennedy listened gravely. He flattered reporters by calling them by their first names, not on television, of course, but wherever he encountered them elsewhere. He consulted with columnists, also very flattering, when he wanted to straighten them out on policy or their interpretation of a development. For *A Day in the Life of the President,* he permitted two reporters to observe him at work in his office from early morning until after dark. He sparked off such ideas, and they made good copy, feature stories, and picture packages. The television audience saw Mrs. Kennedy conducting a tour of the White House and, in her breathless-sounding voice, recalling the history of its rooms and objects and the changes she had made. A voracious reader of periodicals, Kennedy knew exactly what was being written about him and his Administration. When I asked Salinger who had germinated the idea for a particular story about Kennedy, he replied, "The President. If he keeps on like this, I'll go into the books as the greatest Press Secretary in history." Part of a Press Secretary's job is to enhance the Boss's image.

These efforts were entirely legitimate. Kennedy was not interested in publicity for its own sake alone. He worked to engrave an attractive picture of himself in public consciousness because popularity increases a President's effectiveness, helping him in whatever he may be striving to do. Franklin D. Roosevelt's air of jaunty confidence and his warm voice coming into American homes in the broadcast "fireside chats" helped to restore a measure of hope during the frightening days of the Great Depression. Even his up-tilted cigarette holder, his hallmark, was a subliminal conditioner, selling the slogan that "Happy Days Are Here Again." Because Harry S. Truman used earthy language and threatened to bloody the nose of a Washington music critic who gave Margaret Truman's singing an unflattering notice, the President came to be regarded as "a scrappy little guy," and Americans like scrappy little guys. Truman enhanced this image when he conceded in 1948 that all the visible factors favored the election of Thomas E. Dewey, but then stuck out his jaw and said, "Just the same, I'm going to beat him in November." Kennedy followed one of the most popular Presidents in history, Dwight D. Eisenhower, who retained the affection of the electorate, although largely oblivious to his public image. He made no serious effort to correct the picture of him as a kindly, honest, well-meaning but fumble-fingered Chief Executive, an image built up through countless cartoons and cruel jokes.

John F. Kennedy, recognizing his priceless endowment of charm and personality, exploited it continually. He had other and more important gifts, of course, steely resolve and a high sense of purpose, for example, but they were not so easy to project as charm, nor as readily marketable.

Yet, the armory of Kennedy's sterling qualities could not obscure the fact that his record up to the summer of 1963 was, at best, a spotty one. In his campaign for the Presidency, he had exhorted the voters to "join me in getting this country moving again." Three years later, he could point to little in the way of startling breakthroughs to progress. It is true that the "missile gap," another major pillar of his campaign, had disappeared magically, but little credit could be derived from this, because the "missile gap" had never existed except as a campaign argument. One golden October day in Illinois, Kennedy read a newspaper report indicating that the U-2 Case and the cancellation of Eisenhower's proposed visit to Japan, among other developments, had lowered American prestige around the world. Kennedy's eyes glistened. "What a hell of a story," he said. "I'm going to hit this hard." Thus, as soon as his writers could fashion a speech, Kennedy deplored the low estate to which American prestige had fallen. But ahead of him lay an even more damaging blow to the prestige of his country, the Bay of Pigs.

As for Congress, after the customary honeymoon with a new President, conservative Democrats resumed voting with Republicans and throwing roadblocks in the path of his legislative program. The Hill had rebuffed him on a farm bill, a general school assistance bill, legislation to create a Department of Urban Affairs, and numerous requests (twenty-seven, the Republicans claimed) for standby powers. Kennedy blew up, or appeared to, when Congress rejected his program of health assistance for the aged. The outburst was untypical and may have been a ploy. He now could use "Medicare" as a major campaign issue in 1964, giving the Republicans the lion's share of discredit for the defeat of his bill. Only the politicians, Washington correspondents, and persons who read the *Congressional Quarterly* and make a hobby of compiling box scores on legislation knew, in the autumn of 1963, that there had been no action in either house on nearly 40 percent of the President's proposals.

True or not, Kennedy's political opponents explained this mulishness by asserting that the President and his "Irish Mafia" tried to ram legislation through Congress by twisting arms and knocking heads together. Someone observed, and not entirely facetiously, "When the Kennedys want something, they come at you with brass knuckles."

And also when they didn't want something.

Without warning, and against the policies of the Administration, Big Steel suddenly announced price increases. In this instance, Kennedy's anger was not feigned. He moved immediately to force the companies to rescind the increases. Regardless of one's philosophy with respect to government control on business, what followed was nothing less than awe-inspiring. Kennedy marshaled all the immense power of the Federal government, and it rolled like a juggernaut against the companies. Overnight, they capitulated.

Soon, and not alone because of this action, Kennedy was being labeled "antibusiness." He denied it. One night in his office, he said to me, "I've had a lot of business leaders here, and they sit there, right where you're sitting, and I say to them, 'All right, you tell me what I should do about the economy.' You should hear some of the kookie ideas they come up with." He described one captain of industry as "that ass." He dismissed the businessmen's proposals with the phrase "and all that jazz," along with some barnyard terms.

The economy, although big, was mushy. Soft spots persisted. In his campaign speeches about "getting this country moving again," he had criticized the previous Administration on grounds that the growth-rate of the economy had slowed down. He had promised to reaccelerate it. Some economists said he had simply set his sights too high, and they found nothing alarming in the state of the economy. A sharp break in the stock market gave the President's critics the opportunity to call it "the Kennedy market." He wryly observed that Wall Street never used that term when prices rose, and he repeated his denials that he was "antibusiness." Wall Street twitted him with a sarcasm—"Want to take a small fortune out of the market? Bring a big fortune there."

Even more troublesome than these matters was the increasingly dangerous situation developing in the Southern states. The Negroes had become restive, and their earlier enthusiasm for Kennedy had turned, in large measure, to sour disillusionment. This was understandable. A strong civil rights plank had been written into the Democratic platform of 1960. Kennedy had given every indication that, if elected, he would bring the moral weight of the Presidency to bear to improve the condition of Negroes. A phrase, "with the stroke of a pen," returned to haunt him. Discrimination in housing, he had said in speeches, could be eliminated "with the stroke of a pen." But after 18 months in office, the Presidential pen had not scratched paper. The reason had been political; legislation considered more important lay before Congress, and until signs of progress could be seen there, the applecart should not be tipped over by antagonizing Southern congressmen. Explaining this, a top government official said to me, ". . . and so you just have to sit here for the time being and take your lumps on this civil rights thing."

True, James Meredith had been enrolled in the University of Mississippi after Federal marshals repelled a mob with tear gas. But it took Federal troops to keep Meredith there. On the following day, the university campus became another Little Rock. Meredith was one Negro. The millions waited with growing impatience for Washington to move on the broad fronts—housing, jobs, public facilities, the schools. Dr. Martin Luther King was to write, "Eventually, the President would set political considerations aside and rise to the level of his own unswerving moral commitment. But this was still in the future." *

And then, in the summer of 1963, Dr. King took the bit in his teeth. Suddenly, hundreds of Negroes, and perhaps thousands at the peak of the demonstrations, came boiling out of two staging areas, a church and a park, and surged into the business district of Birmingham, Alabama. The demonstrations were nonviolent. However, they snarled traffic, and business suffered simply because shoppers preferred to stay out of the troubled streets. Soon, newspaper photographs were flashing around the world showing powerful streams of water from fire hoses felling the demonstrators, and worse, of snarling police dogs on leashes lunging at them. Parenthetically, this was not the first time

* Martin Luther King, Jr., *Why We Can't Wait* (New York: Harper & Row, 1964), p. 8.

the dogs had been used in Birmingham to fend off trouble in the streets. In an earlier flare-up, police had brought them to a bus station where a mob of whites threatened some Freedom Riders.

Generally, the Southern segregationist pleads his case with great shrewdness and plausibility. However, I had been in Birmingham several days before I was told about the use of dogs against white men. And there was little a Yankee reporter could say when a Southerner asked, quietly but bitterly, "How come you fellows didn't take a million pictures of the dogs when *that* happened?"

Birmingham, in my opinion, forced Kennedy's hand. Thereafter, he and the Attorney General began moving purposefully to find solutions. The President invited Southern businessmen, clergymen, and other groups to Washington to talk out their problems and search for accommodations. Some of the best lawyers in the Justice Department, Burke Marshall, Nicholas DeB. Katzenbach and John Doar, took the government's case into Southern courtrooms and confronted Negro demonstrators in the streets. But the murders continued, and the South grew increasingly hostile to the Kennedys. The states that had comprised the Confederacy seethed with anger against them.

These, then, were some of the principal features of the President's domestic record on the eve of another election year.

In foreign policy, too, the ledger showed both credits and debits. However, it takes two to make peace or even agree to take steps that might lead to peace. On balance, therefore, Kennedy's accomplishments in meeting problems of foreign policy could be considered more striking than what he had done with domestic questions.

In June, 1961, Kennedy went to Vienna for a conference with Nikita S. Khrushchev about Berlin. One wonders what manner of man the Soviet Premier expected to find. The dossier on Kennedy in the files of Soviet intelligence could not have been very fat. They would have identified him as a wealthy young intellectual who had written some thoughtful books . . . lived in England when his father was Ambassador to the Court of St. James . . . victim of a number of serious illnesses . . . voting record as a representative and senator inconclusive as to social and economic philosophy . . . good war record as PT boat commander in the Pacific . . . married. . . .

But only a Soviet agent who knew Kennedy well could

have slipped a note in the file about his coolness under pressure and his moral toughness. Khrushchev discovered these qualities for himself. During one of their talks, he suddenly abandoned the amenities of diplomacy. His porcine eyes narrowed, and he grated out, "If you want war over Berlin, you'll get war." Khrushchev may have thought he could shock the President off-balance. If so, the attempt failed. Kennedy replied with icy composure, "It looks like a cold winter."

The two men, having measured each other, went their separate ways without coming any closer to a *détente*.

On the other hand, after the confrontation in Vienna, Khrushchev stopped setting deadlines for the signing of a separate treaty with East Germany. Perhaps, in a negative sense, Kennedy had achieved something.

Next, the East Germans erected the Berlin Wall. The reaction in the United States was mixed. Some Americans argued that the President should have ordered American tanks to demolish it as fast as the wire and bricks went up. Others felt that the wall did not merit running the risk of nuclear war. Kennedy apparently agreed with them, although he had said "Berlin is our big interest."

On the other side of the world, another "big interest" was building up. Kennedy had long been interested in Vietnam. In the winter of 1961, he took action. He wrote a letter to Diem, dated December 14, in which he said, "I have received your recent letter in which you described so cogently the dangerous condition caused by North Vietnam's efforts to take over your country. . . . We shall promptly increase our assistance to your defense effort. . . . I have already given orders to get these programs under way."

This was the second step in the involvement of the United States in Vietnam. Kennedy sent the Vice-President, Lyndon Johnson, to Saigon to declare publicly in a speech to the Vietnamese legislature that a massive infusion of military and financial help would soon be coming to Vietnam from the United States. Eisenhower had taken the first step in this direction. Johnson himself was to take the third, going even farther than his predecessors.

The two most important events of that period, however, developed neither in Europe or the Far East. They came in Cuba.

The Bay of Pigs was a disaster. But the damage it inflicted on Kennedy's prestige was more than counterbalanced when he forced Khrushchev to remove the Russian missiles from the island.

"Nightmare Week" in Washington began on October 15, 1962, after aerial reconnaissance over Cuba brought back photographs of the missile sites. The Russians were working fast. The photograph of a site near Guanajay at first showed nothing but three large bulldozer scars on the ground. Five days later, erectors, revetments, buildings, tents, and vehicles appeared in photographs of the same site. Kennedy and his advisers clearly were in a race against time.

Only the men in the conferences of that week knew precisely what was developing, but an air of foreboding brooded over the White House. Rumors of an invasion of Cuba began circulating. Strange happenings became known; a high official, leaving his office, said to his secretary, "I'm just going down the hall." She didn't see him again for three days. In one of the conferences, Robert Kennedy doodled. He drew five concentric squares encircled by the word "Cuba" scribbled 96 times. In spite of the tension, the sound of the ticking clock, there were moments of tonic humor. William C. Foster, Director of the Arms Control and Disarmament Agency, observed during one of the sessions, "It hasn't been a very good week for disarmament." McGeorge Bundy told me later that when the several possible courses of action were under examination, the President said, "Everybody in this room should pray that *his* proposal is not accepted." What Kennedy meant was that history would not absolve the advisers who persuaded him to take a given course if it led to war with the Russians. In the end, of course, Kennedy alone had to make the decision—invasion, air strikes to take out the missile launchers, a "quarantine," or diplomatic representations in Moscow and the United Nations. After the week of discussion, he said, "All right, we'll go with the blockade." No man ever shouldered a heavier responsibility. Whatever his emotions, Kennedy's marble calm appeared uncracked. A day or so after the "quarantine" was imposed (a "blockade" would have been an act of war), I asked Kenneth O'Donnell, one of the President's most trusted advisers, how he evaluated the situation. "It's hairy," he said, "and it's going to get hairier." An odd synonym for perilous. At about the same time, half-buried beneath the chaotic pyramid of papers that habitually covered Salinger's desk, I noticed a typewritten list of names.

They were persons to be "relocated," a euphemism meaning they would be whisked away to shelters, if the worst, the unthinkable worst, should come to pass. The days and nights were haunted by an eerie unreality. They reminded me of the last days before Pearl Harbor, reading the undeniable portents as they came to me in the Far East. Everything had seemed unreal then, too.

Then came the incredible Sunday morning when the bells jingled on a teleprinter, signaling something extraordinary, and the machine throbbed into life. It ticked out, "Bulletin-Moscow-Soviet Premier Nikita S. Khrushchev announced today that he will withdraw Russian missiles from Cuba."

The crisis had passed. You could breathe again.

Cuba, like the Berlin Airlift, was a tactical victory, not a strategic one. The island was to remain a Communist outpost. Similarly, all the Airlift accomplished was to show that a big city can be supplied by air; it did not alter nor diminish the basic threat to West Berlin and to world peace.

Nevertheless, on the graph of Kennedy's fortunes, Cuba seemed to mark a turning point, the beginning of an upswing that he and "the Mafia" hoped would reach the crest in 1964.

Developments on all sides were strengthening the President's position. The Senate ratified the nuclear test ban treaty. Evidence accumulated that the Peace Corps was a far greater success than anyone had expected. The Corps idea had not originated with Kennedy, but he perceived its possibilities and set it in motion. Skepticism gradually changed to admiration, expressed in a reference to Sargent Shriver, the Director—"They handed Sarge a lemon, and he's made lemonade out of it." It even was reported that, despite Cuba, Khrushchev was anxious to see Kennedy again at a summit and that feelers had been extended from Moscow.

In Congress, Larry O'Brien was shepherding a meaty package of legislation, bills on education, mental health, civil rights, conservation, mass transit, youth employment, etc. The possibility of a tax cut loomed, although at Kennedy's behest big money was going into new weapons, more Polaris submarines, more planes for the Strategic Air Command. Ted Sorensen predicted "a brilliant record" for the President when Congress finished in 1963. In spite of Sorensen's giant brain, this had to be taken with a grain of salt. For he was less than wholly objective. There had been an axiom during Kennedy's years in the Senate, "When Kennedy hurts, Sorensen bleeds." Even so, it appeared that Kennedy would go into the 1964 campaign with an arsenal of arguments based on his record.

In party politics, too, events seemed to be shaping up exactly as Kennedy and the Democratic captains hoped they might. He watched with keen interest the efforts of a dedicated band of conservative Republicans to capture the GOP nomination for Senator Barry Goldwater. Polls kept indicating that Richard Nixon was leading in the race for it; Kennedy felt certain he could defeat Nixon again, and by a convincing margin. Governors Nelson Rockefeller of New York and George Romney of Michigan would be much tougher. But if Kennedy could have nominated his opponent, he would have chosen Goldwater. The two men were friendly. It was simply that Kennedy felt that Goldwater's positions on domestic and foreign questions would make him the easiest Republican to beat.

On November 12, Kennedy held a three-hour meeting to plan the strategy for what might be called his precampaign campaign. He would begin his "nonpolitical" forays with Texas. There were two reasons. Texas was one of the states he won by an eyelash in 1960, and he needed to build up his position there. Meanwhile, the liberal and conservative Democrats in Texas were at each other's throats. The latter had voted heavily against him in 1960. Now, unless he could restore some semblance of unity, he could easily lose Texas. California would be next on his list. The 1960 race there had been so close that the result became known only after all the absentee ballots were counted, two days after the election, and then it was Nixon by 35,000 votes out of 6,500,000 votes. From California, the itinerary would take the President to Ohio and Wisconsin, both of which had surprised the Kennedys by going to Nixon. Kennedy had beaten Senator Hubert Humphrey in the Wisconsin primary, which seemed to indicate that the point had been reached in political evolution where Protestant midwestern farmers would vote for a Catholic for President. Analyzing the Wisconsin vote, one of "the Mafia" had observed, "I guess the rich Catholics in Milwaukee thought they had done their duty by Jack in the primary." The inference, of course, was that those who were wealthy and conservative had deserted Kennedy in the national election.

The President brought to the November 12 meeting a piece of good news—Mrs. Kennedy had told him she wanted to go with him on these trips. Her husband and his advisers were delighted. A politician's wife almost always is an invaluable asset to him, especially when she is beautiful and dresses tastefully. Previously, Jacqueline Kennedy had seemed shy. When her husband campaigned in the New Hampshire primary, she had kept herself in the background. To the inevitable reporter's question, "What do you think of your husband as a campaigner, Mrs. Kennedy?" she would gulp and say, "Well, he's terrific." She seemed ill at ease. She may have made her first hesitant effort to play a part in campaigning at Green Bay, Wisconsin. At least, this was the first I can recall seeing. She had remained near the airplane, watching her husband shaking hands with a welcoming group of his supporters there. Then she began walking toward the wire barrier at the airfield where a small crowd had gathered. She walked slowly, as though forcing herself to go, held out her hand, and said, in a small voice, "I am Mrs. Kennedy." Applause broke out, and a thicket of hands was extended toward her. Her husband beamed.

The planning for the Texas trip had been going on for months. Something always seemed to postpone it. O'Donnell had been in touch with Governor John Connally, Jr., several times. I have been told that the Governor did not want Kennedy to come into Texas, and so he fobbed off O'Donnell with one reason or another. Connally and Senator Ralph Yarborough were on opposite sides in the conservative-liberal feuding, and being seen in Texas with the President would rub off some luster on the Senator. Finally, Connally capitulated on condition, my informant says, that he would control all the arrangements for the President's appearances in Texas.

The dates were to be November 21 and 22, and the itinerary would take Kennedy to San Antonio, Houston, Fort Worth, Dallas, and Austin. Thereafter, he was to go to the LBJ ranch for a little leisure. In accordance with standard procedure, O'Donnell notified the Secret Service of this about three weeks before the departure, and the planning began. Providing security for the President stood highest among the components of the plans.

At about 11 A.M., November 21, the Presidential party boarded "Air Force One," his specially-equipped airplane, and the flight began. Destination—Texas.

3

On November 8, two weeks before the President was to appear in Dallas, Winston G. Lawson, an agent attached to the White House Secret Service detail, asked the Protective Research Section to run a check on one of its most important files.

The PRS is an arm of the Secret Service. It has a specific responsibility—to keep under surveillance persons who have been adjudged potentially dangerous to the safety of the President of the United States. In the PRS files are studies and data on assassinations of heads of state and conspiracies to assassinate that reach far back into history, including the one that took place during the ides of March at the base of Pompey's statue in Rome. They would probably also show that a man named Joseph Zangara became obsessed with the desire to kill a chief of state, and he is said to have considered three. Nearest at hand was the King of Italy. But Zangara emigrated to the United States in 1932, whereupon Herbert Hoover, who was then in the White House, replaced the King in Zangara's fevered brain. However, having discovered the inclemency of the Washington winters, Zangara moved to Florida, and he was in Miami when Franklin D. Roosevelt, the President-elect, came there to deliver a speech. Zangara aimed a pistol at Roosevelt, but just as he pulled the trigger, a woman grabbed his arm, causing the bullet to strike down Anton J. Cermak, the Mayor of Chicago. No doubt even more exotic histories than these can be found in the PRS records.

The organization maintains a liaison with the FBI, the CIA, the State Department and other Federal agencies. Much information also comes to the PRS from state and local authorities. When it receives a report indicating that someone represents a genuine threat to the President's safety, PRS immediately notifies the White House Secret Service detail and the White House police. If the case ap-

24

pears to be unusually dangerous, an alert is flashed to the Secret Service field office in the area where the suspected man or woman is known to be. Imprisonment or confinement in a mental institution may follow. But if the individual remains at large, the PRS puts a card on him in its "trip index" file. In planning a Presidential trip, it is standard procedure to check this file.

Agent Lawson had been designated White House advance man for Kennedy's appearance in Dallas. In this assignment, he would work with the agent in charge of the Secret Service field office there, Forrest V. Sorrels, and the Dallas police. Both Lawson and Sorrels had had experience in preparing for Presidential travels. The work involved security, the route for the motorcade, timetables, examining the various possible sites for Kennedy's speech, etc.

Thus, two weeks in advance, Lawson asked the PRS to check the "trip index" files for the Dallas-Fort Worth area and for Texas as a whole. In no more than ten minutes he received the answer—two persons evaluated as dangerous in Houston, which was on the President's itinerary, and none in Dallas.

The name Lee Harvey Oswald did not appear among the PRS cards. The agency knew nothing about him.

The State Department and the FBI, however, knew a great deal about Oswald. He was a man who had defected to the Soviet Union, who had expressed hatred and contempt for the United States, who liked guns and had been trained in the Marines to use them, and who was now employed in a building overlooking the route to be taken by Kennedy's open car. It would seem that a man with such a background should have been eminently eligible for a place in the PRS "trip index" files. In itself, of course, Oswald's record did not automatically identify him as a potential threat to the President. And there is the difficulty. Threats are leveled against every President, usually by cranks or by eccentrics who are not sufficiently demented to be committed to a mental hospital. What yardstick should be used? Nevertheless, if the data on Oswald in the files of other government agencies had been collated and passed on to the PRS, the story of November 22, 1963, would have been entirely different. Or rather, there would have been no story. "Drastic action," as it was to be described later, would have been taken. Why this was not done can only be explained by the often uncoordinated gears in a monstrous bureaucracy.

Before he went to Dallas, Agent Lawson made a note of the incident involving Adlai Stevenson in the city on October 24. Stevenson had been jeered during his speech, then jostled, and bopped on the head by a placard in a woman's hand. Characteristically, he said he was certain the woman had been jostled and had swatted him unintentionally. Stevenson, however, advised Kennedy not to go to Dallas. Subsequently, he withdrew the warning. In Dallas, Lawson learned that the "Stevenson incident" had been recorded on live television. He arranged to have photographs made from the film that showed clearly recognizable persons who had participated in the melee. The pictures were to be distributed to Secret Service agents for use while Kennedy was in Dallas.

In the planning, three sad ironies are visible, three sad it-might-have-been's. Originally, Kennedy's Texas visit was to have been telescoped into a single day. Therefore, Governor Connally objected to a slow-moving motorcade, not because he feared for the President's safety, but because motorcades are tiring, and he thought this would be asking too much of Kennedy. In that event, Kennedy would have been whisked in and out of the city over well-guarded freeways. But when the schedule was extended to two days, Connally withdrew his objections. Second, in the early planning, Kennedy was to have delivered his Dallas speech at a dinner. Then he would have passed the Texas Book Depository Building after the workday ended and its doors had been closed for the night. And third, Lawson and Sorrels inspected three buildings as possible sites for the President's luncheon speech. They were the Women's Building, Market Hall, and the Trade Mart. Of these, the Trade Mart was newest and handsomest. It presented greater security problems, but the White House was informed on November 14 that these could be overcome (more than two hundred officers, plus eight Secret Service agents, were to have been stationed in and around the building), and Kenneth O'Donnell gave the go-ahead to arrange for the luncheon to be held in the Trade Mart. Had either of the other buildings been selected, Kennedy's car would not have passed beneath Oswald's sixth-floor window.

To John F. Kennedy, the possibility of assassination was an inevitable fact in a President's life. He accepted it as just one of the several unpleasant consequences of being the Chief Executive, such as continually being shadowed by the Secret Service and having to eat banquet chicken. He sometimes spoke about falling victim to an assassin, but he did not dwell on the possibility. With a curious prescience, he once said there was nothing anybody could do about a man in a tall building aiming a powerful rifle through the cross hairs of a telescopic sight. Indeed, he repeated it on the morning of the day he died.

Kennedy perhaps had better reason than the majority of his predecessors for considering the possibility that he might not live out his term. He was no believer in astrology, but those who were eagerly called his attention to the so-called "20-Year Curse," that strange cycle in which, at regular intervals for a century, six Presidents had died in office. They were William Henry Harrison (1840), Abraham Lincoln (1860), James A. Garfield (1880), William McKinley (1900), Warren G. Harding (1920), and Franklin D. Roosevelt (1940). Kennedy's election in 1960 coincided with the next date in the cycle. He knew it, but he simply found it an interesting fact of history. He laughed and said, "I'll take my chances." *

His cool and realistic attitude came from the simple fact that, like any President, he wanted maximum exposure to the people, to multitudes—the more the better. The size of the crowds might be a gauge of his popularity and therefore the degree of support for his programs. He was the leader of his party. Through frequent public appearances, he hoped to enhance his chances for reelection and to pull other Democrats into office on his coattails. Thus, Kennedy craved to confront large numbers of people, and he often felt impelled to plunge into their midst, shaking hands and feeling other hands tugging at his clothing. On such occasions, it would have been easy to assassinate him, especially if the assailant had been prepared to lose his own life.

There is a photograph, taken at close range, that shows Kennedy in swim trunks just after having come out of the

* Harrison, like Kennedy, may have had a premonition of death. Three months before he died, he closed a speech in Cincinnati with the words "Perhaps this may be the last time I may have the pleasure of speaking to you on earth or seeing you. I will bid you farewell; if forever, fare thee well." He was sixty-eight and apparently in good health.

27

surf at Malibu Beach in California. Women are hanging on both arms. Other bathers are pressing close to the President, reaching to shake hands. He is grinning. He loves it. If any swim-suited Secret Service agents were guarding him at that moment, I was unable to recognize them. He may have decided on the spur of the moment to plunge into the ocean and simply left them behind. In any case, as he walked across the beach, unclad and surrounded by people, he could have been killed with a penknife or a pair of scissors.

The only way to provide total protection for a President would be to immure him in a fortress. It was characteristic of Kennedy to dismiss the danger with a laugh. Referring to James Rowley, the square-jawed chief of the Secret Service, Kennedy said, "Jim Rowley is very efficient—he's never lost a President."

The crowds in Texas were fantastic in size. They jammed the airports, lined the streets for miles waiting for the President's motorcade, and thronged in such numbers into the outdoor areas where he was to speak that they swamped the facilities—and advance arrangements went by the boards. Kennedy preferred to speak outdoors; inside, he said, the audience necessarily would be limited. The reception in San Antonio, the first stop, might have been predictable because of the presence there of so many "viva voters," people of Latin American origin. Probably because they considered Kennedy a member of a minority group, like themselves, he held a special place in their affections. This had been apparent in California when he campaigned for the Presidency. "Viva Jack," their placards had said. Even more impressive than the 250,000 in San Antonio were the 5,000 in Fort Worth, because they gathered in a parking lot across from the Hotel Texas in the rain and while it was yet dark on the morning of November 22. They were mainly workmen, union men who responded to Kennedy's social and economic philosophies, unlike the growing number of conservatives in Texas. Kennedy was anything but the darling of the Establishment in Texas, and Frank Cormier correctly reported to The Associated Press, "There was little evidence that Democratic party workers had turned on the steam to organize mammoth welcomes." Mammoth they were, nevertheless. Perhaps the President had been right when he said, referring to the factional fighting in the state, "Feuds make for

28

crowds." Perhaps many were simply curious to see how Ralph Yarborough, the liberal Senator, and Governor Connally, the conservative, would react when brought together by Kennedy's visit. Whatever the answer, in Houston, Kennedy asked Dave Powers, a White House assistant and member of "the Mafia," to estimate the size of the crowd there. Powers replied that it looked to him to be about equal to the turnout when Kennedy had visited the Space Center on an earlier occasion, plus, Powers added, "about one hundred thousand extra who came to see Mrs. Kennedy."

At each airport arrival, the President broke protocol to let the people see her first. When the doors of "Air Force One" opened, he beckoned her to precede him down the ramp. She wore a white wool suit with a black bow tie belt, white gloves, and a round white hat, all accentuating the black hair framing her face. Women shrieked, "Jackie! Jackie!" Apparently enjoying the reception, she decided to go beyond waving to the crowds in the streets and shaking the hands of welcoming committees; she wrote a few sentences in Spanish, memorized them, and made a speech to the League of United Latin American Citizens in Fort Worth. After her husband addressed the organization, he said, "And now I would like my wife to say a few words." As a political campaigner, she was an unqualified success.

But appearances, the dimensions and warmth of the receptions that day, were probably deceiving. They were one-sided. Wherever Kennedy went, placards rose: "The Cuban Revolution was not betrayed in Cuba only" and "Relax, they're still 90 miles away." That was one jagged issue to throw in his face.

Other placards reflected more generalized antipathies: "We need a new ex-President" and "Lock the door in '64 on JFK and LBJ." Here were the voices of the conservatives and segregationists (who apparently still thought of Johnson as the New Dealer of the 1930's). The Populists disappeared after 1908, and although the tradition lingered a few years longer in Texas, oil, insurance, new business, and new money were causing it to disappear there, too. Rural communities tend toward conservatism everywhere. The racial problem was probably not so acute as in the Deep South, but in East Texas, near the Louisiana and Arkansas line, Kennedy's civil rights moves aroused the same hostility as it had in those states. The Far Right in Texas, as in Southern California, found much to worry about

29

with Kennedy in the White House. Its members asserted that he was backing a Red for leadership in the Congo, and they found it outrageous that Yugoslav fighter pilots were being trained in the United States. That these pilots might some day be fighting Russians could not be conceived; the reported split between Tito and the Kremlin, they knew, was merely a Communist plot to hoodwink innocent Americans, and the "silent, slanted, slippery press," as a Rightist pamphlet described it, was a willing tool in the hands of the plotters. The placard that struck Adlai Stevenson's bald head reflected the sentiments of this group toward the American policy that continued to keep an ambassador to the United Nations.

About a week before the assassination, I had been traveling around Texas, trying to assess the outlook there for Kennedy in 1964. He had won by a scanty 45,000 votes in 1960. The combination of hostilities built up since then made it appear doubtful that he would do even that well in 1964.

While the President was speaking in San Antonio and Houston, Richard Nixon was downgrading his chances in Dallas. Nixon addressed the executives of some soft drink firms that were represented by his New York law firm. "Kennedy's stock in Texas is considerably lower than in 1960," he said, "and Vice-President Lyndon Johnson may not be able to help him, because his position is weaker." Partisan talk of course, grist for the mill. However, remembering my own findings in Texas, I think it contained a measure of fact. How much will never be known.

Johnson found himself in an odd position with respect to his fellow Texans. He had entered Congress as a supporter of Franklin D. Roosevelt. Then, during Eisenhower's eight years in office, Johnson had tended to go along with the President and, like Eisenhower, considered himself a middle-of-the-roader. Thus, in the eyes of the liberals, Johnson had become a creature of the conservatives. As for the extreme Right, there is no middle of the road. He was trying to remain aloof from the Connally-Yarborough feuding. But the Senator wouldn't permit this. In the makeup of the San Antonio motorcade, Yarborough was placed in the limousine with the Vice-President and Mrs. Johnson. Instead, he walked away from them and stepped into a car with Representative Albert Thomas. The action was duly noted by the large press corps covering the President's trip.

Neither principal in the feud seemed disposed to assist Kennedy in the bridge-building, which was one of the purposes of going into Texas. It became known that Connally had omitted Yarborough from the guest list for the Presidential reception in Austin. On the flight from Washington, a reporter asked the Senator for a comment on this, and Yarborough replied, "Governor Connally is so terribly undereducated politically, how could you expect anything else?"

The reporter to whom he said this was a member of what is known as "the pool." Since only a limited number of reporters and photographers can be accommodated on such flights, it is the responsibility of "the poolers" to report to the main body of correspondents who fly ahead of the Presidential plane in the press plane. Thus, Yarborough's remark was duly relayed to the whole corps on the ground in San Antonio.

After Kennedy's appearance in that city, both the Governor and Senator said the feud had miraculously disappeared. "I don't know where all this got started," said Connally. "He's going to be received. We have no problems. He's on the platform. He's being treated with the respect a United States Senator deserves." And Yarborough echoed, "All is harmony."

This was for public consumption. Nobody believed it, including Kennedy. By the time he reached Fort Worth, a few minutes after midnight—and even at that hour, another crowd stood waiting to see him—he knew he had had a good day in Texas. He also knew he had not built the bridge between the gut-fighters.

It had been a long, tiring day, and now he was looking ahead to the next and perhaps most important hurdle in Texas, the day in Dallas. In the hotel in Fort Worth, the President again went over the speech he had prepared for the audience in the Trade Mart. He meant to speak bluntly. To meet an issue squarely had paid dividends in Texas before; in 1960, he had confronted an audience of Protestant clergymen on the question of whether his Catholicism would affect his decisions if he became President. He may not have changed many minds, but the nation applauded a brave gesture. Now he was about to challenge extremism in Dallas, the city that my Texas friend, Bill Barnard, once described as "the Vatican of the Extreme Right." Kennedy's message was to be unmistakeable.

The notion that this nation is headed for defeat through deficits, or that strength is but a matter of slogans, is nothing but just plain nonsense.

Voices are heard in the land, voices preaching doctrines wholly unsuited to the '60's, doctrines which apparently assume that words will suffice without weapons, that vituperation is as good as victory, and that peace is a sign of weakness.

We cannot expect that everyone, to use the phrase of a decade ago, "will talk sense to the American people." But we can hope that fewer people will listen to nonsense . . . or else those who confuse rhetoric with reality and the plausible with the possible will gain the popular ascendancy with their seemingly swift and simple solutions to every world problem.

Well, that would be telling them: "confuse rhetoric with reality . . . seemingly swift and simple solutions"—these are the hallmarks of extremists at either end of the spectrum.

Kennedy was to speak in the square near the hotel in the morning and then appear again at a breakfast. He told Mrs. Kennedy she need not attend the first meeting but to be ready for the second at 9:15. They said good night, and he turned out the lights and closed his eyes. In the adjoining room, Mrs. Kennedy—maidless for the moment —drew from her bags a pink suit and blue blouse, a handbag matching the blouse, low-heeled shoes, and a pink pillbox hat—her costume for Friday, November 22.

Rain began to fall in Fort Worth.

In Dallas, meanwhile, the presses were rolling in the Dallas *Morning News* building. They made a sound like muffled thunder, and the newsprint raced through the huge machines at blinding speed, printing and assembling, folding, and then exiting on a conveyor belt as a finished product. Page 14 was gulping an unusual amount of ink. The entire page was covered by an advertisement bordered in black like a death notice and captioned in large black letters, WELCOME MR. KENNEDY. Underneath, it asked 12 questions, each beginning with WHY. A sampling tells the tenor of the whole.

WHY have you scrapped the Monroe Doctrine in favor of the "Spirit of Moscow"?

WHY have you ordered or permitted your brother

Bobby, the Attorney-General, to go soft on Communists, fellow-travellers, and ultra-leftists in America, while permitting him to persecute loyal Americans who criticize you, your administration, and your leadership?

WHY did you host, salute and entertain Tito—Moscow's Trojan Horse—just a short time after our sworn enemy, Khrushchev, embraced the Yugoslav Dictator as a great hero and leader of Communism?

At the bottom of the page, "The American Fact-Finding Committee" was listed as sponsor of the ad with the signature "Bernard Weissman, Chairman."

Weissman, a carpet salesman, was to tell the Warren Commission that he had become concerned about American foreign policy and interested in conservative organizations while he was in the Army, stationed in Germany. "The American Fact-Finding Committee" was strictly *ad hoc,* according to his testimony, organized for the purpose of putting the advertisement in the Dallas *Morning News.* He and three or four associates had no difficulty collecting $1,463 to pay for the ad.

The testimony would be particularly intriguing as to the reasons for inserting the ad. The record would show Weissman explaining:

Well, after the Stevenson incident, it was felt that a demonstration would be entirely out of order because we didn't want anything to happen in the way of physical violence to President Kennedy when he came to Dallas.

So far so good. Now prepare for a surprise.

But we thought the conservatives in Dallas—I was told—were a pretty downtrodden lot after that . . . we felt that we had to do something to build up the morale of the conservative element in Dallas. So we hit upon the idea of the ad.

Apart from that—

We were, you might say—at least I personally—this is my reason—I was sick and tired of seeing America as a weak sister all the time. And this is

33

especially in the field of foreign affairs, where it seemed that our administration, whether it be the Eisenhower or the Kennedy administration, both of them had no set stable foreign policy. We were constantly losing ground all over the world. We were going to conference tables with everything to lose and nothing to gain and coming away by losing.

Kennedy had been dead on target when he wrote in his speech of the mentality in which "peace is a sign of weakness" and of "their seemingly swift and simple solutions to every world problem."

Here it could be found *in toto* in the words of one "downtrodden conservative."

The President dismissed the ad as typical of the "nut country" into which his itinerary was taking him. What did greatly irritate him, however, when he wakened in the morning, were newspaper reports emphasizing the feuding between Democrats evidenced in part by Yarborough's neat maneuvers to avoid riding in the same car with Lyndon Johnson. Other stories said the effect of the Presidential visit had been to fire the flames of controversy between the factions and widen the "Democratic split" in Texas.

Since Kennedy concerned himself very little over the possibility of being assassinated, he probably paid scant attention to the newspapers' reports of the thoroughness of the preparations to protect him in Dallas. The Chief of Police, Jesse Curry, had called in more than one hundred off-duty officers. Some, although the newspapers did not publish the fact, were to mingle with the crowds along the route of the motorcade to watch for anything that might appear to be a prelude to hostile action. Love Field, the airport, was to be heavily guarded with riflemen stationed on the roofs of buildings overlooking the spot where Kennedy would leave "Air Force One" to enter his car. It is unlikely that many persons in Dallas were thinking of assassination at the time; they feared an incident, an attempt to embarrass the President and the many persons in Dallas who were trying to improve the city's image. The police had infiltrated organizations of extremists. Thus, they had learned some students were painting anti-Kennedy placards, and they checked out a man in another city who had said he intended to "embarrass" the President in Dallas. He admitted having said this but told the Dallas de-

34

tective who questioned him, "I won't even be in Dallas. I was just popping off." The Dallas papers quoted a Republican leader as calling for a "civilized nonpartisan" welcome for the President. The prevailing sentiment in Dallas, plus the unusual precautions taken by the police, seemed to insure such a welcome.

While Kennedy slept, nine Secret Service agents left the hotel and went out, looking for food. It had been a long, tiring day for them, too, and they had eaten on the run when they ate at all. Now, with the President safely locked away in the hotel, they were off-duty until eight o'clock in the morning, although technically on call at all times. Because of the late hour, they were directed to the Press Club in Fort Worth. The fact that they went there, where reporters would be sure to see them, instead of finding some obscure hole-in-the-wall, is evidence that they did not expect to violate any regulations in a way that would imperil the safety of the President. They found no food at the Press Club, but they did find beer and mixed drinks. A section of the Secret Service regulations reads:

> . . . all members of the White House detail and special agents cooperating with them on Presidential and similar protective assignments are subject to call for official duty at any time while in travel status. Therefore, the use of intoxicating liquor of any kind, including beer and wine, by members of the White House detail and special agents cooperating with them, or by special agents on similar assignments, while they are in travel status, is prohibited.

The agents who drank at the Press Club violated this part of the regulations. Some went on from the Press Club, still looking for food. Some were in bed before 2:00 A.M., and most of them by 3:00. One stayed out until five o'clock.

The question later arose: Were any of the agents less alert or agile, when confronted by crisis, as a result of their night out in Fort Worth? Chief Rowley thought not and refrained from disciplining them.

The assassin, ideally positioned, would be waiting, waiting for the image of a man to float into view through the cross hairs of a telescopic sight on his rifle.

The cards were stacked against the Secret Service agents, against Dallas, and against the world.

4

In the time zones of the United States, Washington is one hour ahead of Dallas. Because of this, on the morning of Thursday, November 21, fate decreed an eerie coincidence. Two events, separated then by half a continent but soon to be related, took place in the same span of minutes, just as Kennedy was leaving for Texas.

"Air Force One" lifted into the skies over Washington a few minutes after 11:00 A.M. It carried the President, Mrs. Kennedy, members of the White House staff, and a large company of Texas congressmen.

In Dallas, a few minutes after 10:00 A.M., Lee Oswald asked a seemingly innocent question. He spoke to Wesley Frazier, a fellow workman in the Texas Book Depository Building, and said, "Could I ride home with you tonight?" Frazier replied, "Sure." He would be able to fix the time exactly, because he usually took a short break from his work at 10:00 A.M., and it was during this daily breather that Oswald spoke to him.

"Home," in this instance, meant Frazier's home in Irving, a suburb of Dallas, about 15 miles from the Book Building. He lived with his sister, Mrs. Linnie Mae Randle, and her husband. Oswald lived in a rooming house in Dallas. He was semiestranged from his Russian wife, Marina Nikolaevna, and she had been a guest in the home of a friend in Irving for the past two months. The Oswalds had two small children. He visited his family on weekends, riding to Irving with Frazier on Friday and returning with him on Monday morning. He did not tell Frazier why he was varying the routine now, making it Thursday instead of Friday.

The two men left the Book Building at about 4:55. As usual, little conversation took place between them on the way to Irving. Frazier knew very little about his weekend passenger. Yes, Oswald had been in the Marines. Yes, he had been in Germany, and he preferred Germans to the

36

French because the French would cheat Americans whenever they could. (A longish statement for Oswald.) He also had lived in Russia and took pride in his command of the language, but he didn't tell Frazier that. He kept his thoughts to himself and discouraged conversation with his monosyllabic answers to questions on most topics. With one exception—Oswald's two infant daughters, June and Rachel. Whenever Frazier asked about the babies, Oswald's thin, inscrutable features lit up, and he would talk animatedly about how he enjoyed playing with them.

During the drive that day, Frazier asked Oswald why he was going to see his wife and children on Thursday. Oswald apparently was prepared for the question. "To get some curtain rods," he replied promptly. This was a lie. There were curtains in the room where he lived at 1026 North Beckley Street in Dallas. He probably had another pat answer ready in case Frazier were to ask him why he could not wait until Friday to get the curtain rods.

Frazier parked his automobile in the carport of his sister's home on Westfield Street in Irving at about 5:25.

Oswald walked a half block to 2515 West Fifth, the home of Mrs. Ruth Paine, who had separated from her husband. Mrs. Paine, a Quaker, had befriended both Oswalds. She had arranged for him to meet Roy Truly, the manager of the Book Building, when Oswald was out of work. She felt sorry for Marina because Oswald was unemployed so often. A few weeks before the birth of Marina's second child, and while Oswald was absent on some mysterious errand, Mrs. Paine suggested that Marina would be better off in her four-room house in Irving. Oswald's relief checks could not provide very well for his wife and two daughters. Nothing was said about rent. But Ruth Paine was studying Russian, and by practicing the language with Marina, she saved the expense of taking lessons. It was a convenient arrangement for both women, especially for Marina. Mrs. Paine was to say, "I thought Marina a wonderful person. We were both young mothers and liked to talk about families and housework. I thought that I could teach her English, and she could help me with my Russian."

The Dallas-Irving arrangement suited Marina quite well, but it was by no means satisfactory to her husband. He telephoned her every day and sometimes twice. The baby, born in October, seemed to delight him, and weekends in Irving were, or seemed to be, pleasant. Mrs. Paine had the impression that Oswald was trying to hold his family together. Then came a serious clash between Marina and her husband.

Mrs. Paine organized a birthday party for one of her children for November 17. Marina knew that Michael Paine, Ruth's husband, would attend the party, and she knew that Oswald did not like him. Mrs. Paine heard her speak on the telephone to Oswald and tell him not to come to Irving that weekend. She said the house would be crowded because of the party and that it would not be convenient for Mrs. Paine to have him there, too. Marina went a step farther. Aside from the party, she suggested that perhaps he should not visit her every weekend, that perhaps it made things difficult for Mrs. Paine to have all four Oswalds under her roof from Friday night to Monday morning. Oswald replied, according to Marina, "As you wish. If you don't want me to come, I won't."

Marina's attitudes toward her husband evidently changed capriciously. Having told him to remain in Dallas that weekend and implied that she would welcome longer intervals between his visits, she then seemed to feel sorry for him. Or perhaps it was remorse. In any case, on the following day, she decided to cheer him up with a telephone call. Mrs. Paine dialed the number of the rooming house in Dallas. She was surprised to be told that no one named Lee Oswald lived there. "Who? Sorry. Never heard of him."

But there was an "O.H. Lee" at the rooming house—for Oswald, reversing his names, was hiding his identity under an alias.

As this narrative will develop more fully in a subsequent chapter, Oswald lived in a fantasy world, a cops-and-robbers world in which he used fictitious names, lied about himself, and was forever running—running from or toward what?

On Monday after the birthday party, he had telephoned Marina, and she told him she had tried to talk to him on the weekend. Thus, the fact came out that he was now "O.H. Lee." Marina's Slavic temper flared. She was furious with him. To her, this was another instance of what she called his "foolishness," a decided understatement, considering the dangerous nature of some previous shenanigans. They quarreled bitterly over the telephone. Marina ended it by slamming down the receiver. He had not telephoned again during the week.

38

Consequently, both women were surprised when he came to the house on Thursday, November 21. Ruth Paine was not overly fond of Oswald, but she always tried to be pleasant when he visited in her home. Simply to say something, she now remarked, "Our President is coming tomorrow." Oswald replied, "Oh, yeah," and left her. On finding him there a day earlier than usual, Mrs. Paine immediately jumped to the conclusion that he had come to patch up Monday's fight with his wife. So did Marina. In fact, he had others matters in mind. A reconciliation may have been one of his purposes. Or it may have been a cover story, a mask.

For a while, he advanced no explanation for having come to Irving, unannounced, on Thursday. He became unusually attentive to his wife. He helped her with some housework, washed diapers, and played outdoors with his children. Then he came to the point. He said he had been lonely, not having seen her for two weeks. He said he was sorry about "O.H. Lee" and begged her to forgive him.

Marina's response was a frosty silence. Oswald began pleading more earnestly. He was tired of living alone. He wanted her and the children with him all the time. He ventured the thought that living apart had been the source of their quarrels, overlooking the fact that they had fought physically in the times when they were living together. Once, he had blackened her eye in a fit of jealous rage. On another occasion, she had thrust him into the bathroom and locked the door. Now he said that if she would came back to him, he would rent an apartment in Dallas on the following Monday. He begged his wife not to be angry with him, saying it "upset" him to see her angry.

She remained silent, unbending. He might as well have been pleading with an alabaster sphinx. He shifted to new ground. Bitterly, he said she preferred her friends, especially Ruth Paine, to him. He repeated the accusation several times. She must come back to him, to the new life he could promise her in Dallas.

Marina broke her silence then. She said she would prefer to continue the Dallas-Irving arrangement until after Christmas and New Year, roughly another six weeks. He could visit his family on weekends. But, she said, they were saving money by living in Ruth Paine's home, and she wanted to wait until after the holidays before making the change. The mention of money brought her to another point. Her manner seemed to soften, and she made a wifely request. She needed a washing machine. The birth of Rachel had enlarged the problem of handling the laundry. Oswald probably took this to be the harbinger of an armistice, and he promptly agreed to buy the machine for her. Whereupon, in the next breath, Marina reversed her position. She said, "Thank you. But it would be better if you bought something for yourself. I will manage."

With this deft feminine twist of the dagger, she appeared to tell Oswald she neither needed nor wanted him. She rebuffed him completely.

The shabby, and yet pathetic, domestic scene on the night of November 21 holds elements of mystery. It is sometimes asserted that it unhinged Oswald's reason, that he went mad then, or soon afterward, and in his madness planned the dreadful action to be taken the next day. The Warren Commission would examine this possibility. The evidence, however, does not support the hypothesis.

It points, on the contrary, to the probability that a well-conceived plan had been forming in his mind during the week before he saw Marina in Irving. Why did he come there a day early? Was it to get something he would take into the Book Building on Friday morning? He lied to Frazier about needing curtain rods for his room, a strong indication that he had visualized the shape and dimensions of the package he intended to take to Dallas. Unless the package were closely examined, it might very well have been mistaken for a sheaf of curtain rods. Oswald had hit on a rather ingenious disguise for a long and largely tubular package. Was this the act of a careful plotter or an example of a madman's cunning? Further, although the discovery had not yet been made, a map of Dallas lay in a drawer in Oswald's room. It bristled with x's. They traced the route the President would take, showing he would pass the Book Building. X, as in the old gangster films, marked the spot. Telling Marina he would rent an apartment on *Monday* may have been a red herring, a device to divert suspicion from himself. Marina's memory, of course, could be faulty. And finally, after Oswald's arrest, Federal officers were to find him most adroit in answering certain questions and alert in parrying or refusing to answer others. His behavior before and after November 22 does not suggest that he was demented. Then what is the explanation?

The mystery sealed in Oswald's grave mocks history.

At about 6:30, the three adults sat down to dinner.

When they finished, Marina and Ruth Paine washed and put away the dishes. Then they bathed their children and prepared to put them to bed. The work kept them busy more than an hour. Where was Lee Oswald during that time? Marina and Mrs. Paine would testify they did not know. They assumed, if they thought of him at all, that while they were busy in one part of the house, he was in the other rooms. An electric light burning in the garage may be a clue to his whereabouts.

The Oswald's few possessions were stored in Ruth Paine's garage. Among them, lying on the floor and wrapped in a brown-and-green blanket, was his rifle, a long, high-powered Italian carbine. Marina had taken a snapshot of her husband holding the rifle in one hand and a pistol in the other. The weapon was easily disassembled and assembled. An expert, using no other tool than a dime, could do it in ten minutes. The rifle would not be found in the blanket on Friday.

At about nine o'clock, Mrs. Paine went out to the garage to paint some wooden blocks, toys for the children. She found the light burning. She had not been there herself, but someone obviously had left it on, a common happenstance. It did not occur to her to wonder who had been in the garage or why.

During the early evening, Oswald sat watching an old World War II movie on television. Then he went to bed. Marina entered the bedroom some time later. She could not see her husband in the darkness, but she had the impression that he was not asleep, that his eyes were wide open.

Oswald left the house on Friday morning before either his wife or Ruth Paine arose. To Marina's surprise, she found his wedding ring in a cup on the dresser. He had never before taken the ring off his finger. Even more intriguing, she found his wallet in a drawer of the dresser, and her eyes widened when she counted the money in the wallet—$170. He may have left the money as a peace offering, perhaps for the washing machine they had discussed. But why had he left the ring? What did that mean?,

Shortly after seven o'clock, Linnie Mae Randle saw Oswald cross the street and walk toward the carport beside her home. He carried a package several feet in length, a brown paper package sealed with strips of tape. He opened the rear door of Wesley Frazier's car and gently

41

laid the package inside. Mrs. Randle could not see whether he placed it on the floor or the back seat.

A moment later, her mother, a house guest, suddenly said, "Who's that?" She saw a man's face in the kitchen window. Frazier looked up from his coffee. "Oh, that's Lee," he said. Frazier felt no curiosity about it then, but he would recall later that this was the only time Oswald ever approached the Randle home before they set off for Dallas. Usually, he would see Oswald walking toward him on the sidewalk when he backed out of the driveway. Otherwise, Frazier would toot the horn in front of Ruth Paine's house to summon Oswald.

As they opened the doors of the car that morning, Frazier caught sight of the brown paper bundle in the corner of the back seat on Oswald's side. "What's the package, Lee?"

"Curtain rods," Oswald said.

"That's right," Frazier said. "You told me yesterday."

They rode several miles in the customary silence. Frazier broke it with a question, "Where's your lunch today?"

"Going to buy it," Oswald replied.

The men in the Book Building could buy sandwiches and other food from a caterer who came around in mid-morning. But nobody ever saw Oswald patronizing him. He brought his lunch with him when he left Irving on Mondays. On other days, when he came from the rooming house, he might buy potato chips from a machine, or perhaps nothing at all, at noon. He ate very little, and he was frugal to the point of austerity.

It had rained during the night. Passing cars splattered the windshield of Frazier's car with sludge, and the wipers had little effect. He had to drive a little more slowly than usual. Nonetheless, he rolled into the parking lot near the Book Building in good time. He sat behind the wheel for a minute or two, racing his motor on the theory that it would start more readily in the afternoon.

Oswald did not wait for him. Usually, they walked together to the back door of the Book Building. But on that Friday morning, he immediately stepped out of the car, picked up the package on the back seat, and strode off. Frazier did not attempt to overtake Oswald. He liked to watch the big diesel locomotives switching cars around and assembling trains in the nearby railroad yards. Frazier's watch told him it was not yet eight o'clock, and so he loitered, looking at the railroading. When he turned toward the Book Building, Oswald was well ahead of him. Frazier saw him disappear through the back door.

Lee Oswald was so withdrawn and self-effacing at work, such a cipher in the whole human equation, that none of the men in the Book Building would remember much about his movements on the morning of November 22. Roy Truly, the supervisor, found Oswald already at work pulling books from the bins on the ground floor when he entered the building. Truly said, "Good morning, Lee," and Oswald replied, "Good morning, sir." Others would testify that they also saw Oswald filling the orders for books when they came to work. Nobody would recall seeing him carrying the brown paper package. It would have taken Oswald only a minute to ride the elevator to the sixth floor and hide it in an out-of-the-way corner beneath the jumble of boxes and cartons.

In four and a half hours the President of the United States would come into sight, and the view from the sixth floor would be excellent.

5

A misty rain was falling, and clouds glowered in the morning sky when John F. Kennedy came out of the Hotel Texas in Fort Worth and stepped across the street toward the parking lot. He wore neither topcoat nor hat. (The apostle of "vigah" had scorned both even in the winter winds of New Hampshire, Wisconsin, and West Virginia in his 1960 campaign, impressing the voters with the image of a rugged young candidate.) He wore a dark gray, two-button suit, a gray shirt with thin stripes, and a blue tie flecked with lighter blue squares. In spite of a reasonable night's sleep, he was still weary from the rigors of Thursday, but he could always bounce back in the morning, tapping reserves of vitality. When he saw the mass of people in the parking lot, his face lit up, and the smile, like a sunburst, crinkled the corners of his eyes. The time was 8:45. The crowd, mainly workmen, had been gather-

43

ing for more than an hour. Moisture dripped from the construction workers' hard hats. A few of the reporters followed the President outdoors, but the majority, knowing they could keep him in view and hear his words on the loudspeaker, elected to remain in the hotel. Looking down from windows on the upper floors, they estimated the audience at about five thousand. The scene would make a colorful touch—because in a sense, this was a better tribute to Kennedy than the bigger but organized receptions when they sat down to write the report of his day in Dallas and Fort Worth. In less than four hours, the tableau in the parking lot would be only a footnote to history.

The crowd cheered, laughing and clapping as the President approached the microphone. There were several shouts, "Where's Jackie?" Kennedy knew what to say, not too much at that hour, but not too little either, inasmuch as they had paid him a genuine compliment in assembling in these circumstances. He thanked them for coming. Then he said, "Mrs. Kennedy is organizing herself. It takes her longer, but of course, she looks better than we do when she's finished." Laughter and applause rose again. When it died away, he became serious and moved into the main theme of what he intended to say. It echoed 1960, only now the general line was "We are going forward." He perpetrated one of his little tricks. His audience would know that if the Federal government rained money on Houston, some of the drops would fall on Fort Worth and affect their pay envelopes, too. And so Kennedy deliberately misstated himself, pretending to fluff a line. Referring to missiles and the Space Center in Houston, he said the United States would soon be "firing the largest payroll into space—er, I meant to say pay *load*, not payroll." The sly dodge had been used in Houston, too, and for the same reason. He again thanked the crowd for coming. With that, he returned to the hotel, where another audience, 2,500 guests, awaited him at a breakfast sponsored by the Fort Worth Chamber of Commerce. Two big turnouts before nine o'clock . . . things were going better than he expected . . . to the politician, alert for omens in the sky, it augured well . . . Friday was going to be a good day, and then he could relax on Lyndon Johnson's ranch.

While Kennedy was speaking in Fort Worth, Gordon Shanklin, chief of the FBI detail in Dallas, called his agents into a conference. For the second time, he said that if any of them had information about persons in Dallas who could be considered potentially dangerous to the safety of the President or Vice-President, they should report it at once to the Secret Service and confirm the report in writing. Shanklin had an uneasy premonition. A week earlier, he had made the same statement to the agents and issued the same order.

Nobody spoke up.

Among the agents present was James Patrick Hosty, Jr. He had a dossier on Lee Oswald. He had interviewed Marina and Ruth Paine. The case had been transferred to him from New Orleans FBI agents, so he knew that Oswald had tried to defect to Russia and had championed Fidel Castro in New Orleans. Mrs. Paine, somewhat reluctantly, had told Hosty that Oswald now had a job in the Texas Book Depository Building. Hosty had verified this with a discreet telephone call to the personnel department. So he knew the President would pass Oswald's place of employment. However, Oswald was not in a "sensitive" job, that is in a position where his work might provide him with intelligence of value to Moscow or Havana. He was not concerned otherwise with Oswald; certainly it did not occur to Hosty that Oswald might be a potential assassin. These were the narrow interpretations of the areas of responsibility in government information-gathering agencies on November 22, 1963.

Kennedy returned to the Hotel Texas while Shanklin was admonishing his agents. The President had told Mrs. Kennedy to appear at the breakfast at 9:15. She entered on the dot. The audience rose in a storm of applause. She flashed her brilliant smile. She was beginning to understand how much she could help her husband in his campaigns.

When the applause ended, the chairman asked everyone to remain standing for the prayer that opened the meeting. A photographer caught a curious picture. It shows the President, Lyndon Johnson, and Governor Connally standing together, heads bowed, eyes closed. Through some accident of lighting, or perhaps in developing the negative of the photograph, a crescent-shaped aureole like a halo glows above Kennedy's head. He would have been vastly amused to see it. With some vintage Kennedy jest, he would have punctured the idea that he had earned a halo. Not just yet, anyway. Or he might have said, referring to

45

the Republican TV team, "Of course. Everybody can see it except Ev and Charley."

In a strange flash of prescience, something impelled him to return that morning to the possibility of being assassinated. He noted how easy it would be for a killer to shoot him from a high building or amid one of the moiling crowds. It was not the first time his thoughts had flickered around the specter, but it would be the last.

O'Brien and O'Donnell, preparing for another strenuous day, remained upstairs in the hotel and watched the proceedings on television. They began to grin when boots were presented to the President and Mrs. Kennedy, plus a wide-brim Texas hat. They knew that all such totems of American politics left him cold, and they were interested to see how he would meet the problem. Sure enough, he said nobody would notice the hat if he wore it in Texas, but he invited everyone present to "come to Washington Monday, and I'll put it on in the White House for you." The Mafia upstairs belly-laughed.

Around ten o'clock, Roy Kellerman, special agent in charge of the Secret Service for the Texas trip, approached O'Donnell with a weather report and a question. He had been talking with Winston Lawson, the Secret Service advance man, who was at Love Field. Lawson reported the rain. The question was whether to raise the "bubble top" on the Presidential limousine, a blue Lincoln Continental that had been flown from Washington to San Antonio and from there to Dallas.

The "bubble top" was composed of sections of clear plastic glass designed to protect the occupants of the car during inclement weather. It was not bulletproof. The thought seems never to have occurred to anyone, in all the years since Presidents began riding in automobiles, that a bulletproof "bubble top" would be a sensible precaution.

While Lawson waited on the telephone, Kellerman checked with O'Donnell. "Mr. O'Donnell," he said, "the weather—it's raining a little in Dallas—predictions of clearing up. Do you desire to have the 'bubble top' on the President's car, or would you desire to have it removed for this parade over to the Trade Mart?"

"If the weather is clear and it isn't raining," O'Donnell said, "have that 'bubble top' off."

The "bubble top" would not have stopped the bullets. But the sight of them shattering the plastic and the noise made inside the top would have removed any doubt that

46

someone had fired at the President. In fact, the Secret Service men in the limousine did not immediately identify the explosion as a rifle shot. Oswald had time to get off his second and third shots.

Kellerman relayed the order to Lawson. The consequences of this minor matter could not be foreseen.

The President and his wife went upstairs to their suite after the breakfast and prepared to leave for Dallas. Before the departure, however, he made a gesture that would go down well in Texas and with Democrats everywhere. He telephoned John Nance Garner in Uvalde and congratulated him on his ninety-fifth birthday. (The Kennedys are meticulous about such amenities.) Garner was the Vice-President in Franklin D. Roosevelt's first Administration. Drawing on that experience, he had strongly advised Lyndon Johnson not to accept the nomination for Vice-President when Kennedy offered it to him in Los Angeles in 1960. The old man had used a decidedly earthy figure of speech to describe the office.

The Presidential party left the hotel at 10:35 and traveled by automobile to Carswell Air Force Base on the outskirts of Fort Worth. The base is named for a Texas war hero, Major Horace Carswell. His body lies in Rose Hill Cemetery. Lee Oswald's mother had purchased a family plot in that cemetery.

The flight from Fort Worth to Dallas was so short that the passengers on "Air Force One" barely had time to fasten seat belts before the plane's heavy landing gear went down with a thud and then eased it onto the runway. Clustered around the buildings at some distance from the main terminal, another large crowd awaited the President. Looking closely, you could have spotted men on the roofs of the airport buildings armed with rifles and watching the people below.

The Vice-Presidential plane and the press plane had arrived a little while before. (The President and Vice-President travel in separate aircraft, just in case. . . .) A reception line stretched from the foot of the ramp to the point where the motorcade, automobiles and police motorcycles, already had formed. Each car had a special function.

At 11:37, the door of "Air Force One" slid open. Mrs. Kennedy appeared, a bright pink figure against the silver and blue fuselage. Several thousand people struggled to see, pressing tight against the wire fences, craning, lifting cameras. Teen-age girls and young women invariably assembled in hordes wherever Kennedy went. The reporters long since had divided them into categories, the "jumpers," "runners," "touchers," and "repeaters." The "repeaters" were hysterical females of indeterminate ages who clutched at Kennedy and then sprinted ahead of his car or line of march to touch him a second time. All were shriekers. Their shrieks rose to a crescendo at Love Field, but not for the President. "Jackie! Jackie!" they cried.

Kennedy and his wife passed along the reception line, shaking hands. In the silly mummery of politics, protocol decreed that Johnson and Connally and their wives, who had stood in reception lines at San Antonio, Houston, and Fort Worth, must also be in the one at Dallas, beaming for the benefit of potential voters and local politicians. A bouquet of roses, bloodred roses, was presented to Mrs. Kennedy, and she carried the flowers in the crook of her left arm as she walked slowly, shaking hands. In the reception line, she came to a silver-haired woman in a wheelchair. The man standing beside it said, "This is Mrs. Dunbar, Mrs. Annie S. Dunbar. She is eighty-five and a loyal Democrat, and she has never seen a President." Mrs. Kennedy extended her white-gloved hand, smiling warmly. The President said, "It's so nice to meet you, Mrs. Dunbar. We need all the loyal Democrats we can get." He might have added, "especially in Dallas County," but he was too astute for that. Many of those waiting behind the wire fence may have come out to see his wife, but *quand même,* they were there. (Kennedy had been taking French lessons in the thought that one of these days he would be able to deal with Charles de Gaulle in his own language, not realizing that De Gaulle speaks so elliptically that not even the French can always understand the deeper meaning of what he is saying.) Together, they walked to the wire fence, shaking the hands outstretched to him there. Jacqueline Kennedy was accustomed to the ritual now.

The weather had turned warm. The clouds had broken, and the puddles of rain on the apron at the airport mirrored the bright sunshine. Obviously, the "bubble top" would not be needed.

Walking toward the blue limousine, Kennedy's eyes narrowed. A quizzical expression came over his face without wholly erasing his smile. Perhaps he caught sight of the placard carried by a man in the crowd, "Help JFK Stamp Out Democracy." And the bumper stickers, "Which Kennedy Do You Hate the Most?" And the billboard, "Impeach Earl Warren." And the "Wanted For Treason" circulars distributed in Dallas that day; they showed Kennedy in profile and front view, like the "wanted" posters on bulletin boards in post offices. Well, he was not unaware of the hostility toward him in Dallas, and for that very reason, he had insisted on going there, disregarding the warnings of his friends, some of whom expressed deep apprehension. It echoed now in a congressman's jape, "Well, I'm taking a chance. I didn't bring my bulletproof vest."

He cupped his hand on his wife's elbow, assisting her into the limousine. She sat in the rear on the left, with her husband on her right. Nellie Connally, a Texas beauty, took the jump seat in front of Mrs. Kennedy. The Governor jackknifed his long, lean frame into the jump seat in front of the President. William R. Greer, a Secret Service agent, was behind the wheel, and his boss on the trip, Roy Kellerman, took the other front seat.

Those assigned to vehicles following the President and Vice-President quickly took their places. Once a motorcade starts moving, you are either on board or left behind.

A Presidential motorcade is organized so as to attempt to reconcile two conflicting purposes—to provide the President with the maximum amount of exposure to spectators, while minimizing the danger inherent in this. The one in Dallas conformed to that pattern, except that Kennedy himself, in two aspects, reduced the normal safeguards set up to provide a little protection.

This was the lineup of vehicles: motorcycle police—pilot car—command car—Presidential limousine—Secret Service security car, or "follow-up"—Vice-Presidential car —"follow-up" car—VIP car—"wire car"—buses and other cars—motorcycle police.

The pilot car held a position about a quarter-mile ahead of the command car. The detectives riding in it were to watch for any sign of trouble ahead. Moreover, when the pilot car came into view, the policemen patrolling the route would know approximately how soon the President would pass. They tensed up when they saw the pilot car, and the plainclothesmen mingling in the crowds became doubly alert.

Next in line came the command car. It stayed about five car-lengths ahead of the Presidential limousine. In case the lead vehicles reported signs of trouble ahead, orders would be radioed from the command car on the necessary measures to be taken. Jesse Curry, the Dallas Chief of Police, was driving. Sorrels and Lawson, of the Secret Service, and Dallas County Sheriff J. E. Decker, manned the command car.

Kennedy's car followed it. In compliance with his orders, no Secret Service agents were riding on the small running boards in the rear and on each side of him. Maximum exposure. Further, Kennedy dispensed with another precaution in the interests of being seen; he ordered two motorcycle policemen, who normally would have been riding beside his position in the car, to stay a little behind him. The human shield, a Secret Service agent and a motorcycle policeman, would have interfered in some degree with the view of a man sighting a rifle from an upper floor in the Book Building. But it wasn't there that day.

An arsenal rode behind the President in the next car. An automatic rifle and a shotgun lay on the floor. Each of the six Secret Service agents carried a .38 caliber pistol. This was a follow-up car.

If the President stopped, or if the police should be unable to restrain the crowds, the agents in the follow-up car would quickly surround the President's limousine, facing outward toward the people. These agents are physically tough, quick as cats, and they have no choice but to unhesitatingly strong-arm citizens who may be merely trying to get out of their path.

All the agents and policemen have orders to scan the upper floor windows of buildings along the route, watching for bombs, hand grenades, or even a hurtling flowerpot. In the spring of 1958, the Secret Service uncovered a plot to kill President Eisenhower in this fashion. Grenades were to be lobbed into his car from the windows of a building. The agents traced two grenades to a post office box rented under a fictitious name. (Another Oswald?) The city where the attempt was to have been made never has been identified.

Lyndon Johnson's car came next in line. He sat on the right with Mrs. Johnson in the middle and Senator Yarborough on the left. The Vice-Presidential follow-up car rode close behind Johnson, and the duties of the agents in it were identical with those in the Presidential follow-up.

In the hope that some Presidential luster will rub off on them, congressmen and local politicians insist on being as close as possible to him in a motorcade. Theirs is the VIP car.

The "wire car" is provided for the use of reporters for the principal wire services, the Associated Press and United Press International. The pressure for speed on these reporters is far more acute than it is on newspaper staffmen, whose next deadline may be hours away. Minutes, and even fractions of minutss, may be critical in the intense competition between the two wire services. So the "wire car" is equipped with a radio telephone that is cradled beneath the dash board. Theoretically, a reporter can pick it up, give the operator the number of his office, and be dictating in a matter of seconds. Theoretically, he doesn't monopolize the phone, holding it longer than necessary to get a bigger jump on his opposition. The reporters in the "wire car" that day were Jack Bell of The Associated Press and Merriman Smith of United Press International. They had a healthy respect for each other.

In the remainder of the procession in Dallas came the cars and buses carrying photographers, the main body of reporters, and White House aides. More motorcycle policemen brought up the rear.

Radio communication was the nexus for the whole lengthy procession.

At approximately 11:50, the police sirens snarled, and the motorcade rolled out from Love Field into Mockingbird Lane.

At that moment in the advertising department of the Dallas *Morning News*, a sleazy character who called himself Jack Ruby was writing the ads himself for his two nude-girl emporia, the Carousel in downtown Dallas and the Vegas farther out. James P. Hosty, Jr., of the FBI, was staking out a good place on Main Street to see the President. Marina Oswald, watching the scenes on television, saw the motorcade leave the airfield. A tremendous throng, ten and twelve deep, probably the largest to greet Kennedy in Texas, massed on both sides of the parade route. The workmen in the Book Building prepared to go downstairs for a quick lunch before the President's car slowed to negotiate the sharp turn from Houston Street into Elm, directly in front of the building. A man named Abraham Zapruder, standing across the street, checked his movie camera. He wanted very much to have some good footage on the President and Mrs. Kennedy for his film library at home. The frames of film would soon capture

51

an historic tragedy and become a vital segment in the effort to fix responsibility for it.

And Lee Oswald, left alone on the sixth floor, was now free to arrange the cartons for concealment and for a rifle rest, reassemble the Italian carbine, and quietly raise a window.

Dallas at high noon, November 22, 1963.

6

In the first mile or so along the route, only clusters of people stood on the curbs waiting to see the President, a handful here, a handful there. To the professional crowd-watchers in the motorcade, Kennedy's people and the political writers, they appeared neither friendly nor unfriendly. The point was that they were few in numbers. Was Dallas about to give Kennedy the back of its hand?

A group of girls at the intersection of Lomo Alto and Lemmon streets held a homemade sign, and when they saw the caravan approaching, they began waving it, frantically. The sign read, "Please, Mr. President, stop and shake our hands." It caught Kennedy's eye. He grinned and told Greer to stop the car. Instantly, Kellerman stepped out of the front seat, and the agents in the follow-up car surrounded the limousine, although the potentiality of danger from a covey of schoolgirls was almost nil. The girls, shrieking, reached past the agents, clutching at the President's hands, while others ran to the left side of the car and tried to touch his wife's. He was in his element. And as a politician with a keen sense of newspaper values, he was aware that the photographers were snapping pictures that would look good in the late editions of the afternoon papers. It may have reminded him of a similar photograph taken in Michigan on a rainy day during the 1960 campaign. Running behind schedule as usual, he had told his lieutenants at the airport to get him into town as rapidly as possible. The car was starting to accelerate on the highway when he saw a placard waved by a man standing in front of a supermarket. The sign read, "Shake my hand, and you've got my vote." The driver hit the brakes, and the car, careening on the wet concrete, skidded to a stop. Kennedy, without hat or coat, walked through the downpour and gripped the man's hand. "Well," he said, "do I get your vote?" The man replied, "You sure do, Senator. Yes, sir." That photograph of the dripping candidate smiling at the sign had made the front pages with the caption, "Jack's singin' in the rain." The girls on the outskirts of Dallas were too young to vote, but they would tell their parents and anyone who would listen that they had shaken hands with the President, and he was just wonderful, and Jackie was even more beautiful than in her pictures. They might not change their parents' opinion of him, but you never knew. . . . Kennedy was overlooking no opportunity to pick up a vote here, another one there, in Texas.

A little farther along the route, he stopped the motorcade a second time. Now it was to speak to a nun shepherding some smaller children.

The agents noted both stops and the times in their logs.

In the Book Building, Charles Givens was retrieving his package of cigarettes on the sixth floor, and Lee Oswald was asking him to close the gates of the elevator when he went downstairs, indicating that he would follow Givens shortly.

Kennedy passed through a sparsely settled part of the city, semi-business, semi-residential. Strings of triangular pennons fluttered in front of the used car lots. A few people turned to look, and some waved. There were others in front of the stores. Beyond were some small dwellings. The procession turned into Turtle Creek Boulevard, passing a green and lovely park on the left and more houses on the right. Still very few spectators. Kenneth O'Donnell, riding with Dave Powers in the follow-up car, felt a pang of apprehension.

It vanished in a wink. Near the City Hall, the edges of a vast throng came into view. The motorcade turned into Main Street, and even O'Donnell, a seasoned politician who was accustomed to crowds, gaped in astonishment. The wide avenue was a seething mass of people packed so tightly that only a narrow channel, slightly left of the center line, remained open. The police were struggling to keep it clear. Those on motorcycles revved up their motors, making them backfire, trying to move people out of the path of the cars. The command car was like an ice-breaker clearing a channel for the limousine. The roaring of thousands upon thousands of Texans drowned out the racket of the motorcycles and echoed and reechoed between the skyscrapers like the pounding of heavy surf. The agents stepped down from the running boards of the follow-up car to walk beside the President and Mrs. Kennedy. Behind them, some excited spectators broke through, nearly stopping the car carrying Lyndon Johnson, his wife, and Yarborough. Rufus Youngblood, another agent, quickly moved to a position between the Vice-President and the people. A teen-aged boy slipped through the police and approached Kennedy's car from the rear. The agents grabbed him and literally hurled him back into the crowd. The storm of applause and excitement was deafening.

O'Donnell had been standing up in the follow-up car but as it neared the turn from Main into Houston, he sat down, relaxing against the jump seat. He felt good. He has recalled his thoughts in the warm glow of that moment: "This proves that the average person in Dallas is no different from people in any other American city"—"They like and respect the President"—"There's a noisy minority against him, but they don't represent Dallas"—"It will be an eye-opener for the polls and some congressmen who think Kennedy is unpopular here when they read about his reception today." Dallas was the climax of an already successful trip through Texas.

The people waiting in Dealey Plaza, standing beside and in front of the Book Building and hanging out of the windows of the Dal-Tex Building and the County Records Building nearby, could not yet see the parade. But the roaring Niagara on Main Street told them it was not far away. Some had followed the President's progress, listening to portable radios, from the time he left Love Field, and they knew he was coming down Main Street. Only minutes now.

Bonnie Rae Williams finished his chicken sandwich on the sixth floor of the Book Building. He thought he was alone there. He wanted to be with his pals when the President passed, and so he went down to the fifth floor.

A number of people in the plaza below could have told Williams the sixth floor was not deserted.

Bob Edwards, a college student temporarily working in Dallas, nudged his companion, Ronald Fischer, a county

54

auditor. "Look at that guy there in that window," he said. He directed Fischer's attention to the southeast corner window on the sixth floor. Fischer saw the man, medium-sized, thin-faced, thinning hair. What struck both Edwards and Fischer as odd was that the man in the window was standing absolutely still. He seemed rigid. Moreover, he was not looking up Houston toward the corner where Kennedy would appear. He was facing to the right of a pine oak tree in front of the Book Building. Edwards and Fischer noticed the stacks of boxes behind the window arranged in a rough semicircle behind the thin-faced man, and Edwards said, jokingly, "I wonder who he's hiding from, crowded in among all those boxes."

The thunder on Main Street, laced with the crackle and backfiring of the motorcycles, came nearer.

The figure in the sixth-floor window also intrigued the curiosity of a young man named Arnold Rowland. He was eighteen, a recent graduate of high school and a recent bridegroom. He said to his wife, Barbara, "Boy, you can't say the Secret Service isn't on the ball. Look at the guy with the rifle up there."

"Where?"

"Right up there."

A commotion in the plaza distracted the attention of the young couple just then. It appeared that a man was having an epileptic seizure. When Rowland looked toward the window again, he could not see the man. He had seen the rifle, almost the whole length of it, from the stock to the end of the long barrel. He recognized it as a high-powered rifle. And he saw that it was equipped with a telescopic sight. The man was holding it diagonally across his chest, in the position called "port arms" on the parade ground.

Only a few feet from the Rowlands there was a policeman. It did not occur to them to call his attention to the figure in the window. They assumed that both men were arms of the law.

The barking motorcycles turned into Houston, and then the pilot car appeared. "Keep back, folks," said a policeman in the plaza. "They're coming."

Howard Brennan, a steam fitter, had seated himself on a low concrete wall directly in front of the Book Building. When he came there, he had noticed the clock on the roof of the building and had synchronized his watch with it: 12:14. The windows had been opened on several floors, and Brennan saw men in them looking down into the

55

plaza. One caught Brennan's attention. He was holding a rifle. The distance from Brennan's position on the wall to the sixth floor of the Book Building would be measured and found to be 120 feet. He would give an accurate description of the man with the rifle.

A fifteen-year-old boy, Amos Euins, also saw him, but he thought the long object was a section of pipe.

Shouting exploded on Houston Street. Slowly rounding the turn came the big blue limousine.

A gust of wind tugged at Jacqueline Kennedy's pink pillbox hat, and she quickly steadied it with her left hand. A zephyr ruffled her husband's thick hair, but he didn't bother to smooth it. The noonday sun made him squint.

"He sure did get himself a Texas tan."

"Look at Jackie's outfit. Isn't she a doll?"

"Hi, Governor!"

"Here comes Lyndon Johnson. Hey, Lyndon!"

Kennedy, Connally, and Mrs. Connally turned their heads to the left, admiring the crowd in the plaza. Everyone in the motorcade thought Main Street would see the end of the crowds, but here was another. Dave Powers, coaching Jacqueline Kennedy in the technique of political parading, had told her she must always face in the direction opposite from where her husband was looking, otherwise the people on one side of the car would see only the backs of their heads. So now she was looking to her right.

Mrs. Jean Lollis Hill aimed a Polaroid camera. "Hey," she cried, "look this way. We want to take your picture."

Slowly down Houston . . . speed, 11.2 miles per hour . . . approaching the Book Building.

Powers saw the clock on top of the Book Building and remarked to O'Donnell that it was almost 12:30, the scheduled time of arrival at the Trade Mart. Not too bad, considering that Kennedy invariably ran late.

The turn from Houston into Elm Street is sharp, almost a u-turn because of a concrete abutment. Greer had to slow for it and spin the wheel hard to the left to negotiate it.

Kellerman also saw the clock and noted in his log, 12:30. From the command car, Forrest Sorrels radioed the Trade Mart that the President would be there in five minutes. Only five more minutes.

James Altgens, an Associated Press photographer, raised his camera, ready to start shooting. Abraham Zapruder touched the trigger on his movie camera, and the motor began whirring.

The limousine passed the tree in front of the Book Building. It started down the slope on Elm Street, heading toward a railroad underpass. Nellie Connally turned and said to Mrs. Kennedy, "We're almost there." She twisted around to her right toward Kennedy and said, "Mr. President, you can't say that Dallas doesn't love you."

"That's very obvious," he replied.

The tree no longer interfered with the view from the sixth floor. The President's car floated, a slow-moving image, into the crosshairs of the telescopic sight. The man in the window put the point where they intersected on the President's head. He would have seen the President, smiling, raise his hand to wave to a small boy on his right.

Then, amid the sounds of shouting and clapping, there was another sound.

A flock of pigeons fluttered upward as one from the roof of the Book Building.

Kennedy clutched his throat convulsively with his left hand. He seemed to stiffen. The smile faded from his face. He canted slightly to his left, toward his wife. Kellerman thought he heard him say, "My God, I'm hit."

Jacqueline Kennedy glanced at her husband. A strange expression came over his face. He swayed slightly. She put her hand on his left arm, just below the shoulder.

Jim Altgens' camera froze the dreadful instant on film . . . the hand at the throat . . . the white glove on his arm . . . two Secret Service agents on the follow-up car looking backward toward the Book Building.

If Kennedy heard the shot at all, he heard it after he was wounded in the back of the neck and throat. The bullet, ripping the air at 1,800 feet per second, outraced the speed of sound.

The many other faces in Altgens' picture reflect no signs of comprehension, no awareness of what has happened. Some Negroes near the main entrance to the Book Building are still smiling. The agents on the left running boards of the follow-up car appear to be scanning the people on the grassy knoll ahead and to the right of them. So do two white-helmeted motorcycle policemen riding just behind the President's car. Lady Bird Johnson, riding in the third car, appears to be looking at the people in and around the pine oak tree. A Negro woman in the window of a building across the street stares toward the upper floors of the

Book Building. A white man leans against a traffic sign on the corner, face upraised, as though something above has attracted his attention, too.

There had been a sound. It is altogether probable that only Kennedy knew the significance of the explosion.

"It sounded like a firecracker"—"a cherry bomb"—"just a kind of a pop"—"It sounded like a cannon"—"It was like the small cannon they shoot off at a football game when they score a touchdown"—"I thought they must be giving him a 21-gun salute."

Connally, Yarborough, Jack Bell, and others who are familiar with hunting rifles were to recall that they immediately identified the explosion as a rifle shot.

Where had it come from?

The sound ricocheted. It bounced between the nearby structures like a hard-hit golf ball. Thus, some would claim it came from the railroad underpass directly ahead of the motorcade. To others, it came from the knoll on the right of the limousine. Connally, two agents in the follow-up car, and a few other persons in the Plaza turned their eyes to the upper floors of the Book Building.

Howard Brennan was one of these. There was the same figure in the sixth floor window. There was the rifle. Brennan saw him take aim. And then—

Crack-bang. Crack-bang.

Perhaps five seconds elapsed after the first shot. The second and third came in quick succession, almost together.

A bullet shattered the upper right side of the President's skull. Blood and bits of brain tissue and bone spattered the car. They even reached Greer and Kellerman in the front seat.

Kennedy slumped to his left, toward his wife. She cradled him in her arms and cried out in agony. "Oh, no! My God, they have shot my husband. Jack! Jack! I love you."

O'Donnell, only a few feet behind the limousine, clearly saw the hideous head wound. He blessed himself. "In the name of the Father, of the Son, and of the Holy Ghost. Amen." He understood at once that he had seen death take the President.

"When he was hit, his face went blank. No smile. No frown. Nothing. He fell over on Jackie's knees. There was blood all over her and everything. I was weak. I had to sit down." Alan Smith, fourteen, had skipped school to see the President, and the limousine was just passing him.

58

In a split second, primeval instincts gripped the witnesses in the plaza and directed their actions, the instinct to flee, to seek shelter, to protect, the instinct simply to scream.

A man pulled a woman in an orange-colored dress to the ground and covered her with his body. Others, like soldiers under artillery fire, pressed themselves against the earth. A man lay on the grass, beating it with his fists, striking back savagely at something he could not see. A woman shrieked, "They're shooting the President from the bushes," and Abraham Zapruder, blinded by tears, was moaning, "They killed him. They killed him." A dazed motorcycle policeman, James Chaney, kept repeating, "His head exploded in blood." Without knowing the direction of the bullets, people sought shelter behind the low concrete wall or the pine oak tree or huddled in doorways. A tall Negro swept a little girl into his arms and ran. Panic drove others to run, fanning out in all directions from the plaza. Those farther back in the motorcade could see the sudden scattering. They had heard the sound of the gunfire, and now they saw men and women, like the pigeons winging upward from the roof of the Book Building, sprinting away from the plaza. Bob Jackson, a Dallas *Times-Herald* photographer, saw something more, the barrel of a rifle being withdrawn from the sixth-floor window. "There's the gun," he gasped.

Unconscious of what she was doing, Jacqueline Kennedy rose in the back seat, climbed to the rear section of the limousine, and began crawling on hands and knees, reaching for something. She would never remember what it was nor why she was doing this. Of all the horrors to be inflicted on her, this at least would be blotted from memory and buried deep in her subconscious.

She might have fallen beneath the wheels of the follow-up car and been killed or seriously injured. For in the same fraction of a second, Kellerman said to Greer, "Let's get out of here. We're hit." He stood erect, microphone in hand, and radioed to the command car, "We're hit. Get us to a hospital immediately." The limousine was in low gear. Greer jammed the accelerator to the floorboard, and the car leaped forward in a surge of power.

This sudden burst of speed almost certainly would have pulled the President's wife off the back of the car but for the lightning-fast reflexes of Clint Hill, the agent riding on the left front running board of the follow-up car. At the sound of the shots, Hill instinctively jumped, raced toward the rear running board of the President's car, and grabbed the handhold. His foot missed the running board, but he hung on against the strong acceleration and pulled himself up towards Mrs. Kennedy. His hand touched hers. Hill pushed her back into the seat and sat above her on the top of the seat to shield her. She stared at him with a pleading expression in her luminous dark eyes. Through some telepathy, Hill understood. He took off his coat and draped it over the President's head.

Another agent, Rufus Youngblood, also reacted instantly to the sound of the shots. He was in the front seat of the Vice-President's car. He reached back, struck Johnson smartly on the shoulder, and snapped, "Get down." Then Youngblood threw himself into the back seat, pushed Johnson down, and sat on him.

In the President's car, John Connally felt something strike him in the back. It felt as though a strong man with a big fist had hit him. He did not hear the sound of the shot, and at first, he felt no pain. Then he saw blood oozing through his shirt, and the red stain spreading to his belt line. "Oh, no, no, no," he shouted. "They're going to kill us all." Nellie Connally pulled him into her lap, not knowing whether he had been killed. When she saw him move, she said, "It's all right. Be still."

They both heard the sound of the slug shattering Kennedy's head. Blood flecked their clothing.

In response to Kellerman's message to the command car, Jesse Curry radioed to the pilot car, "Go to the hospital. Parkland Hospital. Have them stand by." Seconds later, Curry again spoke into the transmitter. "It looks like the President has been hit. Have Parkland stand by." The radioed reply, words gurgling through a metallic larynx, told him, "They have been notified."

The lead cars in the motorcade raced beneath the railroad underpass and swept onto Stemmons Freeway. Sirens shrieked. The hospital was about four miles from the point where the bullets struck down Kennedy. Faster! Faster! At the peak speed, Greer must have been doing between 70 and 80 miles per hour, and he could not have slowed very much on the curves, for at 12:35, he brought the limousine to a lurching stop at the emergency entrance of Parkland. Lyndon Johnson's car came right behind it. The reporters in the "wire car" were out and running before it stopped.

Connally, still conscious but in agony now, had to be taken from the jump seat before the President could be removed. He summoned a reserve of strength to help the attendants as they lifted him and shouldered him to a stretcher. Mrs. Connally and then Mrs. Kennedy leaped out.

Gently, yet with swift expertise, the hospital attendants lifted the President's long, muscular body and transferred him to the wheeled stretcher. Clint Hill's coat covered the lacerated head. Jack Bell mentally noted that Kennedy's business suit was scarcely rumpled.

"Is he dead?" Bell asked, speaking to a Secret Service agent.

"I don't know, but I don't think so."

In the front seat of the blue limousine, a soft felt hat, which Kennedy seldom wore, lay beside the Governor's light gray Texas rancher's hat. A tattered cluster of asters was on the floor of the back seat, and three roses, twisted and torn, lay in a pool of blood.

The mind could record the scene like a movie camera. But the enormity of its meaning, and the shocking suddenness, placed it beyond comprehension, beyond acceptance.

Only a little more than five minutes earlier, Kennedy had been pulsing with life, his bronzed features aglow with pleasure and satisfaction over his reception in Dallas. His russet brown hair had gleamed in the sunshine. He had been smiling and waving to the people in Dealey Plaza, and the last wave was for a small boy there. Now the Dallas parade would have been over, completed without incident, without any of the ugly incidents that Lyndon Johnson and Adlai Stevenson had encountered in the city. Now for the luncheon speech at the Trade Mart; it was mordant, but the atmosphere seemed right for it. If Jackie had told him she would need a few minutes to "organize herself" before taking her place at the head table, so much the better; he could repeat the line that tickled the men in the parking lot at Fort Worth and add, "Nobody notices what Lyndon and I wear." When he felt good, as he did now, his humor was an artesian well. Yes, it had been a good day, a fine day, so far. *Allons voir si les roses sont rouges.*

Barely more than five minutes ago. . . .

And now only a pale spark of life flickered, and Jacqueline Kennedy's roses were stained with a darker red.

The brutal, frightening word about the gunfire in Deal-

61

ey Plaza swiftly reached the world outside Dallas. When the reporters in the "wire car" heard the rifle crack, they instantly recognized the sound for what it was. It was Merriman Smith's luck to be riding in the front seat with the radio telephone close at hand. (They alternated places at each stop, and Jack Bell was to have been up front on the return drive to Love Field.) Smith grabbed the transmitter and quickly reached his office. He began dictating. All he knew was that shots had been fired, not that Kennedy had been wounded, but even this was news of transcendent importance. He dictated three sentences. To Bell, frantic to get the phone and report to his office, this was an eternity. No doubt, in the interests of accuracy, and also to keep Bell from using the phone for as long as possible, Smith then said, "Did you get that? Read it back to me. I can't hear you." At that point, what the correspondents were to describe as "some jostling" broke out in the car. The struggle over the phone might have caused a serious accident, for by that time, the driver was gunning the motor for all it was worth, trying to overtake the speeding Presidential car. Smith, knowing his bulletin was well away, finally surrendered the transmitter. Bell's cup of gall and wormwood now overflowed; the operator rang his Dallas office, but before he could speak to anyone, the phone went dead.

Bell could not know it, but the word of the shooting, and worse than that, already had reached the AP's Dallas bureau.

Jim Altgens, the photographer, had run to a telephone after making his pictures and seeing Kennedy's car hurtle down Elm Street. Robert Johnson, the Dallas chief of bureau, took Altgens' call.

Altgens gasped, "Bob, the President has been shot!"

"What? How do you know?"

"I saw it. There was blood on his face. Mrs. Kennedy jumped up and grabbed him and cried, 'Oh, no!' And then the motorcade raced out on the freeway."

"You saw that?" Johnson already had rolled a sheet of paper in his typewriter and was writing.

"Yes. I was shooting pictures, and I saw it. If I could have turned away, I would have."

"Bulletin," Johnson yelled.

Across the main trunk wires, breaking in on reports partially transmitted, came the dreadful words:

BULLETIN

DALLAS, NOV. 22 (AP)—PRESIDENT KEN-
NEDY WAS SHOT TODAY JUST AS HIS MO-
TORCADE LEFT DOWNTOWN DALLAS. MRS.
KENNEDY JUMPED UP AND GRABBED MR.
KENNEDY. SHE CRIED, "OH, NO!" THE MO-
TORCADE SPED ON.

From Parkland Hospital, Bell telephoned Johnson, who read the bulletin to him. No time had been lost, and the inexorable wire service demand for speed had been satisfied.

Peter Lisagor, of the Chicago *Daily News,* also was having telephone trouble. Rushing into the hospital, he asked the receptionist near the front entrance if she would call Chicago for him. She tried. But, blinded by tears, she could only fumble with the dial while sobbing, "Why Dallas? Why Dallas?"

But for all the swiftness of teletypes and telephones, they were not the first to convey the fearful news to the world outside Dallas. In New York, a shortwave radio expert was twisting the dials of his equipment. Suddenly he heard a mystifying conversation:

"Is he hit bad?"

"He's dead."

"What! How do you know?"

"I saw the side of his head blown off."

Then the radio went dead. This must have taken place in the last minute or so before the President's limousine reached the dock at Parkland Hospital. The man in New York had accidentally tuned in on the frequency used by the Secret Service during the motorcade. He telephoned a friend on a New York newspaper and asked if the paper had any news of an incident involving Kennedy in Dallas. To his immense relief, he was advised that the President was about to begin speaking at the Trade Mart luncheon.

Meanwhile, the surgeons were making the first swift moves in a battle that could not be won.

Dr. Malcolm Perry was having lunch in the cafeteria when he heard himself paged, along with the word "stat." At Parkland, it meant "emergency" a twice-told tale there, as it is in most hospitals. But when Perry answered the telephone, he was told, "The President has been shot. They are taking him into Trauma One now." This is an emergency room where persons are taken who have been severely injured or who are at the point of death from an illness. The news about the President spread like wildfire through the hospital. Perry ran down the corridor toward the Trauma rooms.

Trauma One is small, windowless, with gray tiles. When the surgeon burst through the doors, he saw the President on the wheeled stretcher in the center of the room. He had already been stripped to the waist. His shoes had been removed, but not the steel brace that supported his back. Perry ripped off his plaid jacket and let it fall on the floor. Nurses snapped the surgical gloves on his hands.

Another surgeon, Dr. Charles James Carrico, had preceded Perry. He was already setting up the procedure designed to help the stricken man's breathing. In the next few minutes, 12 doctors, all specialists, crowded into Trauma One.

The President's eyes were open, pupils dilated, but not focused and not reacting to light. Beneath the tan, his color was ashy-blue. Carrico heard sounds in his chest which he took to be weak heart beats. Slight reflexive movements of the chest and abdominal muscles seemed to indicate the effort to breathe.

The odds against saving Kennedy's life were overwhelming, and they all knew it.

In Trauma Two, surgeons and attendants were preparing the Governor for surgery. They found multiple wounds, the most dangerous one in his chest.

Lyndon Johnson entered Parkland close behind the two stretchers. He appeared to be clutching his chest with one hand. The reporters, remembering his heart attack in 1955, gasped when they saw him. Perhaps in the excitement, he had been stricken a second time. The odd position of his arm and hand also gave rise to an erroneous report that he had been wounded. In fact, he was physically all right.

Rufus Youngblood, the agent who had forced Johnson to take cover in the motorcade, was concerned about the potentialities, wide and frightening, of the gunfire in Dallas. Nobody yet knew who had shot at the motorcade. Or why. Were the events in the city a first step in a conspiracy, activating a plot to overthrow the government of the United States? If so, the Vice-President now became the prime target of the assassins. Youngblood hastened Johnson and his wife into another room in the hospital and drew the blinds. He curtly refused to permit Johnson to go into the corridor to see Jacqueline Kennedy and inquire about the condition of the President.

The possibility of a conspiracy caused one of the most untoward incidents of November 22. A man in a business suit attempted to enter Trauma One. A Secret Service agent slugged him, and he crumpled on the floor, yanking from his pocket his credentials as an agent of the FBI.

Mrs. Kennedy had followed the stretcher into Trauma One. She had seen the worst, and whatever might come now, she determined to remain near her husband. Dr. Kemp Clark, a neurosurgeon, noticed her and said softly, "We could make you comfortable in a room where you can rest."

"No," she said firmly. "No, thank you."

A chair was found and placed just outside the doors of the room. The ordeal of waiting began for her.

7

Jacqueline Kennedy huddled on a chair, a forlorn, crumpled figure, clothes splotched with her husband's blood. The chair had been placed in the corridor to the left of the doors of Trauma One. Inside, the ancient struggle of man against death was approaching its climax. She was dry-eyed. She appeared to be dazed, but she wasn't. She was listening to the sounds behind the doors. So long as the low-toned voices of the specialists came to her from inside the room, she could cling to a thread of hope. The voices, terse and urgent, would tell her that her husband was still alive.

"Adrenal insufficiency . . . the hydrocortisone is here."

The weather in Washington was clear and warm, a fine autumn day, and the rhythms of government slowed, as they usually do when the President is out of town. Moreover, six members of his Cabinet were absent too, flying to Japan. It was, so it seemed in the capital, the beginning of a long, quiet weekend. On Capitol Hill, Edward M. Kennedy, the youngest member of the Senate, was presiding over a half-empty chamber and a droning discussion of Federal library services. Teddy in the Senate, Bob in the Justice Department, Jack in the White House. The distance between these three buildings is about a mile, and somebody had dubbed it "the Kennedys' miracle mile." Democratic politicians, reading newspaper reports of the Texas reception for the President, breathed easier. The front pages in Washington featured another interesting political tidbit: The Attorney General said he did not plan to resign in order to manage the President's campaign for reelection in 1964. "Right now, I plan to stay on this job at least through the election," he said. "I'm not sure what will happen after that. Of course, something could happen between now and then. . . ."

Jacqueline Kennedy heard the voices, "Blood, type O-negative . . . getting a faint pulse."

Could it be? Could it possibly be that he will live? She rose from the chair and entered the emergency room. They were doing something to his throat. She remembered that he had clutched his throat in the car. And they were operating some kind of hand-pump with rubber tubes. They were working over him and that meant he was still alive. She returned to the corridor and the anguish of waiting.

The silver and blue jetliner carrying the six Cabinet members and their wives was almost two hours west of Honolulu and about 1,200 miles from Wake Island. Dean Rusk, the Secretary of State, was in the forward compartment, the area normally reserved for the President. The plane was so equipped that if necessary, the Secretary could speak directly to Washington. Pierre Salinger opened his attaché case and drew out a document on economic relations with Japan. He found it heavy going. His thoughts drifted to another task. Kennedy was considering an official visit to Japan. But remembering Eisenhower's experience, the last-minute cancellation after the President had reached Manila, he was withholding a decision until he had more information. Salinger was to take some discreet soundings.

"Tracheotomy tray. . . . Here, I'll hand it to you."

Dr. Perry's first objective was to reconstruct an airway to assist the President's breathing. The throat wound, about the circumference of a pencil, was conveniently situated, and he began the tracheotomy there, enlarging the hole and then making an incision in the windpipe. The green

66

line on the cardiotachyscope quivered, indicating a slight heart action, and the doctors detected a weak pulse in Kennedy's neck and wrist.

"Bennett machine . . . oxygen".

In the darkened room across the corridor, Lyndon Johnson, Lady Bird, and the Secret Service agents waited in silence. For all they knew, both Kennedy and John Connally might be dead, and a monstrous conspiracy to seize the government might be in motion. Kenneth O'Donnell entered and spoke with Johnson, but he knew even less about the condition of the President than Jacqueline Kennedy listening intently to the words coming from Trauma One.

"Infusions . . . chest tubes."

The tubes were inserted to siphon off blood and air in the chest cavity. At the same time, slits were opened in the President's left arm and right leg for infusions of blood and saline solution. He had lost an enormous quantity of blood, perhaps as much as two quarts. A great dark pool of blood covered the floor.

With swift, expert hands, they were doing all they could to save his life, although, except in the strict medical sense, he already was dead.

Jacqueline Kennedy again came into the emergency room and stood, wordless, watching everything. They offered her a sedative, but she refused.

And now the reporters who had been riding in the press bus, too far back in the motorcade to know what had happened, came storming into the hospital. The bus had gone to the Trade Mart, as scheduled, and they learned there that Kennedy and the Governor had both been wounded. No doubt prompted by wishful thinking, the first report at the Trade Mart was that the President's condition was not serious. At the hospital, they crowded into a nurses' classroom, and Malcolm Kilduff, the White House Assistant Press Secretary, came there in answer to their shouted demands. Is he badly wounded? Is he dying? Is he dead? Kilduff could only mumble, "I can't say. I just can't say."

Only minutes had elapsed since the shattering explosions on Elm Street, but in such moments, time has no meaning. It all seemed long ago.

At "Hickory Hill," Robert Kennedy's estate in Virginia, the telephone rang. He was in a luncheon conference with Robert Morgenthau, United States Attorney for the Southern District of New York, and Morgenthau's chief deputy,

Silvio Mollo. Since the weather was so pleasant, the luncheon table had been set up in the patio, and they sat in the sunshine munching tuna sandwiches. Ethel Kennedy answered the telephone and said her husband was in conference. The operator replied that the call was urgent—J. Edgar Hoover. The Attorney General picked up the extension phone beside the swimming pool. His wife saw him press his hand over his mouth, compulsively, and his eyes widen with horror. She hurried to him. A long moment passed before he could speak. Then, choking out the words, he said, "Jack's been shot. It may be fatal." She put her arms around him.

In the Senate press gallery, Richard Riedel, press liaison officer, was looking at the AP teleprinter. Suddenly it coughed, chattering unevenly, and the bulletin from Dallas broke into the news story that had been moving. Riedel ripped the copy from the machine and raced down to the Senate floor. He first encountered Senators Wayne Morse of Oregon and Spessard Holland of Florida and said, "The AP says the President's been shot in Dallas." He hurried to the dais and whispered to Teddy Kennedy. Without a word, Kennedy swept up a handful of papers and fled the chamber.

On the jetliner streaking across the Pacific, Salinger was doggedly trying to digest the report on Japanese-American trade relations when he was summoned to the forward compartment. He found the other cabinet members there with the Secretary of State, Douglas Dillon of the Treasury, Orville Freeman of Agriculture, Stewart Udall of Interior, Luther Hodges of Commerce, and Willard Wirtz of Labor. Rusk was holding a sheet of yellow paper. Salinger recognized it as teleprinter copy. The teleprinter was part of the miraculous communications equipment on the plane.

The words were badly garbled, little better than hieroglyphics, but they told only too much. Shots had been fired at Kennedy in Dallas.

The machine stuttered out more words. KENNEDY WOUNDED. . . . PERHAPS SERIOUSLY WOUNDED. . . . PERHAPS FATALLY WOUNDED.

The fateful progression, the inexorable descent into darkness.

Orville Freeman quickly offered a thought that might help. "A man can live when he is shot through the head," he said. "I ought to know." He had been an officer in the

68

Marines in the Pacific during World War II, and a sniper's bullet had left him speechless in the hospital for eight months.

They nodded. They wanted to believe him.

Salinger said the plane should turn back immediately. Rusk agreed but said he wanted more information from the White House. Salinger went at once to the communications cabin. In a matter of seconds, across nearly 6,000 miles of water and land, he was speaking with the White House Situation Room. He used his code name and the President's. "This is Wayside," he said. "Can you give me the latest situation on Lancer?"

The distant voice verified the report that had reached them on the plane that Kennedy and Connally had been wounded. Nothing more.

Salinger said the plane would return to Honolulu and asked to be kept advised of any further information from Dallas.

Father Oscar L. Huber, pastor of the Holy Trinity Church in Dallas, had gone to the corner of Lemmon and Reagan streets, three blocks from his rectory, to see the President pass. He had shared the pleasure of the nuns and schoolchildren gathered there. Only a few minutes later, the shocking report came to the rectory, where he was sitting down to lunch. "Shooting on Elm Street. . . . Kennedy crumpled toward his wife. . . . there was a wild dash to Parkland Hospital." The hospital was in Father Huber's parish, and a Catholic President might need him. He went upstairs to get his purple stole—and the holy oil, in case (the unthinkable) it should become necessary to administer the last sacrament. Another priest, the Reverend James Thompson, jumped into the car with Father Huber, and they started for the hospital. Perhaps, in the excitement, the report had been exaggerated. In moments of stress, people so easily become confused. Yes, that could be the explanation.

Marina Oswald had been watching the events on television. She could not understand when the excited words, the broken phrases, half-gasped, came over the air. Ruth Paine translated. Next came the staccato report that sent a tingle of horror through Marina. The shots were believed to have been fired from the Texas Book Depository Building. Without a word, Marina ran out to the garage. The green and brown blanket lay on the floor in the usual place. She did not look inside it.

A motorcycle policeman burst into the Book Building, drawing his gun as he came through the doors. Roy Truly followed him. Both elevators were upstairs somewhere. The policeman didn't wait. He raced up the steps. On the second floor, he found a man beside a vending machine, a bottle of pop in his hand. Lee Harvey Oswald looked utterly composed, blank-faced, as though he had seen nothing, heard nothing, and was totally unaware of the turmoil just outside the building.

The officer, pistol in hand, advanced toward him. To Truly, he snapped, "Does this man belong here?"

"Yes. He works here."

They left Oswald and began climbing the stairs, rushing to the roof.

In the hospital, the moments ticked away.

Dr. Perry, hoping to stimulate heart action, was massaging the President's chest. He clenched his fist and rolled it back and forth, back and forth. If only the fluttering pulse would steady and grow stronger. . . .

Only a few yards away, surrounded by Secret Service agents, Lyndon Johnson and his wife stood beside the wall, waiting. Time had stopped. Only driblets of information came to them.

Then Emory Roberts of the White House detail, as Johnson would recall later, entered and told them he understood Kennedy was sinking. Roberts advised a speedy departure for Washington. Johnson asked about Connally and was told that he too had been wounded but that his condition was not serious. Neither Mrs. Kennedy nor Mrs. Connally had been hit, the agent said. Johnson asked if he could see them. Rufus Youngblood told the Vice-President he could not leave the room.

Under the enormous strain of uncertainty, uncertainty about the meaning and sinister potentialities of the attack, Johnson thought about his daughters. "Tell the children to get a Secret Service man with them," he said.

Kenneth O'Donnell came into the room. His bleak, pinched expression warned them before he spoke that he had all but abandoned hope. "It's very, very serious," he said, "in my opinion, probably fatal. I haven't been able to get a definite opinion. As soon as I can, I'll let you know."

Johnson asked, "How about Mrs. Kennedy."

O'Donnell said she had stationed herself just outside the emergency room. She would not budge from there. Johnson had considered the advisability of getting away from the hospital, but now he said, "I don't want to go off and leave Mrs. Kennedy in that state." O'Donnell nodded and went out to rejoin Jacqueline Kennedy.

At that point, since he could not leave the room, Johnson told his wife to go and see "Jackie and Nellie."

Lady Bird's memories of these last moments have been recorded in a statement she dictated, partly to relieve her own emotions and also for the use of the Warren Commission. It reads:

> People came and went—Kenny O'Donnell, Congressman Thornberry, Congressman Jack Brooks. Always there was Rufe right there, Emory Roberts, Jack Kivett, Lem Johns and Woody Taylor. There was talk about where we would go—back to Washington, to the plane, to our house. People spoke how widespread this may be. Through it all, Lyndon was remarkably calm and quiet. Every face that came in, you searched for the answers you must know. I think the face I kept seeing it on was the face of Kenneth O'Donnell, who loved him so much.
>
> It was Lyndon who thought of it first, although I wasn't going to leave without doing it. He said, 'You had better see if you can see Jackie and Nellie.' We didn't know what had happened to John. I asked the Secret Service if I could be taken to them. They began to lead me up one corridor, backstairs, and down another.
>
> Suddenly, I found myself face to face with Jackie in a small hall. I think it was right outside the operating room. You always think of her—or someone like her—as being insulated, protected; she was quite alone. I don't think I ever saw anyone so much alone in my life. I went up to her, put my arms around her and said something to her. I am sure it was something like, "God help us all," because my feelings for her were too tumultuous to put into words.

Reporters saw Mrs. Johnson. Remembering the odd position of his arm when he entered the hospital, apparently clutching his chest, they called to her, "How's Lyndon?" "He's fine," she said. The Secret Service agents pushed them away before they could ask further questions. They had been told that Connally's condition was "good, but

71

he's not out of the woods," that the President was "alive but in critical condition."

It was 12:57.

In Trauma One, the specialists saw no further activity on the cardiotachyscope. The spectral green bar stood still, straight and still. Kennedy's heart had stopped.

Perry paid no attention. He continued the chest massage. Clark said, "It's too late, Mac."

They shut off the valves of the oxygen machine. Too late for oxygen, too late for infusions, too late for surgical skills. Perry stepped back from the table. His arms dropped, and his fist opened. They brought a clean sheet and shrouded the still form from head to toe. Since the head wound was certified as the cause of death, it fell to the neurosurgeon, Dr. Clark, to certify the time of death. He fixed it at 1:00 P.M.

Jacqueline Kennedy entered. She walked with a firm step, shoulders rigid, head high, a Roman matron, stony-faced against the ancient sorrow of widowhood. She approached the table. The sheet was withdrawn from her husband's face. She knelt and clasped his right hand in hers. She heard Father Huber's voice intoning the rite of absolution: *"Si vivis, ego te absolvo a peccatis tuis.* If you are living, I absolve you from your sins. In the name of the Father and of the Son and of the Holy Ghost." With holy oil, he traced the sign of the cross on the cold forehead. "Eternal rest, grant unto him, O Lord."

Jacqueline Kennedy responded, "And let perpetual light shine on him."

She rose to her feet. She had slipped her wedding ring from her finger. Now she placed it on his lifeless hand. Ten years had passed since the day when he, all thumbs, had placed it on hers. "With this ring I thee wed, in death as in life." She stood looking at his face, and then she turned away, and they covered it with the sheet.

"I am sorry," said Father Huber. "You have my deepest sympathy."

"Thank you."

"I am convinced that his soul had not left his body. This was a valid last sacrament."

"Thank you for taking care of the President."

It was finished, irrevocably ended, her ten years of marriage, his 1,037 days in the White House, the unforgettable Kennedy Era.

8

First, there is shock. Grief comes after the numbness of shock, as pain comes after the anesthetic wears off. It is possible to act, to behave adequately on a reflexive level of consciousness while one is still stunned by overwhelming tragedy, to do what must be done without looking back.

And so it was in that numbing moment for the men at Parkland Hospital, the men in Washington, the men in the airplane high over the Pacific, the people who had been close to John F. Kennedy, and those on the perimeter of his world, the reporters, many of whom, while professionally critical at times, nonetheless held him in deep affection. The time for grief was not yet. Mechanically, almost like robots, they moved to discharge inescapable duties. Emergency measures must be taken, if indeed a conspiracy, directed from within or without the nation, was afoot. The Vice-President must be shielded and safely returned to Washington. The Cabinet must be called into session. The American people and the world must be notified. The Armed Forces must be alerted. Sorrow must wait.

Father Huber emerged from the hospital and walked toward his car. A group of reporters surrounded him, and they asked one question, "Is he dead?"

Sadly, the priest nodded. "Yes," he said. "He is dead."

His words set off another flurry of bulletins. The report was not official of course. Mechanically, as they dictated, the reporters noted this. The official word would come from a member of the White House staff.

In a sense, the official word already had gone out.

Clint Hill, of the White House detail, obtained the address of a funeral home not far from the hospital. He telephoned and found himself speaking to the undertaker, Vernon B. Oneal. "This is a legitimate call," Hill said. "Load a coffin into your hearse, get a police escort, and get over to Parkland as fast as humanly possible. *It's for the President of the United States.*"

The urgency in Hill's voice dispelled any fleeting thought that the call might be a macaber jest, the work of a Kennedy-hating crank. Hearing the words, anyone in Oneal's position would have been startled, and perhaps for this reason, he automatically said what he would have said in response to a routine call for a casket, "What type of casket do you want?"

"The best you have."

O'Donnell brought the word to Johnson. "He's gone," he said. There was no further reason for Johnson to remain in the hospital. "You ought to get out of here as fast as possible," O'Donnell said. Johnson again asked about Mrs. Kennedy. Would she leave with them? Dully, O'Donnell said she would not leave until her husband's body could be taken to the plane, that on no account would she leave "Jack" behind. Again, the specter of conspiracy grimaced in the darkened room. Dallas seemed electric with danger. Johnson must be spirited out of the city at once. Briefly, they considered moving "Air Force One" and "Air Force Two" to the Strategic Air Command base at Carswell, thus evading the snipers who might be posted on the route to Love Field. But the plan would have involved more complications, and possibly greater danger, therefore, than making a dash for the Dallas airport. "I am in your hands," Johnson said to O'Donnell.

Whether they discussed which plane Johnson should take would remain unclear. In Johnson's recollection, it was agreed that he should fly to Washington in "Air Force One," the Presidential aircraft. O'Donnell would recall no such discussion. The tensions inevitably inherent in the transfer of power were to be aggravated by this misunderstanding, trivial as it may seem against the enormity of the assassination.

O'Donnell left Johnson. Outside in the corridor, Malcolm Kilduff was waiting for him. Kilduff asked whether he should now notify the reporters, who were clamoring for information, that the President had died. Or would O'Donnell tell them?

"You're going to have to make the announcement," O'Donnell replied. "But you'd better check it with Johnson."

Kilduff was taken to the Vice-President. Johnson said he should make the announcement, but on second thought, since nobody knew what lay behind the shooting, he in-

74

structed Kilduff to withhold it until he and Mrs. Johnson had left the hospital for Love Field.

It was about 1:20.

Measures imposing unusually tight security had been in effect at the airport for nearly an hour by that time. The agents and police there, having heard the radioed exchanges between the agents in the motorcade at the moment of the shooting, had taken immediate action. Several thousand people had gathered to see the President's departure. The radioed reports from downtown Dallas brought many more. All were cleared from the buildings and the parking lots nearby. The area bristled with guns. Tension gripped the guards. For all they knew, the next attack might strike at the airport.

In Parkland, they were ready to leave. Outside the hospital, two unmarked police cars waited, motors idling. Jesse Curry, the Chief of Police, sat behind the wheel of one car. A group of agents surrounded the Vice-President, another group shielded Lady Bird, hustling them through the corridor to the hospital doors.

Youngblood, fully in charge, directed the Vice-President into the car with Curry. He put Mrs. Johnson into the second car. He ordered Johnson to sit on the floor, below window level. He put Representative Homer Thornberry in the front seat beside Curry and stationed himself in back, shielding Johnson. Just as the car started to move out, Representative Albert Thomas pounded on the door. They opened it and put him in the back seat. Johnson was now completely covered. A bullet would have to pass through a screen of bodies before it could strike him. Ringed with motorcycle policemen, the cars swept out of the hospital driveway. Parkland Hospital, forever marked in history now, faded out of sight.

Kilduff watched until the cars reached the freeway. Seeing him, the reporters crowded around, demanding information. He pushed through them, and they followed him to the classroom where the others, the majority, were waiting.

It was 1:33 when he entered the room.

His eyes were red and swollen. An unlit cigarette trembled in one hand. The other held a slip of paper. He glanced at it and read the terse communiqué:

"President John F. Kennedy died at approximately 1 P.M. Central Standard Time today here in Dallas. He died of a gunshot wound in the brain."

The words, stark and brutally direct, seemed imprinted in the air.

In seconds, they reached the communications cabin on the airplane racing toward Honolulu. They came in the form of a message addressed to Pierre Salinger. It read:

"Situation Room relays following to Wayside. Have report quoting Kilduff in Dallas that the President is dead. He died about 35 minutes ago. New Subject: Front Office desires plane to return to Washington with no stop in Dallas."

Salinger has described the scene that ensued:

> There was a cumulative cry of anguish from the passengers. I was standing at the front of the aisle, sobbing. My wife, Nancy, came up and held me, tears rushing down her face. Other wives reached for their husbands, and the aisle was clogged. I wished I had been with him in Dallas.*

No one on the plane had been closer to Kennedy than his Press Secretary. Salinger could recall the distant autumn of 1959, when, having joined Kennedy's entourage in California, he conducted the Senator to a Democratic luncheon in Oakland. Only a handful of guests had appeared; more than half the luncheon tables were vacant. The party hierarchy had made it clear to Kennedy that he was not welcome in the state, and besides, at that point, he appeared to be the longest of long shots among the contenders for the nomination in 1960. So, he had found the politician's nightmare, a half-empty hall. Visibly depressed, Kennedy shambled through a lackluster press conference and then delivered a soggy speech. Salinger's debut had been less than auspicious. Later, they had been able to laugh about the fiasco. "Anyway, Mr. President, you can't say I didn't get the reporters there." "Yes, and considering what they had to write about, I wish you hadn't."

No time for memories now. No time for thoughts of the shining past. The brutal exigencies of the immediate present pressed in on Salinger.

He sat down to compose a statement on behalf of the Cabinet members that he would read to the reporters who would be awaiting the plane in Honolulu.

* Pierre Salinger; *With Kennedy* (Garden City, N.Y.: Doubleday & Company, Inc., 1966, p. 8.

Dean Rusk telephoned the State Department and spoke with George Ball, the Undersecretary. What problems, what unsettled questions of foreign policy might take on a new urgency as a result of the assassination? Rusk wanted a survey, nation by nation, on his desk by Saturday morning.

No time for shock in the Pentagon.

Here, the possibility that the assassination was only the first step in a plot of as yet unknown dimensions weighed more heavily than in any other arm of the government. Here was the nerve center of the communications complex linking the Secretary of Defense, Robert S. McNamara, with American military installations around the world, with radar networks, bombers in the air, and Polaris submarines carrying nuclear-tipped missiles.

Like the gauges that measure the velocity of a hurricane, there were five gradations of emergency action, calibrations of the estimated danger from abroad. DEFCON FIVE called for routine watchfulness, DEFCON ONE would signal an all-out war alert. The Joint Chiefs of Staff had standby authority to signal any one of these. For the moment, however, the Pentagon ordered no change. It sent a message to all commands informing them of the assassination and instructing them to be especially alert. The message was informative, and the routine posture remained in effect. More than 600 heavy and medium bombers, about half the total force of the Strategic Air Command, warmed up on runways. Other aircraft rose in the skies. Anti-aircraft missiles were deployed to firing points. Overseas, some commanders on their own initiative ordered unusual precautions. The shots in Dallas activated a vast assemblage of men and machines.

On Capitol Hill, Frederick Brown Harris, the Senate Chaplain, mounted the rostrum. "We gaze at a vacant place against the sky," he said. And he recalled the words spoken on the morning of Abraham Lincoln's death, 98 years earlier: "God reigns, and the government lives in Washington." They were spoken by Representative James Garfield of Ohio. Now they linked the assassinations of three Presidents. The records show no reason for adjournment of the Senate on November 22, 1963. It simply stopped.

Time itself seemed to stop in every nook and corner of the United States.

There is probably not an American, man or woman,

who will ever forget exactly where he was and what he was doing at the moment when he learned that John F. Kennedy had died.

A man in New York, late for lunch, left his office and stepped out into Fifth Avenue. He noticed that the traffic was unusually light. On Fridays in summer and autumn, the streets are choked with drivers leaving the city for the weekend. Now they seemed curiously empty. Then, wherever he looked, he saw groups of people crowded around parked automobiles, listening to the radios. Near him, another group ringed a young Negro who was holding a transistor radio in his hand. The voice on the radio was saying: ". . . a hidden sniper shot President Kennedy in downtown Dallas today. . . . condition reported very grave. . . . a gigantic manhunt is on in Dallas for the— hold it! A flash is coming in from The Associated Press. . . . . President Kennedy is dead! We repeat, the President of the United States is dead. . . . A White House spokesman in Dallas announces that he died at 1 P.M. Central Standard Time . . . Mrs. Kennedy was at his side when —" The Negro snapped off his transistor. Tears coursed slowly down his cheeks. The man who had come down for lunch did not go to a restaurant. He returned to his office, high above Manhattan, and drew a bottle from a cabinet and began drinking.

On the streets, men and women alike sobbed openly. Some simply stood, stupefied, no longer listening to the staccato voices that sounded unceasingly on the radios. Church bells tolled, and the churches began to fill. People dropped to their knees, praying, and strangers spoke to each other seeking surcease. Telephone switchboards lit up like Christmas trees in newspaper offices and radio and television stations. In the bars, people drank mechanically. Liquor didn't help. They speculated. Who could have done it? Why? Those who knew Dallas said it was probably the same crowd that had roughed up Lyndon Johnson and Adlai Stevenson. Those who knew the South said it had to be some crazy racist. A flag dropped to half-staff, and the sight of this, for some reason, hit people harder than the torrent of words spewing out of Dallas.

The scene repeated itself in countless streets and churches and halls and homes across America.

The Boston Symphony broke off a Handel concerto to play a funeral march by Beethoven. The gong sounded in the New York Stock Exchange, suspending trading. Hundreds of football games to have been played Saturday were postponed. Race tracks closed. Theaters posted signs canceling Friday-night performances. Sessions in the United Nations came to a halt, and outside, all flags fell to half-staff. Television and radio networks announced that they were withdrawing all entertainment programs and commercials from their schedules to devote full time to covering the developments related to the assassination; normal programming would not be resumed until after the funeral. (Would anything ever be normal again?) The waves of grief all but paralyzed the nation.

In Washington, a strange phenomenon began taking shape. Crowds formed in front of the White House and stood, peering through the high iron fence. They were silent, speechless, simply staring.

The word had come to Robert Kennedy from J. Edgar Hoover. Now he was pacing the lawn at "Hickory Hill" shoulders slumped, staring at the grass. Broumis, his big, black Newfoundland, kept pace with him and kept looking into his master's face, questioningly. They walked slowly, the man and his dog, back and forth across the lawn as the afternoon shadows lengthened. Then, characteristically, he responded to his need to be active—and there were things to be done. He would take charge now, as he had done so often in clearing the path for his brother. A member of the family must go to Hyannis Port to be with his mother when she informed Joseph P. Kennedy, who had been felled by a stroke. Teddy and Eunice should do that. Little Caroline was in the home of one of her friends, playing. She must be brought back at once to the White House, where she would be safe. Poor kids. Both were to have birthday parties in a few days. Caroline would be six on the 27th and John-John three on the 25th. For days, Caroline had been talking about her birthday. How could you have birthday parties now? How could you not?

From his office, knowing only that his brother had been wounded, Teddy Kennedy tried to telephone the White House, then "Hickory Hill," then other government offices. His telephones, mysteriously, seemed to have gone dead. In fact, the phones were operating, but as the news spread, the circuits in Washington became so overloaded that the dial tone was slow to sound. He felt walled in, frantic. He hurried home. His beautiful wife, Joan, was not there. She had gone to the hairdresser. All telephones

79

were dead in the house, too. He tried another house nearby. The same. Finally, in the home of still another neighbor, he heard the familiar metallic humming in the receiver, and he got through to the White House. They read Malcolm Kilduff's statement to him.

Joan Kennedy came out from under the dryer in Elizabeth Arden's. An attendant began combing and setting her blond hair. The salon seemed unnaturally quiet. What little conversation she heard was in muted voice. She wondered why, but nobody told her. When she went into the street, she saw a knot of people clustered in the doorway of a television salesroom. She stopped there and listened. . . .

In spite of the all-pervasive voice of modern communications, there were some that day who did not hear, within minutes, that the President had been assassinated. Rose Kennedy was on the golf course at Hyannis Port. She finished the round and went home and prepared to plunge into an afternoon of planning for Thanksgiving, the annual bedlam. They were all expected, three sons and their wives, three daughters and their husbands, relatives, a horde of shrieking, towheaded children, the whole uproarious clan. At least two turkeys would be consumed, possibly three. No doubt, they would play touch football on the grounds between the houses on the estate, and not even the President of the United States would be handled gently in the blocking and running. They made a fetish of winning at everything, the Kennedys. Or they might go sailing, in which case it was more than likely that some one of them would be pushed, fully clothed, into Nantucket Sound. Rose Kennedy had reared a boisterous brood.

She entered the house and found her niece, Ann Gargan, in tears.

There is a photograph taken in London in the late 1930's, when the father of the clan was Ambassador to the Court of St. James. It shows three of his children, Joe Jr., Kathleen, and Jack, walking arm in arm to the House of Commons. Two had gone. Joe lost his life flying a bomber in World War II. Kathleen was killed in an airplane crash. Twice, without warning, children had been taken from Rose Kennedy. And now Jack, the third figure in the photograph. Her chiseled features, regal and strong, settled into sternness, and she raised her chin. She thought of her husband, napping upstairs. Should she waken him and tell him that they had lost another son? The question was no sooner asked than answered. She decided to wait. Sometime, he must be told, but not yet. She telephoned his doctor in Boston and asked if her husband could survive the shock. The physician said he believed so. Nonetheless, she determined to wait until the next morning. After a night's rest, he might be in better condition to bear the blow. Quietly, the television sets were unplugged. They would persuade him to watch a movie in the projection room in the house before he went to bed that night. Teddy arrived. He found his mother composed, fully in control of her emotions. He would recall, "She has this tremendous inner strength, and she helped us more than we could help her."

About an hour later, the telephone rang. Lyndon Johnson, using the radiophone on "Air Force One," asked if he could speak with Rose Kennedy. When she answered, he said, "I wish to God there was something I could do. I just wanted you to know that." He paused and said, "Hold on just a second. Lady Bird wants to speak with you." Mrs. Johnson was sobbing. "We feel as if the heart had been cut out of us," she said. "Our love and our prayers are with you."

This was only one of Johnson's many calls that afternoon. The moment he boarded "Air Force One" and found the radiophone operative, he began using it. He entered the stateroom, decorated with paintings chosen by Jacqueline Kennedy and her husband, and sat down on the bed with the telephone beside him. It was his airplane now, with or without the formality of being sworn in. (The Constitution provides, "In case of the removal of the President, or of his death . . . the powers and duties of the said office . . . shall devolve on the Vice-President.") Johnson began calling Washington. He spoke with Kennedy's special aide, McGeorge Bundy, with his own aides, and to others in the capital. He dictated the gist of these conversations to his secretary, Marie Fehmer. Restless, a whirring dynamo in the quietest of times, Johnson was supercharged now.

Uppermost in his mind, apparently, was the question of being sworn in as President. When and where. He asked the opinions of the three Texas congressmen on the plane, Albert Thomas, Homer Thornberry, and Jack Brooks. Two advised holding the ceremony immediately. Johnson telephoned Robert Kennedy at "Hickory Hill." He first offered condolences. Then, he spoke of the possibility of a conspiracy and said that because of this, he had been advised to take the oath immediately. He asked if the Attorney General had any objections.

Johnson's critics were to point to this and some of his other actions on the plane as evidence of his alleged insensibility to the feelings of the slain President's family and aides. Less than an hour had elapsed since death had taken him. Yet, the Nuclear Age permits so little time for the life-or-death decision. And if the assassination was in fact the product of a conspiracy, it was desirable, and perhaps imperative, for Johnson to take the reigns of government at once. The transition of power, never a pleasant moment for those surrendering it to the new group, could not wait.

"Who can swear me in?" Johnson asked.

In the overriding shock and chaos of the first hours of that Friday afternoon, nobody around him could answer his question. Nor could the Attorney General when Johnson put it to him. Kennedy telephoned his deputy, Nicholas DeB. Katzenbach, and Katzenbach replied that anyone who administers oaths under Federal or state law could conduct the ceremony. (In the dead of night, Calvin Coolidge was awakened and advised that Warren G. Harding had died. "Are you still a Justice of the Peace?" he asked his father, who nodded. "Then I want you to swear me in," Coolidge said. He took the oath, witnessed by neighbors watching through the windows of the house in Plymouth, Vermont.)

As Vice-President, Johnson had worked hard to obtain an appointment to the Federal bench for a friend, Sarah T. Hughes, a tiny, sweet-faced woman of sixty-seven. He thought of her now as the person he wanted to administer the oath and began trying by telephone to track her down in Dallas.

Everybody he called seemed to be absent from his office. Some had gone to the Trade Mart. The whereabouts of others, who were probably simply milling through the streets, was unknown. One of the unhappiest absentees in the city was Jack Kreuger, the managing editor of the Dallas *Morning News*. Kreuger had been sitting on a jury. When the news of the assassination reached the courtroom, everyone assumed the hearings would be recessed. It was not to be. The aged Federal judge delivered a homily on the continuity of the nation, the government, and the courts and said the hearings would go forward. Kreuger, frantic, with the biggest story of his life breaking less than a mile from his newspaper, remained locked up throughout the afternoon until the customary hour of adjournment.

Leaving messages all over Dallas, Johnson eventually reached Judge Hughes. She said it would take her 20 to 30 minutes to drive to Love Field.

Somebody on the plane raised the question of the actual wording of the oath. Where could it be found? Again, no doubt dazed by the enormity and swiftness of what they had been through, memories failed. The Constitution is published in *The World Alamanac,* for one thing, but nobody thought of going into the airport terminal to get a copy. Another telephone call went to the Department of Justice. Katzenbach dictated the language of the oath to Marie Fehmer, and she typed it on a card.

Now they settled down to wait for the arrival of Judge Hughes and of John F. Kennedy's widow.

"Air Force One," baking in the sun for nearly two hours, was becoming an oven.

At Parkland Hospital, Jacqueline Kennedy's ordeal was being protracted, partly because of her insistence on staying with "Jack," and partly through an effort to apply red tape in proceedings that should have been made as simple as possible.

Oneal, the undertaker, rolled up to the loading dock at the hospital in a white hearse bringing a heavy bronze casket. Agents and newspapermen helped place it on a cart. They began wheeling it along the corridor toward Trauma One. Jacqueline Kennedy was still near the emergency room, alternately pacing the hall and then resuming her post on the chair beside the doors. In the thought that the sight of the casket might be too much for her, might sweep her over the breaking point, O'Donnell and Dave Powers tried to persuade her to go into another room. The strategem failed. Having endured so much, the appearance of the coffin would not add to the anguish. They urged her to leave now, to go to the airplane. There was no further reason for her to wait. She refused. She would not leave until the coffin was taken out. Presumably, that would be only a few minutes.

Before Oneal closed the coffin, she stood beside it, gazing at her husband's face. She went outside, expecting them to follow with the bronze casket.

Unaccountably, nothing happened. The minutes multiplied.

A man had entered and identified himself as Earl Rose, the Dallas County Medical Examiner. He said the body could not be removed until he had performed an autopsy. The Kennedy men were dumbfounded. Horrified at the prospect of further delay and its effect on Mrs. Kennedy, they protested, "This is the President of the United States!"

Rose replied that the law was the law and a homicide was a homicide, and the law stipulated that when a homicide had been committed in Dallas County, the autopsy must be performed there. He remained unmoved in the face of arguments and pleading. Until he performed the autopsy, the body of the President could not be taken from the hospital. The rules were not to be waived on any account.

Technically, he was right. But the assassination of a President was no routine homicide, and Rose must have had some glimmer of sympathy for the raddled emotions of Jacqueline Kennedy and the men with her, some understanding of their intense desire to quit the scene of the tragedy at once. If so, he did not exhibit it. He remained adamant.

The dispute grew more heated. They sought higher authority to overrule Rose. Telephone calls were placed for the Attorney General of Texas, Waggoner Carr, who could not be found, and for Henry Wade, the District Attorney. Wade is a quiet, cool-headed, sensible lawyer who tempers the rules with common sense. He advised Rose to step aside.

In the corridor, Jacqueline Kennedy was murmuring half to herself, "Why can't I take my husband back to Washington?"

By this time, the Kennedy men had reached the end of the rope. O'Donnell signaled Powers and O'Brien, Roy Kellerman, and the other agents that they were going. They surrounded the cart and pushed it through the doors and into the corridor. They literally shoved aside Rose and others at the scene, some of whom were merely trying to get out of the way. Recalling the fracas in his testimony before the Warren Commission, O'Brien would say, dryly, "My recollection is that we paid little attention to them."

Jacqueline Kennedy walked behind the coffin with her gloved hand touching it. They came out to the loading dock, placed it in the white hearse, and set off for the airfield.

Lifting the heavy burden up the steps of the ramp presented a serious problem. They were carrying nearly 1,000 pounds, and there was room on the ramp for only a few hands. Somehow, they struggled up to the door of the plane and wrestled the coffin inside. Four seats had been removed from a compartment in the rear, and they maneuvered the coffin into this space. A desk and two chairs remained in the compartment. For the moment, nobody sat in the chairs. They stood, looking at the coffin, looking at each other.

Jacqueline Kennedy said, "It's so hot."

O'Donnell told General Godfrey McHugh to go to the cockpit and order an immediate takeoff. By the time the General returned, the jet engines were whining. Then the sound died away. Puzzled, McHugh retraced his steps. The pilot, Colonel Jim Swindal, told him Kilduff had countermanded the orders to take off. Kilduff? McHugh had no idea the Assistant Press Secretary was aboard. In the corridor, they met. McHugh asked why Kilduff had told the pilot to cut his engines. They all wanted to get out of there immediately. Kilduff shook his head. He said Johnson was on the plane and had made arrangements to be sworn in before departing. A Federal judge was on the way. This was the first inkling the Kennedy men had that Johnson was in "Air Force One." They assumed he and his group had gone to the Vice-Presidential plane as usual. Kilduff said he had been instructed to organize a press "pool" to cover the ceremony and a cameraman to photograph it. McHugh hurried to the rear compartment, bringing this information. Slowly it dawned on them: the Kennedys no longer were in charge; Lyndon Johnson was giving the orders now.

Jacqueline Kennedy sat down on the right of the coffin, in the chair nearest it. Again, she rested her hand on the hard bronze. They urged her to change her clothes, to put away the pink suit, gloves, hose and shoes, all splotched with blood. Hesitantly, she went into the Presidential bedroom, the private compartment furnished with a gold carpet, easy chairs, twin beds, and a telephone. Someone had been sitting on one of the beds. On the other, the clothes she was to have worn in Austin that night were laid out, white dress, white jacket, black shoes.

Johnson and Lady Bird found her there. They tried to

express commiseration and their own sorrow. The effect was not successful. Johnson choked up, stammered, and fell silent. His wife burst into tears. "What if I hadn't been there?" Jacqueline Kennedy said. "I'm so glad I was there."

Johnson told her about his intention of taking the oath of office as soon as Judge Hughes appeared. He asked her to join him when the ceremony was performed. It was not only an act of courtesy; her presence at his side would symbolize transition, continuity in government, and the life of America. Mrs. Johnson asked if she wanted someone to help her change into a fresh costume. She shook her head. Perhaps later. They urged her to rest and left her in the bedroom.

At about 2:30, Judge Hughes boarded the airplane. The word was passed that the ceremony would be held at once.

"If there's anybody else aboard who wants to see this," Johnson said, "tell them to come in." In the next minute or two, 27 persons crowded into the bedroom, all it would hold. Johnson noticed Kennedy's secretary, Mrs. Evelyn Lincoln. He took her hand and kissed it. O'Brien brought what looked like a Bible bound in black leather. In fact, it was a Catholic missal, a prayer book. Judge Hughes did not look at it. It was a matter of no importance. The use of the Bible in administering an oath is a formality, but it is not necessary.

Jacqueline Kennedy and O'Donnell entered. The others made room for her on Johnson's left. Lady Bird was on his right. O'Brien and Rear Admiral George Burkley, the physician, watched from farther back.

In the rear compartment, far from this scene, there was a lonely tableau. Godfrey McHugh remained with the coffin, discharging his last service to his Commander.

Johnson placed his left hand on the prayer book and raised his right. He was so much taller than Judge Hughes that he had to bow his head to look into her eyes. She began, "Do you solemnly swear. . . ."

He responded in a low, firm voice, "I do solemnly swear that I will faithfully execute the office of the President of the United States, and will to the best of my ability, preserve, protect and defend the Constitution of the United States. So help me God."

His expression was more than solemn. Men are always solemn when they take the Presidential oath, with all that it implies. But their features mirror other emotions, too, fleeting signs of anticipation, the flush of victory, the look of determination. None of these are to be found in the official photograph that recorded the swearing in of Lyndon Baines Johnson as the thirty-sixth President. His face sagged in loose folds.

It was 2:38 P.M., two hours and eight minutes since the sudden burst of thunder in Elm Street.

Silence momentarily filled the crowded cabin, and no one moved. The sense of tragedy and history weighed heavily on everyone there. Then Johnson bent down and kissed his wife. He turned to Jacqueline Kennedy and took one of her hands in his. Lady Bird moved to her side and clasped the other.

For Lyndon Johnson, no massed thousands in the Capitol Plaza, no applause, no bands saluting him with "Hail to the Chief," no cameras carrying the scene to the far corners of the earth, no uniformed men parading down Pennsylvania Avenue and saluting him in the Presidential box, no exuberant supporters pumping his hand, no exaltation. He came to office through a curtain of grief.

The others shuffled out of the stateroom. The Dallas officers and those who were to return to Washington in the back-up plane went down the ramp. Seat belts clicked. A reporter's typewriter chattered. Judge Hughes handed the missal and the card with the typed oath, priceless mementos, to a man who has never been identified. Then, she left the plane, and the door thudded, closing. Jim Swindal started the jet engines.

Jesse Curry shook Johnson's hand and, taking his leave from the stateroom, said to Mrs. Kennedy, "God bless you, little lady. You ought to lie down now."

"Thank you," she murmured. "I am fine."

The Johnsons asked her to sit in the forward cabin with them, and she did for a few moments. Then she excused herself and returned to the chair beside her husband's coffin. The Irishmen were there, O'Donnell, O'Brien, Powers, McHugh, stricken men who for her sake were leashing in their emotions.

The whine of the jets rose to a shriek, and the plane lifted toward the sky, leaving behind Elm Street and Parkland Hospital and Dallas and the bright hopes and dreams of John Fitzgerald Kennedy.

9

Night had fallen over Europe, and the darkness of early Saturday covered the Far East when the black news from America flashed around the world. The death of the Chief of State of a major power, by custom, elicits messages of condolence from his opposite numbers in their chancelleries, mini-eulogies that may contain elements of sincerity, but which also represent international good manners and good diplomacy.

In the passing of John F. Kennedy, however, the reaction in many capital cities, and in many more obscure hamlets, was quite extraordinary. To a degree that Americans had not realized and that Kennedy himself could not have comprehended, he had imprinted his image in the minds of people around the globe, the great, which is wholly understandable, and the faceless masses, which is less easy to analyze.

Consider, for example, the behavior of Nikita S. Khrushchev, then Premier of the Soviet Union. After his meeting with Kennedy in Vienna, Khrushchev is supposed to have said, "I think we scared that young man." He learned differently when Kennedy, risking war, forced him to remove the Soviet missiles from Cuba. He would have held Kennedy in utter contempt if indeed he had "scared that young man." Then, when the President caused him a serious loss of face over Cuba (and perhaps ultimately, his job) he would have been justified in regarding Kennedy's death with equanimity.

The amenities of etiquette and diplomacy would have been satisfied by a formal statement from Khrushchev, particularly since his Foreign Secretary, Andrei Gromyko, promptly telephoned the American embassy to convey, formally, the regrets of the Soviet government. Gromyko expressed "shock and the greatest sympathy for the American people." He added, "Official condolences will be conveyed later at the highest level." Khrushchev went well beyond this gesture. He interrupted a tour of the Ukraine and returned at once to Moscow. On Saturday afternoon, dressed in black, he went to Spasso House, the residence of the American Ambassador, Foy Kohler. On a table in an anteroom, the embassy staff had placed a photograph of Kennedy. It was the one in which a trace of sadness tinges the thoughtful expression. (I had often intended to ask him what he was thinking about when the picture was taken, for the sadness is there.) Black crepe draped the photograph in the anteroom. In front of it lay a book in which those who called to express commiseration left their signatures. Khrushchev drew his old-fashioned, gold-rimmed spectacles from the breast pocket of his suit, bent over the book, and signed it, adding the date, November 23. Television cameras recorded the scene, which meant that Khrushchev wanted the Russian people to see it.

He was not finished. With Kohler, he walked into an adjoining room, and they chatted for about 20 minutes. Khrushchev reminisced about "that young man."

On the night before, Moscow radio broke a broadcast of domestic news to announce that Kennedy had been shot. When his death was announced, the radio began playing funeral music, a requiem for an American President. The directors must have known that Khrushchev would not object.

London, too, went beyond the routine gestures.

Sir Alec Douglas-Home, the Prime Minister, was driving to the south coast to spend the weekend in Arundel Castle, the ancestral home of the dukes of Norfolk. At a stop along the road, he learned of the tragedy and turned back for London. "There are times in life," the Prime Minister said, "when mind and life stand still, and one such is now." The words were far more meaningful than those in the official statement issued from 10 Downing Street.

For an hour on Saturday morning, from eleven o'clock until noon, the tones of the great bell in Westminster Abbey echoed in Whitehall. It sounded 60 times, once every minute. This usually is reserved for the last rites of British monarchs when they are interred in the abbey. Now the bell tolled for the great-grandson of an Irish potato farmer.

On the Houses of Parliament, the Union Jack was dropped to half-staff. This, like ringing the abbey bell, usually is done only to pay last respects to royalty or a prime minister.

Winston Churchill, eighty-nine and heavy with years, sat up long past his bedtime, peering at the television with his "Clemmie". The pictures from Dallas and Washington came in steadily. The next day, the old warrior's voice growled. The assassination, he said, "is a monstrous act which had taken from us a great statesman and a wise and valiant man. The loss to the United States and to the world is incalculable. Those who come after Mr. Kennedy must strive the more to achieve the ideals of peace and human happiness and dignity to which his Presidency was dedicated."

Charles de Gaulle, President of France, sounded a martial note and, predictably, the clarion call of duty. He said, "President Kennedy died like a soldier, under fire, for his duty and in the service of his county. In the name of the French people, a friend always of the American people, I salute this great example and this great memory." The Tricolor dropped to half-staff in France.

The President of Venezuela, Romulo Betancourt, first cabled his message to Washington. Then he began reading it to newspapermen who came to his office. Midway, he broke into tears and was unable to finish. An aide read, "With his death, the United States lost one of the best Chiefs of State it has had in this century."

Around the world, in the reaction to the tragedy, respect and admiration for Kennedy seemed to cut through the miasmas of chauvinism and the barriers set up by nationalistic fears and rivalries.

In the Middle East, the Shah of Iran and the King of Jordan sent messages expressing sorrow, while Gamal Abdel Nasser, President of the United Arab Republic, and no friend of theirs, said he was "immensely grieved." In a message addressed to Mrs. Kennedy, he said, "With his death, humanity, progress and peace suffer a loss by no means less great than yours. It is a painful tragedy."

Prince Norodom Sihanouk of Cambodia had proclaimed on the day of the assassination that Communist China was "Cambodia's best friend." Now he ordered anti-American placards stripped from the walls and a three-day moratorium in newspaper attacks on the United States.

In Peking, the heirs to one of the oldest and most glittering civilizations in the world behaved like Neanderthal

90

men. A trade union paper, *Kunjen Jih Pao,* published a cartoon of Kennedy lying face down, blood streaming from his head, with the caption, "Kennedy Bites the Dust." A diplomat of a neutral country said one of his Chinese translators grinned broadly and said, "Very good news. He was a very wicked man." In present Chinese policy, crude and primitive, hatred is a 24-hour assignment, on no account to be relaxed.

Japanese editors knew they had a special angle on the story, and they immediately went after it. At 5:00 A.M., a reporter rapped on the *shoji,* the sliding panel doors, of the home of a man named Hanami Kohei. Kennedy's election to the Presidency had conferred a kind of distinction on Hanami-san. Twenty years earlier, Kennedy and Hanami had tried to kill each other, although, in the impersonal idiocy of war, neither knew the other existed. Lieutenant Hanami was commanding the destroyer *"Amagiri"* ("Heavenly Fog") in the South Pacific, and Lieutenant (Junior Grade) Jack Kennedy, commander of PT-109, had been stalking the Japanese warship. In the darkness, the *"Amagiri"* rammed the flimsy torpedo boat and sliced it in two. A member of Kennedy's crew was badly injured. Kennedy tied a rope around him, took it between his clenched teeth, and swam to an island, towing the wounded sailor. In this incident, Kennedy suffered the injury to his back that remained with him for the rest of his life. Robert Donovan, the Washington correspondent, wrote a book about the episode. He went to Japan to interview Hanami and others who had been involved. "They were apologetic," he said. "They almost made it sound as if they wished Kennedy's boat had sunk the '*Amagiri.*'" He reported this to the President, who was hugely amused. After the war, Hanami also went into politics and also was successful. He was elected Mayor of Shiokawa, his native place.

In the predawn darkness, the reporter told Hanami about Kennedy's death and asked for a statement. The Mayor, in the Japanese tradition, said that death in the service of one's country is the highest honor a man can earn, not a tragedy, and he added simply, "The world has lost an irreplaceable man."

When Robert Kennedy was inducted into the Armed Forces, the Lieutenant, then in the Solomon Islands, wrote him a teasing letter. It is worth recalling, inasmuch as it appears to hint at his feelings about the war. It reads:

The folks sent me a clipping of you taking the oath. The sight of you up there was really moving, particularly as a close examination showed that you had my checked London coat on. I'd like to know what the hell I'm doing out here while you go stroking around in my drape coat, but I suppose that's what we're out here for, so our sisters and younger brothers will be safe and secure—frankly, I don't see it quite that way—at least, if you're going to be safe and secure, that's fine with me, but not in my coat, brother, not in my coat.

Many heads of state and foreign diplomats of course had come to know Kennedy. They had discussed problems and policy with him in Washington and in their own capitals. As everyone did, they had felt the forcefulness of his character, the tough-mindedness, along with his grace and charm. So although national interests are not altered by personal charm, these men felt the loss of a commanding personality, a man they had found to be farsighted and civilized, with whom they could work.

But what is the explanation for the tremendous outpouring of grief among the millions in the world who had not known him personally? Some had caught a glimpse of him during his travels abroad. Some had heard him speak and, without understanding his words, sensed the quality of the man. To the great majority, however, the President was merely an image, a photograph in the local newspaper, a man who had said something that stirred them. The breadth and depth of feeling soon became apparent in newspaper photographs flashing across the oceans into New York.

In Amsterdam, two young women are holding a newspaper, and one is weeping, and the other stares, wide-eyed at the black headlines . . . a picture from Paris shows tears streaming down the cheeks of a craggy-faced street sweeper . . . in Rome, the hammer-and-sickle flag droops at half-staff over the offices of the Communist party . . . in West Berlin, a homemade placard is on a stake driven into the ground near the forbidding Wall, and the placard repeats the words he had spoken in the city, "J.F.K. Ich bin ein Berliner" . . . and the steps of the City Hall in West Berlin are carpeted with flowers.

In saying, "I am a Berliner," he had identified himself with them and pledged his support for their determination to remain free. On the night of his death, the city marched in his memory, a funeral procession that just seemed to start and then grew and grew. It began about midnight. A handful of students, fewer than 100, formed up near the Technical University. Carrying torches, they began to march the three miles or so to the City Hall. There was no music, no funeral dirge. They marched in silence that was broken only by the sound of shuffling feet. It had been drizzling, and the wet streets gleamed in the torchlight. A bell sounded, the Freedom Bell, a gift from the American people to the city where people die in the effort to escape to freedom. It tolled steadily as the procession flowed through the streets. Others rapidly joined the students, falling into step in the slow cadence. By the time they came in sight of the City Hall, more than 60,000 were marching in memory of the man who had said he stood with them.

"We in Berlin have become poorer," said Mayor Willy Brandt. "America has lost its President. A tortured humanity has lost the man so many believed could help us along the road to a just peace and a better life in this world."

It was drizzling in Paris, too. Frenchmen and Americans, ignoring the rain, crowded in front of newspaper offices, reading the pages pasted in the windows. In the Rue de Berri, across the street from the Paris *Herald Tribune*, a clerk in the Hotel California gripped the hands of an American guest. "It is terrible, terrible," he said. "You have the sympathy of everyone in France tonight." In an expensive restaurant on the Champs Elysées, a Spanish waiter dabbed his eyes with his serving napkin and poured out his feelings in his two languages, *"Eso es un chieste malo. Je ne le crois pas. Je n'accepte pas. Mierda!"* ("It's a bad joke. I don't believe it. I reject it. Shit!")

New Ross, County Wexford, is the home in Ireland of the Kennedys. From there, more than a century earlier, Patrick Kennedy had emigrated to America. In his day, the earlier waves of immigrants despised the Irishmen who were settling in Boston and New York and would take any kind of work. Nonetheless, Patrick Kennedy had done well and now "Cousin Jack" had crowned the efforts of all the Kennedys. Only five months before, he had been in New Ross and had visited his cousin Mrs. Mary Ryan. In front of the fireplace in her cottage, the "Widow Ryan" had given him tea. A priest came to the cottage when the news reached New Ross, and they knelt and prayed for

"Cousin Jack", the widow, her daughter Josephine, and the priest. They could hear the knell tolling from Bally-kelly Church, and they prayed for him there. The priest said, "Never again will we see his smiling face."

To be sure, the people in the British Isles and Western Europe could feel a kinship, a rapport, with John Kennedy because his roots were in that part of the world and his political objectives, in the broad sense, were identical with theirs. But the charisma had been felt in places where this had by no means been so.

It is routine, when a big story breaks, for foreign correspondents to go after man-on-the-street reaction. On Gorki Street in Moscow, a reporter joined a group of Russians waiting for a bus. He reported their remarks. "He was a good man. It is always the good who suffer. . . . Who will the next President be? Is he a peaceful man? . . . It is bad for our people, and bad for the American people."

The staffs of two television stations in Rio de Janeiro were on strike. They went back to work, temporarily, in order to broadcast the overpowering news from the United States.

In Katanga Province, the Congolese Cabinet was in session when an excited clerk burst into the conference. They adjourned immediately, went home, and then, bringing their wives, they thronged into the American consulate. "We Bantus mourn the passing of a great chief," the spokesman said.

Americans traveling abroad found feeling for Kennedy in distance places and among people to whom Washington must have seemed more remote than the moon.

Colonel Allen Griffin and his wife, of Monterey, California, were in the Valley of the Kings in Egypt. They returned to their hotel after a morning of sightseeing in Luxor. In the lobby, they saw an Egyptian newspaper with a photograph of Kennedy so large that it all but filled the page. Laughingly, they asked the elevator boy, a Sudanese, "What has our President been doing now?" The youth spoke English, but he did not answer. He turned his face away. When they stepped off the elevator, they saw tears in his eyes.

A statistician from New York City, Justin Spafford, was in Yugoslavia. Kennedy had been dead several days when Spafford set off for Sarajevo, scene of the assassination of Archduke Francis Ferdinand in 1914. He was traveling slowly through Bosnia, where the evidences of Turkish dominion are still to be found. Spafford stopped in a village. A man there, recognizing him for an American, told him in fragmentary English and with gestures what had taken place when the radio brought the news to the village. Pointing to the mosque, he indicated the people had gone into it out of respect for Kennedy. He cupped his hands over his eyes to show that they had wept.

At home, meanwhile, there was a development that would have caused Kennedy to split his sides with laughter. The American Communist party and the John Birch Society found themselves together for once. Both sent messages to his widow.

Robert Welch, founder of the Birch Society, wrote her, "I wish to express our deep sorrow at so untimely a loss to our nation of its youngest elected President and to convey . . . our sincere and heartfelt sympathy in your overwhelming personal loss."

The Communists' message said, "All true Americans, in tribute to your husband, will not only condemn this political [sic] murder, but also will rededicate themselves with greater strength to the struggle for the democratic character of the world."

Needless to say, not all right-wingers endorsed Welch's words; some are reported to have applauded the news of the assassination. And in the Communist lexicon, little value is placed on the words "truth" and "sincerity"; words are used for effect, to twist facts.

And yet, this was not wholly unique. Around the world, groups divided by deep ideological chasms found common cause in mourning John F. Kennedy. His death suffused with meaning the cliché, "without regard for race, creed or color." To which one could add, "without regard to station in life, high or low, rich or poor, intellectual or illiterate." He touched the hearts of millions.

To them, Kennedy symbolized Youth, new ideas, a fresh approach, the New Generation. Indeed, he had sounded that chord himself in his Inaugural Address. "Let the word go forth from this time and place, to friend and foe alike, that the torch has been passed to a new generation of Americans, born in this century, tempered by war, disciplined by a hard and bitter peace. . . ."

It was not only younger Americans but younger men in many lands who had been "tempered by war" and hoped never again to experience it. An even greater host of men and women in the world had been "disciplined by a hard and bitter peace" and yearned for a genuine peace.

Kennedy came to office after more than 20 years of bloodshed, suffering, and fear. The greatest of wars had been fought, only to be followed by the specter of an even greater war in which the new weapons could decimate the human race. A divided Germany, a divided Korea, and a divided Vietnam were the dangerous consequences of East-West conflict, friction points, and no end to the tensions was in sight. The leaders of the major powers during those two decades and more were all aged or aging men, some identified with the Colonial Era, and some, including the Russians, with imperialism, the roots of war. Now, a comparatively young man had taken center-stage, a determined, intelligent, farsighted man who identified himself with the new generation and was expected to explore new avenues and try new methods.

He offered hope, a fresh page, not a mere palimpsest.

It is doubtful that many persons in Bosnia or Shiokawa or the Congo had read the words he spoke at the Inaugural, yet they seemed to sense his purpose and respond to it. He envisioned "a new world of law, where the strong are just and the weak secure and the peace preserved. . . . a new endeavor . . . let us begin."

He had just begun when the bullets cut him down. If there is any meaning in his death it is that, for an hour at least, he drew men together in universal mourning.

10

The police were questioning the employees in the Book Building when the supervisor, Roy Truly, sensed that something was not quite right. Then he identified the cause. "I don't know if it means anything," he said to a policeman, "but I'm missing a man."

The missing man was Lee Harvey Oswald.

Truly had last seen him when M. L. Baker, the patrolman, had rushed into the building a minute or two after

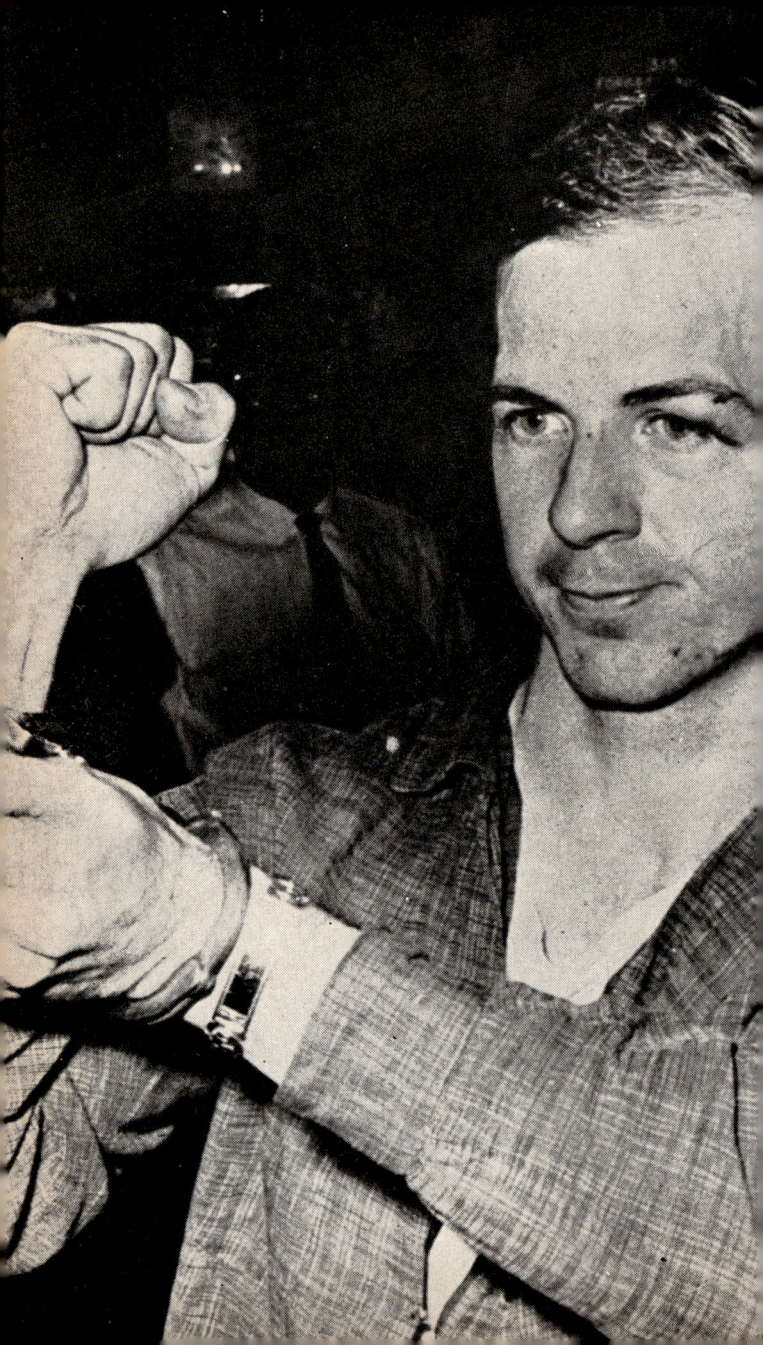

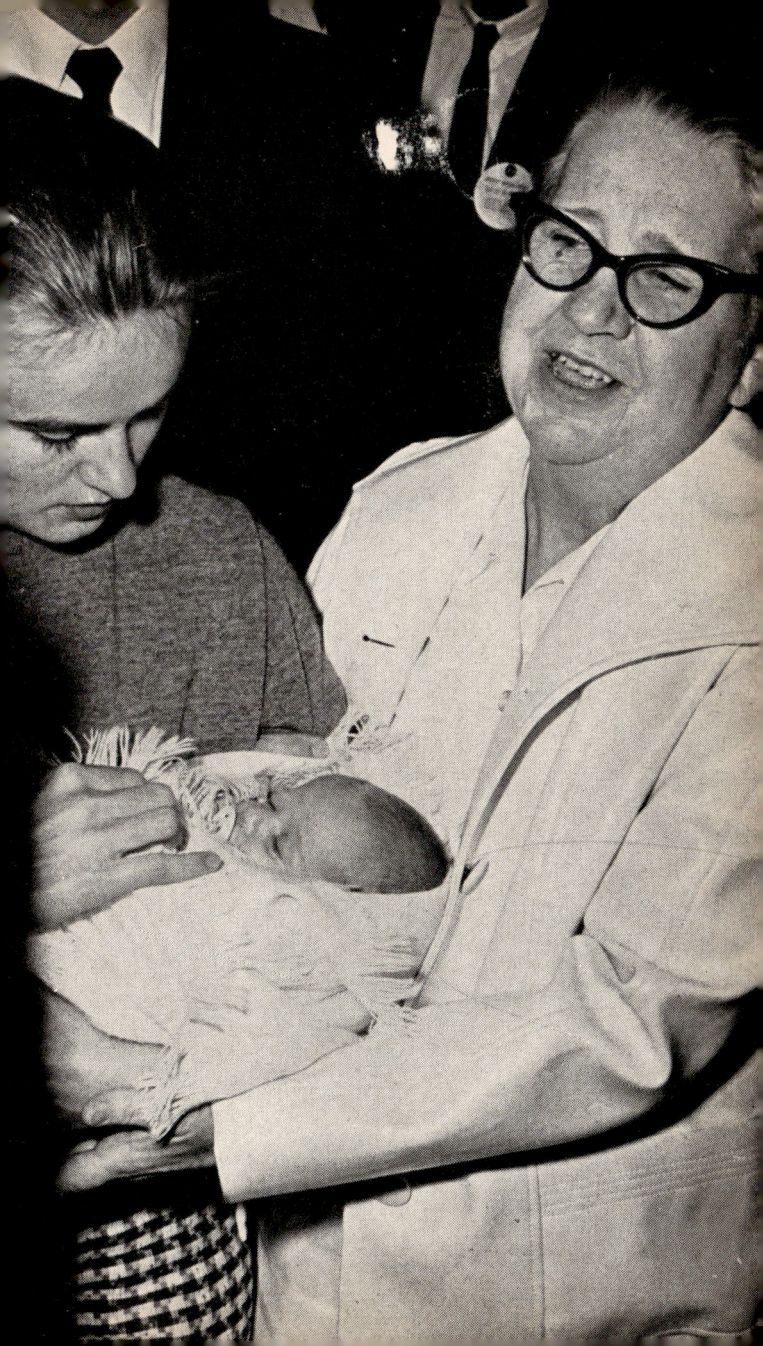

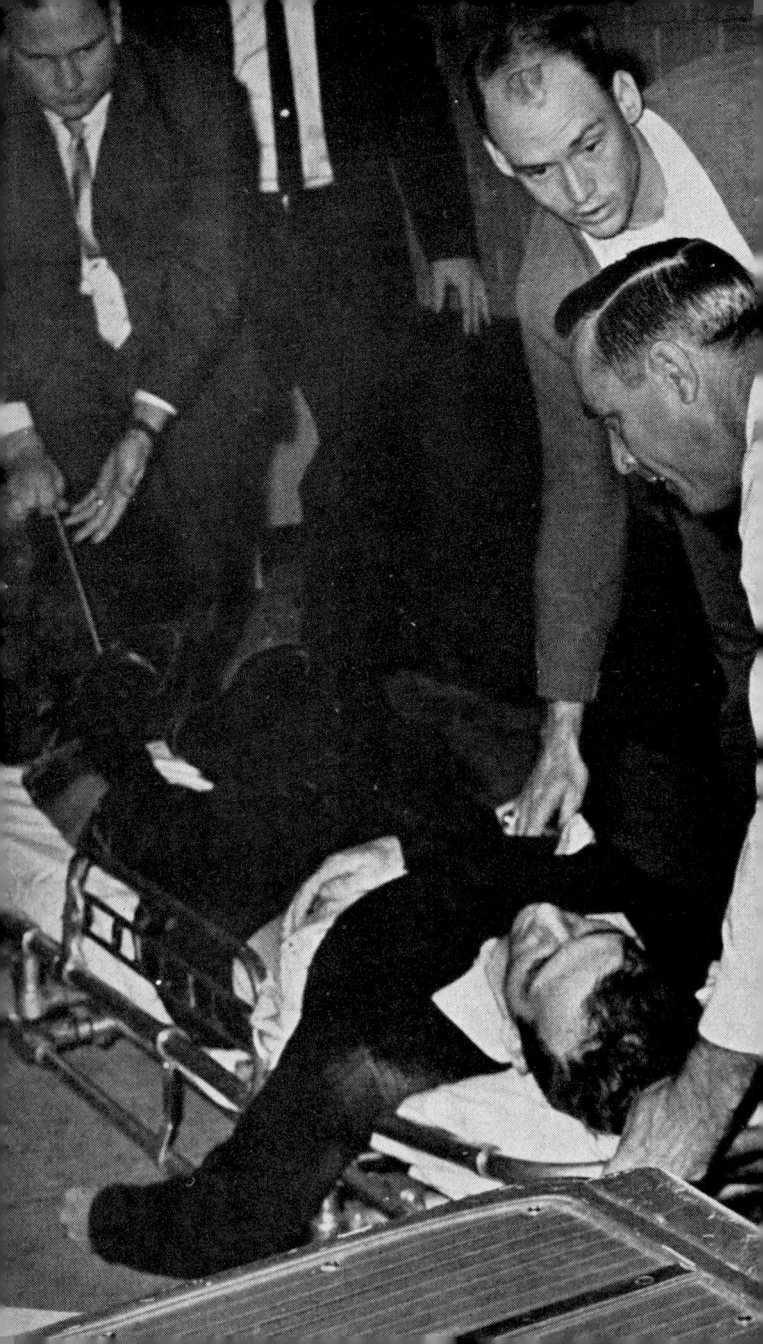

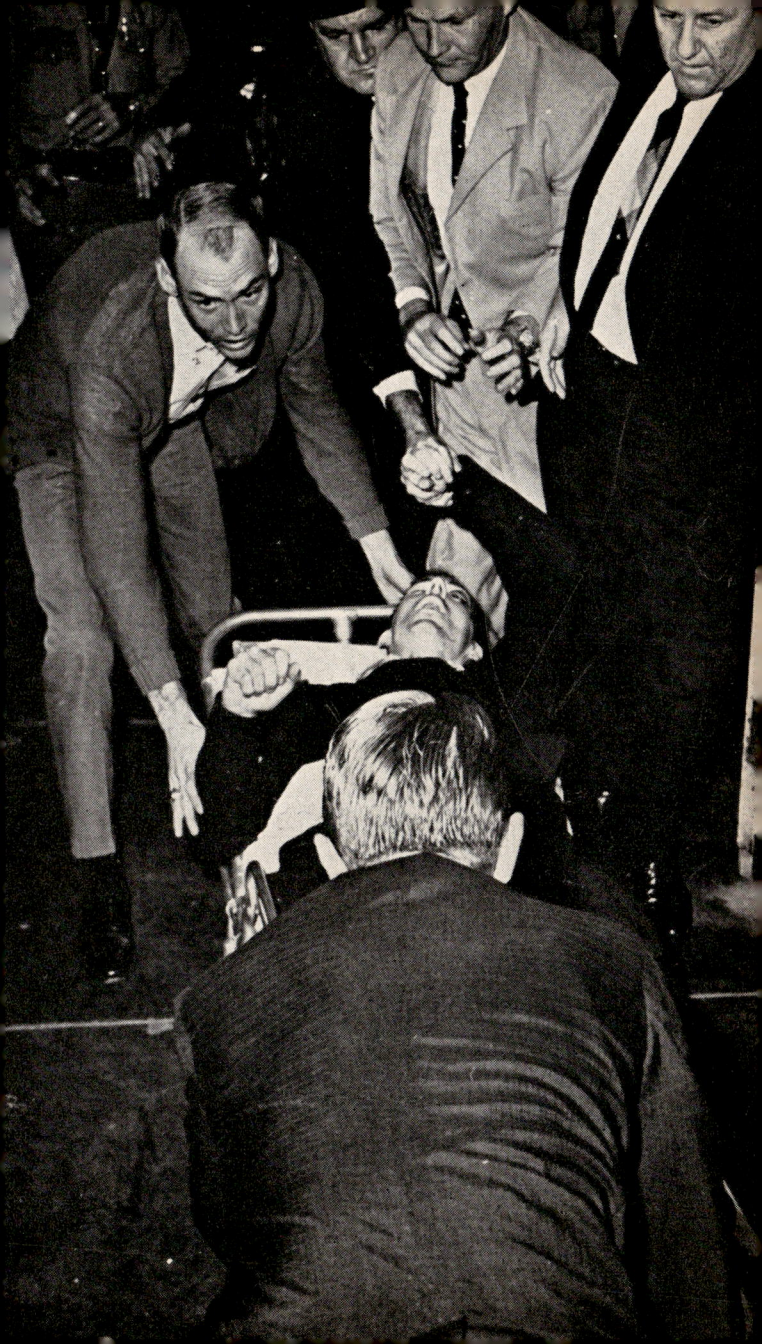

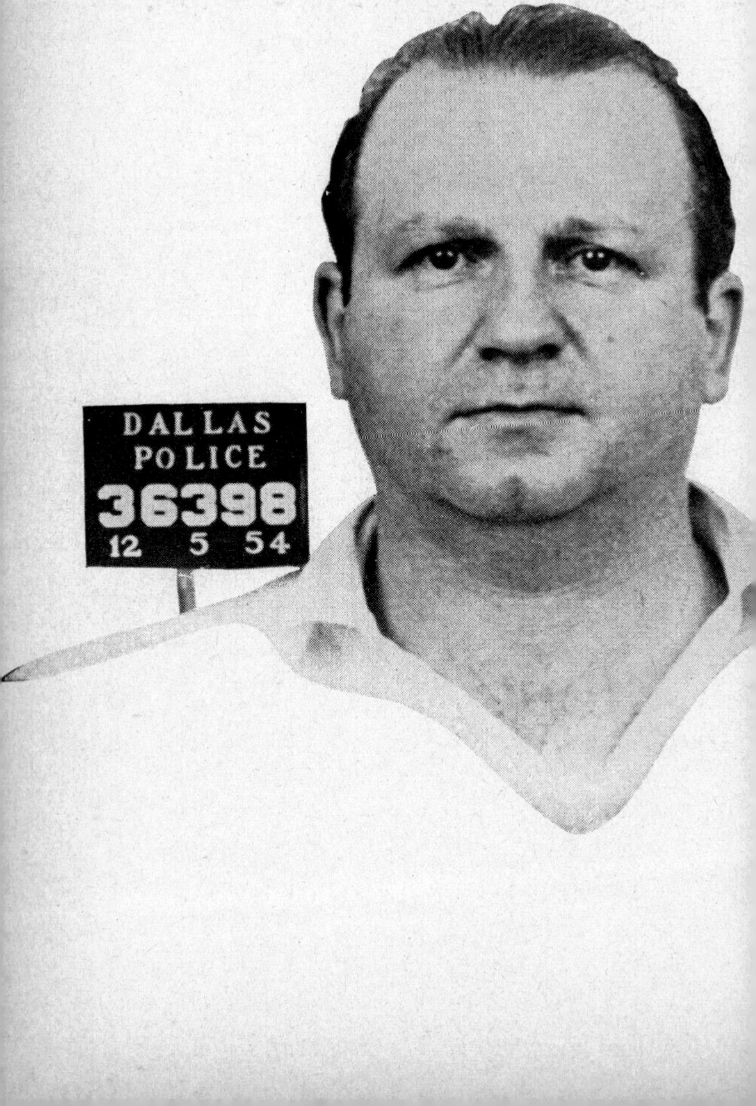
DALLAS
POLICE
36398
12 5 54

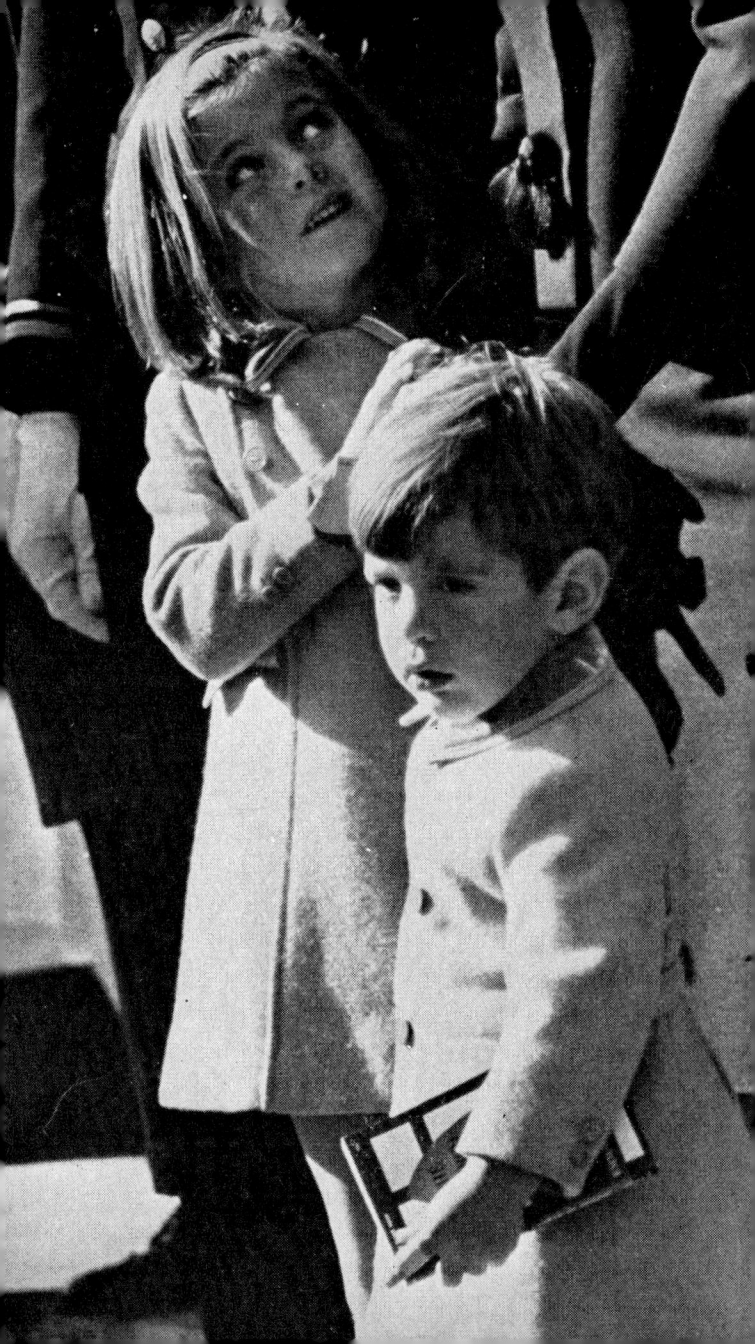

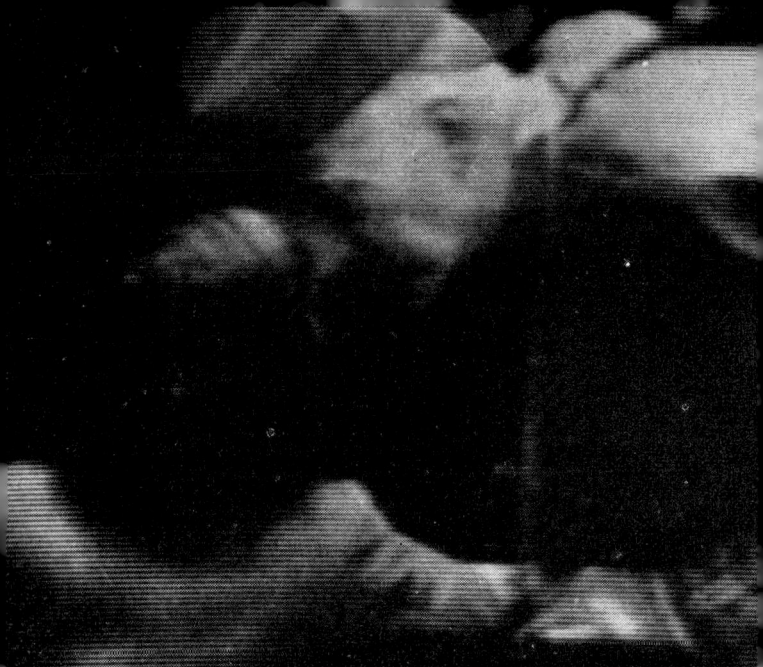

the shooting and found Oswald beside the soft drink vending machine on the second floor. Having been assured that Oswald worked in the building, Baker ran up the steps to the roof, Truly following. They then returned to the ground floor, and the supervisor noted Oswald's absence. Had anyone seen him leave the building? Nobody could remember. He had vanished.

Truly took Oswald's employment application card from the files. It showed his address and telephone number and a few details of his physical appearance.

At 12:45, the police radio dispatcher broadcast an order to patrol cars to pick up "a white male, approximately 30, slender build, height five feet 10 inches, weight 165 pounds." The message was rebroadcast twice again within the next ten minutes. Instructions were issued separately to different radio cars, and one of these went to Officer J. D. Tippit. He was ordered to cruise in the central part of Oak Cliff, a section of Dallas, and at 12:54, he messaged that he was on station and gave his position. All such messages to and from the prowl cars are logged by the dispatcher.

In the Book Building, the questioning of the employees soon developed information that sounded highly important. James Jarman, Jr., Harold Norman, and Bonnie Rae Williams, it will be remembered, watched the President's procession from the fifth floor. They told the officers that they believed the shots came from above them, that they heard a metallic sound that could have been the bolt action of a rifle and heard three thumps on the floor.

Captain Will Fritz and other officers rode the elevators to the sixth floor. Almost immediately, they noted the open window in the southeast corner and the excellent view of Elm Street that it afforded. The arrangement of some small cartons containing the Roller Readers suggested a convenient seat and rifle rest. Unquestionably, they had been moved; the others were stacked in another part of the room. Why? Who? Nobody could say.

At 1:22, the rifle was found. Nearby on the floor was a brown paper bag. Three empty cartridge cases then came to light. The rifle appeared to have been thrust in among a pile of boxes, but with no specific effort to hide it. In the first reports, the weapon was erroneously identified as a Mauser. In fact, it was an Italian Mannlicher-Carcano 6.5 millimetres, with a telescopic sight. It was a cheap gun but not inefficient.

A palm-print, to be identified as Oswald's, was on the underside of the rifle barrel. Two more fingerprints and a palm-print were to be discovered on the cartons and identified as his. The brown paper bag had been fashioned from lengths of coarse paper of the type used in shipping the books.

Where was Lee Harvey Oswald?

In the Book Building, he passed the office of Mrs. Robert Reid, who said to him, "They shot at the President, but maybe they didn't hit him." If Oswald replied, she did not hear what he said. At this point, he was walking toward a stairway leading from the second floor to the front door below. This was at about 12:32, two minutes after the shooting and immediately after Baker and Truly left Oswald at the vending machine.

Seven blocks away, he rapped on the doors of a bus that was stalled in traffic. It was now about 12:40. The driver, C. J. McWatters, had passed a checkpoint a few blocks back on schedule at 12:34, so he could estimate with some accuracy the time when he saw Oswald. It was not a regular stop on the bus route, but McWatters opened the doors. For this very reason, he was more likely to remember Oswald than passengers boarding the bus at a regular stop. But he was not the only person on the bus who could identify Oswald.

He went to the third seat from the front of the bus on the right-hand side. Mrs. Mary Bledsoe, sitting further back, recognized him, and she looked at him with distaste. Oswald had rented a room from her and lived there until October 7, some six weeks earlier—when she had thrown him out of the house. She was to testify that she just didn't like Oswald and told him she would no longer rent to him. On the bus, womanlike, she noticed a hole at the elbow in the right sleeve of the brown sport shirt he was wearing. She also would say that ". . . he looked so bad in his face, and his face was distorted." In the enormity of the events of November 22, memories played tricks, and Mrs. Bledsoe's description of his expression may or may not have been accurate. But she was entirely accurate in her observation about his shirt. When Oswald was arrested, he was wearing a brown sport shirt with a hole in the right sleeve.

The bus was carrying Oswald *toward* the Book Building, in other words in the direction from which he had come. Was this a classic instance of the criminal returning to the scene of the crime? Or had he boarded a bus going in that direction, rather than away from the building, to divert suspicion?

It stopped again in the choked street. A motorist just ahead of the bus jumped out of his car, his face working with excitement and shock, and gasped, "the radio . . . says . . . the President's . . . been shot." Oswald said nothing.

About a block and a half further, when the mass of cars again forced McWatters to stop, Oswald asked him for a transfer and stepped into the street. The transfer, dated, was found in his shirt pocket later. Each bus driver carried a punch that made a distinctive hole in transfers, marking the route. The one in the transfer found on Oswald proved he was on McWatters' bus when the driver said he was and when Mrs. Bledsoe said she saw him.

But Oswald did not use that transfer. For one so frugal, he did something rare. He took a taxi.

He next appeared at the Greyhound Bus Depot, two blocks from the point where he left the bus. He opened the door of a taxi driven by a cabbie named William Whaley. A small incident fixed Oswald's face in Whaley's memory. Just as Oswald sat down in the car, the driver said, a woman leaving the Greyhound station walked to the taxi window and asked Whaley where she could find another cab. Oswald, according to Whaley, politely offered to get out and let her have the cab. However, Whaley assured her others would soon come to the depot, and she declined.

The address of Oswald's rooming house was 1026 North Beckley, but he gave Whaley a different street number. He said he wanted to go to "500 North Beckley," which was about five blocks away. In all probability, this was because Oswald did not want Whaley to know exactly where he went when he left the taxi, a fact the driver would have logged on his tripsheet.

As they started the trip, Whaley said to Oswald. "What the hell do you think happened over there?" Presumably, he meant in the vicinity of the Book Building. Oswald remained silent. To Whaley, this meant that he was one of those fares who dislike talking with cab drivers, and he thought nothing of it. On North Beckley, Oswald told Whaley to stop. He gave the driver a dollar (the fare was 85 cents) and hurried down the street.

A friend had telephoned Oswald's landlady, Mrs. Earlene Roberts, about the shooting on Elm Street, and she was watching television when he entered the house. He seemed to be in a hurry—and he was. He swiftly changed his clothes. He put on a light-colored jacket, and thrust his revolver into a pocket. He was still zipping up the jacket when he passed Mrs. Roberts on the way to the front door. "You're in a big hurry," she said. He did not answer her.

This was at approximately 1:03 P.M., shortly after the sheet was drawn over Kennedy's face in Parkland Hospital.

Oswald was next seen about a mile from his rooming house, walking on Tenth Street in the direction of Jack Ruby's apartment. The two residences were 1.3 miles apart, and Oswald had covered more than half that distance when he was stopped.

The man who stopped him was Patrolman Tippit, driving Car 10. Tippit, following orders, was cruising slowly through the Oak Cliff section. He stopped the car and called to a man wearing a light-colored jacket. Why can never be known, unless it was that Tippit thought the man answered the general description broadcast by the police dispatcher about a half hour earlier. He appeared to speak briefly to Tippit through the car window on the right. Tippit then opened the door beside him, on the left, and started to walk around the front of the car. He took only a few steps. A revolver barked (four times, most witnesses said), and the officer dropped to the street, covered with blood and dying.

One witness was a taxi driver, William Scoggins, who was eating lunch in his cab. He said he saw Car 10 stop, saw the man in the jacket approach it, and heard the shots. He did not see the shooting; shrubbery blocked his view. An instant later, the man reappeared, gun in hand, and came toward Scoggin. Frightened, the cabbie crouched down beside his taxi to hide. He thought he heard the man mutter, "Poor dumb cop" or "Poor damn cop."

Two other witnesses had a clear, close view. Domingo Benavides, driving a truck, was within 25 feet of Car 10. Mrs. Helen Markham, a waitress, was waiting to cross the street about 50 feet from the point where Tippit fell. Benavides used the radio in Car 10 to call the police. "We've had a shooting out here," he said, and located it on Tenth Street near Patton. His call was logged at 1:16 P.M. Mrs.

Markham screamed and ran to Tippit. She gave a description of the killer. At 1:22, a general alarm sent a number of police cars, sirens wailing, into the area around the scene of the murder. The investigative agencies were to report that "at least 12" persons, including the three mentioned, saw the man with the pistol near the point where Tippit was killed. Five of them picked Lee Harvey Oswald out of police lineups.

After the shooting, Oswald reversed his direction. He walked rapidly from Tenth to Jefferson, which parallels it. Then he must have veered off Jefferson for a short distance to cut through a parking lot. His light-colored jacket was found later under a car, and Marina identified it as his.

Then he continued down Jefferson again until he heard police sirens approaching. John Calvin Brewer, manager of a shoe store, had heard radio reports that the President had been shot and now that a policeman had been gunned down in the Oak Cliff area. Brewer also heard the police sirens, and then he saw a man in a t-shirt step into the recessed entrance to the store. A police car that had been coming toward the store made a u-turn and went in the opposite direction.

With that, Brewer saw the man go back out on the sidewalk. Brewer's suspicions were aroused. He saw the man go into the lobby of a movie house, the Texas Theater. Mrs. Julia Postal, the ticket seller, also saw him there. But the sound of the sirens caused her to leave the box office and go out to the sidewalk. Brewer had followed the man in the t-shirt and saw him dash into the theater. He asked Mrs. Postal if the man had bought a ticket. "No, by golly, he didn't," she said. She, too, became suspicious and called the police. At 1:45, a terse message went out over the police radios: "Have information a suspect just went into Texas Theater on West Jefferson." Some 15 officers converged on the theater.

The movie running in the theater was *War Is Hell*. A real drama interrupted the screening.

On orders from an officer, the projectionist cut the film and turned up the house lights. Brewer and some police officers entered from the alley and walked on stage. Brewer spotted the man in the t-shirt in a seat on the right center aisle, toward the rear, and pointed him out to Patrolman M. N. McDonald. The man was Lee Harvey Oswald. He made no effort to run out of the theater. He sat quietly until McDonald, having frisked two men farther front, approached and told him to stand up and raise his hands. Oswald complied. But when the officer moved to frisk him, he lashed out with his left fist, hitting McDonald between the eyes. With his right hand, he pulled the gun from his pocket. McDonald grabbed it, at the same time smashing his fist into Oswald's face. They both fell into the seats. Oswald pulled the trigger on the gun, but it failed to fire. He apparently had loaded it with shells of two different makes, some of which did not exactly fit the firing mechanism, causing it to abort when he tried to shoot McDonald. Oswald fought like a wildcat, grappling with five policemen. As they locked the handcuffs on his wrists, McDonald thought he heard Oswald say, "Well, it's all over now."

At 2:35, on news agency teleprinters across the country, five bells jingled, signaling a bulletin. The machines stopped, stuttered, and then spelled out—

BULLETIN

DALLAS, TEX., NOV. 22 (AP)—DALLAS POLICE TODAY ARRESTED A 24-YEAR-OLD MAN, LEE H. OSWALD, IN CONNECTION WITH THE SLAYING OF A DALLAS POLICE-MAN SHORTLY AFTER PRESIDENT KENNEDY WAS ASSAS-SINATED.

HE ALSO WAS BEING INTERROGATED TO SEE IF HE HAD ANY CONNECTION WITH THE SLAYING OF THE PRESIDENT.

At that moment, on "Air Force One," Lyndon Johnson was saying, "I do solemnly swear. . . ."

In filling out his application for employment in the Book Building, Oswald had given Ruth Paine's address in Irving as his own, not the North Beckley Street rooming house. Shortly before three o'clock, detectives rang the doorbell in Irving and said they wished to question Marina Oswald. They all went to the garage where the Oswalds' possessions were stored. Mrs. Paine translated the questions. They asked if Oswald owned a rifle. Mrs. Paine, un-aware that it had been concealed in the blanket, said, "No." But when she translated the question, Marina said, "Yes." They were standing near the brown and green blan-ket. Marina pointed to it. She said her husband owned a rifle, and she believed he had wrapped it in the blanket. An officer picked up the blanket, and it fell limply across his arm, empty.

Having learned that Oswald had been living in the rooming house under the alias "O.H. Lee," the detectives went there and searched his room. They found a leather holster that fitted his revolver and the city map that was marked with red x's.

At police headquarters, meanwhile, he was shouting denials—to everything. He had not shot either the President or Tippit. He did not own a rifle.

Paraffin tests were made on his hands and cheeks for traces of burned gunpowder. They came up positive from his hands but negative from his face. These tests are not always reliable.

In his billfold, the detectives found a forged Selective Service card. It showed his face but not his name. The name printed there was "Alek J. Hidell." In due course, handwriting experts would trace the rifle from a Chicago sporting goods firm to one "A. Hidell, P.O. Box 2915, Dallas, Texas." The order and the return address on the envelope were certified to be in Lee Oswald's handwriting; so was a mail order to a Los Angeles firm for a revolver. The Chicago company's records showed that the rifle cost $16.78, plus $2.17 for the scope, total—$18.95. They had been mailed to the Dallas post office box on March 13, 1963.

In short order, the scientific techniques and equipment for criminal investigation—ballistics, handwriting analysis, the study of the trajectory of the bullets that struck Kennedy and Connally, microscopic examination of fibers and hairs, fingerprints—came into operation and developed a mass of physical evidence against Oswald. Experts were to testify that the bullets that took the President's life came from Oswald's rifle and that the bullets recovered from Tippit's body were fired by the pistol he was carrying when he was arrested. Fibers and pubic hair together linked the rifle, the blanket, and the shirt he was wearing that day. The web of circumstantial evidence against Oswald tightened.

In all Oswald's actions, and in his answers to the police interrogations, a curious, baffling pattern emerges. Strands of cunning interweave with threads of incredible stupidity. On some points, he gave plausible, though false, explanations. To others, he gave answers that he must have realized would easily be exposed as falsehoods. He contradicted himself, or said he must have made a mistake, or simply refused to answer certain questions.

103

His "curtain rod" story was an ingenious one, considering the length and shape of the package he carried into the Book Building. But he claimed he had not told Frazier the brown paper bag contained curtain rods; he said he had brought his lunch in it, although Frazier recalled that Oswald said he intended to buy lunch. The bag, of course, was far larger than what he would have needed to bring his lunch, which he said was cheese, fruit, and an apple.

When he was asked about the marked city map, he blandly replied that the x's showed places where he had applied for work before he came to the Book Building. He seemed to become excited when they showed him the x on the Book Building. Secret Service Inspector Thomas J. Kelley quoted him as saying, "My God, don't tell me there was a mark where this thing happened!" But he quickly recovered and said, "What about the other marks on the map? I was looking for work and marked the places where I went for jobs or where I heard there were jobs."

They asked him about the snapshot showing him holding the rifle. He sneered—it was a photographic trick, he said, in which his face had been superimposed over the original face in the picture; having worked in photography, he said, he was well acquainted with the technique.

He said he knew no one named A.J. Hidell. When police produced the Selective Service card bearing that name and his picture, Oswald flew into a rage and said, "I've told you all I'm going to tell you about that card. You have the card, and you know as much about it as I do."

"A.J. Hidell" came back to plague Oswald again when United States Postal Inspector H.D. Holmes questioned him. In answer to a question, Oswald told Holmes no one but himself was permitted to receive mail in his Post Office Box 30061 in New Orleans. The Inspector pointed out that the application to rent the box listed Marina Oswald and A.J. Hidell as persons entitled to receive mail through it. Holmes said Oswald replied, "Well, so what? She's my wife, and I see nothing wrong with that, and it could very well be that I did place her name on the application." What about the elusive Mr. Hidell? Holmes' report said, ". . . he simply shrugged his shoulders and stated, 'I don't recall anything about that.'"

In the records of his interrogations, Oswald seems rational, shrewdly picking his way through a mine field of dangerous questions. Yet, some of his lies were so transparent, so easily checked out and found to be false, that it is difficult to understand why he would have implicated himself by uttering them.

For example, why had he used the alias "O.H. Lee" at the rooming house? He hadn't, he said. The landlady must have made a mistake when he told her his first name was "Lee." Had he forgotten that he had signed the rooming house register "O.H. Lee"? Actually, he had given Marina a far more plausible reason for using the alias. He told her that he did not want the landlady and the others in the rooming house to know that he was the Lee Harvey Oswald who had lived in Russia and had tried to defect to the Soviet Union.

Again, Oswald claimed that two fellow workers could establish his whereabouts at the moment of the shooting and shortly afterward. He said he was eating lunch with "Junior" (probably meaning Jarman) when the shots were fired. Later, Oswald said, he spoke with William Shelley, a foreman, who said no more work would be done in the Book Building that day. Oswald gave this conversation as the reason why he went home immediately after the assassination. Both Jarman and Shelley denied seeing him when he said they did.

What about the famous curtain rods? Where were they?

Oswald denied having told Frazier the package held a sheaf of curtain rods. He said he had wrapped his lunch in it. It was pointed out to him that the package was very large, much larger than necessary for sandwiches and some fruit. The interrogators quoted him as replying, "I don't recall. It may have been a small sack or a large sack. You don't always find one that just suits your sandwiches." He said he had placed the package beside him on the front seat of Frazier's car, not in back. When they told Oswald that Frazier said he laid a long parcel on the back seat, the suspect replied, "He must be mistaken, or thinking about some other time when he picked me up."

For no apparent reason, too, Oswald told the officers he had purchased his .38 caliber pistol in New Orleans, whereas they traced it through the mail order to Los Angeles. What was his purpose in this? Or was he simply too stupid to realize that the gun would be traced?

Mocking questions arise on all sides in examining Oswald's erratic behavior before and after he was arrested and in searching for his reasons.

Why did he take no steps to insure that his fingerprints would not be found on the rifle? He could have used

105

gloves. Failing that, and although he was in a great rush to leave the sixth floor, wiping the weapon to erase the prints would have been a matter of mere seconds. Apparently, he simply stuck the gun among the boxes and fled.

What was his ultimate destination after he left the Book Building and then the rooming house? Obviously, he was racing the clock. He took the taxi rather than ride the buses because he seemed to want to get to North Beckley faster than they could take him there. Yet, he walked the five blocks after leaving the taxi, losing time. If he was not covering his tracks, what was the meaning of this and of the unused bus transfer?

Why did he arm himself with the revolver? And where was he going when he met Tippit?

A central question may answer all the others—

Did Oswald have a plan for escaping from Dallas, a scheme that unforeseen circumstances prevented him from carrying out? Did he expect to slip away scot-free? Did he have accomplices waiting for him in Oak Cliff or elsewhere within walking distance to assist the getaway? If so, it might explain why he made no effort to erase his fingerprints from the rifle and why he moved so hastily in the approximately 42 minutes between the time he left the Book Building and the moment when he stumbled into Tippit. It might also explain why he left most of his money, $170, in Marina's room in Irving that morning, keeping less than $15 for himself.

But assuming that Oswald and others had worked out a plan of escape, it was anything but a model of efficiency. He loses time riding the bus, and more time walking from the taxi to his rooming house, where the police might have been staked out and waiting. Then in broad daylight, he walks nearly a mile. Forty-two minutes have elapsed. If he had accomplices with a fast car, they could have been a long way from Dallas in 42 minutes. Moreover, it would seem that they overlooked one important contingency— that he might be apprehended. Otherwise, a much better alibi would have been invented to cover him, with more plausible answers to the interrogators than the ones he gave them. In view of all this, the theory of an organized plot seems ridiculous.

It has been argued that Oswald was simply the patsy in the assassination, the triggerman in a conspiracy with accomplices. But what was their motive and his?

106

Or were the two murders on that dreadful afternoon simply mindless deeds brought about by the vaporings of a twisted brain?

Legally, a person is adjudged sane if he knows the difference between right and wrong and understands the nature and consequences of his act. Some psychologists and legal specialists, however, contend that the definition is too narrow. They believe a person may commit a crime, knowing it to be a crime and punishable by law, and yet, through some murky compulsion, nevertheless may carry out the act.

Oswald, after his arrest, appeared sane in the legal definition.

He certainly recognized that he was in serious trouble. Therefore, he vehemently denied killing the President and Tippit. He tried to lie his way out of the mesh of evidence to the contrary. He was sensible enough to demand a lawyer. The police advised him that this was his right. He then named the man he wanted, a Mr. Abt of New York City. Oswald did not know Abt personally but said he would understand the case, having represented some persons accused under the Smith Act. (The Act, passed in 1950, recognizes the existence of a worldwide Communist conspiracy, with agents in the United States, stipulates certain procedures for meeting the problem, and provides penalties for failure to comply.) Conspiracy! Much would be made of this, especially in Europe where an apolitical assassination could not be envisioned. There, and later for some Americans, there *had* to be a political motive for the death of John Kennedy.

In his questioning, Captain Fritz tried to discover Oswald's feelings about the President and his policies. Oswald was too cagey to be drawn into that. Fritz's report quoted him as saying, "I have no views on the President. My wife and I like the President's family. They are interesting people. I have my own views on the President's national policy. I have a right to express my view, but because of the charges I do not think I should comment further." The report said Oswald also stated, "I am not a malcontent; nothing irritated me about the President."

In the reports, Oswald also is represented as having said he had refused to take a polygraph (lie detector) test for the FBI in 1962 and had no intention of submitting to one now.

All of which would indicate that Oswald knew very well

107

what he was doing under interrogation. Inspector Holmes summarized his impression of him in these words:

> Oswald at no time appeared confused or in doubt as to whether or not he should answer a question. On the contrary, he was quite alert and showed no hesitancy in answering those questions which he wanted to answer, and was quite skillful in parrying those questions which he did not want to answer. I got the impression that he disciplined his mind and reflexes to a state where I personally doubted if he ever would have confessed. He denied emphatically having taken part in or having any knowledge of the shooting of the policeman, Tippit, or of the President, stating that so far as he is concerned, the reason he is in custody was because he 'popped a policeman in the nose in a theater on Jefferson Avenue.'

With respect to the three post office boxes Oswald had rented, the inspector found "in each instance his answers were quick, direct and accurate as reflected on the box rental applications."

Oswald's memory was functioning and so was his reasoning that day. Where discrepancies he could not explain appeared in his story, he said, "I must have forgotten." Or someone else must be mistaken when their version of an incident contradicted his. Or he simply refused to answer.

If the investigating officers' reports were complete and accurate in the statements attributed to Oswald, he was a sane man on November 22, 1963, at least under the legal definition of sanity.

Then what was his motive?

His mother, as will be shown, was to come up with one of the weirdest theories of all.

But the only hope of determining the real facts was to be blotted out by a pistol in the hands of a shoddy eccentric named Jack Ruby.

11

Lee Oswald was barely in handcuffs before it became
abundantly clear that although the Protective Research
Section had no record of his existence, the files of other
Federal agencies bulged with information about him.
Lengthy news reports flooded the wires during the afternoon of November 22, giving detailed background on him.
He had served in the Marine Corps. He had lived and
worked in Russia, attempted to renounce his American citizenship, and had married a Russian woman. From New
Orleans came the information that Oswald had characterized himself as a "Marxist" in a radio panel discussion
over Station WSDU just three months before the assassination. He also listed himself as Secretary of the New Orleans chapter of the "Fair Play For Cuba Committee."
(Marina Oswald was to testify that no such committee existed except in her husband's fevered imagination; he was
its only member.) One news report quoted his exact words
when he defected to Russia. "I have made up my mind.
I'm through," he said as he angrily slapped his American
passport on the desk of an embassy official in Moscow.

Much of this information came from official files, of
course. From the moment when Oswald returned from
Russia with his wife and child, disembarking in New York
on June 13, 1962, he had been under surveillance. The
FBI offices in Dallas and New Orleans both had data on
his activities in those cities. It would seem that the whereabouts of a man with his history—in Dallas and working in
a building the President would pass—would have been
brought to the attention of those responsible for protecting
Kennedy that day. But as has been said, the Dallas FBI
agent, James Hosty, Jr., was to testify that this "meant
nothing" to him. And when he was asked to describe his
reaction on learning that Oswald was accused of the assassination, he replied, "Shock. Complete surprise." Why? "I
had no reason prior to that time to believe that he was ca-

109

pable or potentially an assassin of the President of the United States."

An army of reporters promptly began digging into Oswald's background, going back to his childhood, interviewing his former teachers and acquaintances about his school days.

An odd and somewhat pathetic profile emerged.

Oswald was a loner, a perennial failure, an egotist with small reason for egotism, restless, dissatisfied, highly introverted, quarrelsome, given to fantasies, reaching for some unfathomed objective. In the full sense, he never knew the meaning of loving or being loved. He seems not to have understood that love, and even friendship, entails giving. Oswald, on the whole, was a taker. He gave little, least of all of himself. Consequently, he developed no close relationships and had no close friends. He displayed no interest in other people, his fellow workmen, the people in the rooming house, the group of White Russians in Fort Worth and Dallas who tried to befriend him and Marina. His laconic answers discouraged conversation. Obviously, he loved his two children, and his face would light up with any mention of them. They were his. He had little else in life.

He was not unintelligent. While he was a schoolboy, his I.Q. was tested, and the tests showed it to be slightly above average. He read voraciously, borrowing books from the public libraries. His wife said there were occasions when he read all night, sitting in the bathroom so the light would not disturb her. He is supposed to have come home from grade school and said to his mother, "Why are they teaching me these things? I already know all that." This may have been another of his fantasies; later in life, at least, he liked to consider himself superior.

Oswald was of average size and not unusually strong, but he had physical courage. When challenged, he did not back away from a fight. He had a streak of violence that led him to strike his mother and Marina and pull a knife on two other occasions. He liked firearms, and he had himself photographed in a silly, strutting posture, holding the rifle. Perhaps the weapons reassured him about what the Mexicans call *macho*, maleness in the basic, testicle sense. A Russian woman rejected him before Marina married him. Some of Marina's friends said she told them she found her husband sexually inadequate.

He was neither lazy nor stupid, but he had difficulty in

110

holding even unskilled jobs. He earned little money. In the last 18 months of his life. his earnings averaged less than $200 a month. He managed on that, and even saved, because he lived like an ascetic. He ate little and rented cheap rooms. He spent almost nothing on himself. He was not interested in clothes, automobiles, playing cards, or chasing women.

Then what were the interests and major satisfactions of Lee Harvey Oswald? His children of course, but two infants could hardly fill a man's life to the brim. Ideology, yes, but his knowledge of Marxism was at best superficial; to some who heard him expound on the subject, it seemed only a pose. What were his releases? What did he think about when he went to an empty room in the Y.M.C.A. or a rooming house? Where, deep down, did he really live?

So long as historians study the assassination of John F. Kennedy, they will puzzle over the enigma of Lee Harvey Oswald.

Some, no doubt, will begin the search for the keys to his character and behavior patterns by examining his relations with his mother, to see if the twig was bent in childhood or early youth.

She was born Marguerite Claverie in New Orleans in 1907. When she was 17, she dropped out of high school after one year and went to work as a receptionist in a law firm. She was pretty and popular with men, and she had three husbands. The first, John Pic, left her. She said it was because he didn't want children, and she was pregnant with the first of three sons. Then, she married Robert E. Lee Oswald, an insurance man. He was the father of Robert and Lee Oswald. He dropped dead of a heart attack two months before Lee was born. Lee's birth date was October 18, 1939. Her third husband, Edwin A. Ekdahl, was an electrical engineer. He apparently liked her three sons very much and treated them as though they were his own children. The marriage, however, was anything but successful. There were separations and reconciliations. After one of these, when Ekdahl was about to return to their home, John Pic, the oldest boy, said, "This seemed to really elate Lee. This made him really happy that they were getting back together again." But after three years, Ekdahl sued for divorce. He complained in the suit that his wife nagged him about money, hit and scratched him, and during these flare-ups, threw a bottle, a cookie jar, and a vase at him. She denied the allegations. The jury

111

found Marguerite "guilty of excesses, cruel treatment or outrages" and granted the divorce. She then took the name of her second husband. Her three marriages lasted a total of eight years.

Marguerite Oswald moved frequently, from city to city and from one house to another. She held a succession of jobs and worked hard to care for her sons. Money problems plagued her. Because her work kept her away from home during the days, she put the boys with relatives or in children's homes. For a time, the four lived together in a small house in Fort Worth. It had a single bedroom. The older boys slept on a screened porch. John Pic said later, "Lee slept with my mother until I joined the service in 1950. This would make him approximately 10, well, almost 11 years old."

Signs of Lee's violent nature, or at least of his hair-trigger temper, appeared early.

From watching John play chess with a friend, Hiram Conway, Lee learned the game himself and well enough so that occasionally he defeated the older boys. But he couldn't endure to lose. Conway said, "He'd throw the chess pieces all around, and the older boys would try to hold him off but he'd go kicking their shins and try to bite their hands. " On another occasion, a neighbor said he saw Lee chase John with a knife and then throw it at him.

These incidents might be dismissed as childish tantrums. However, when Lee was in his teens and John Pic had married, there was a family quarrel during which, Pic said, Lee threatened Mrs. Pic with a pocket knife and slapped his mother.

Yet, the boy responded to kindness.

His grades in school were slightly above average, but he was always poor at spelling. When he was in the fourth grade, his teacher, Mrs. Emma Livingston, gave him special attention to help him with this problem. "I felt no necessity for helping the other students because they were going to get help at home," she said. "They had someone to depend on. Evidently, Lee didn't." And so, after school, Mrs. Livingston worked with the boy to improve his spelling. The result, she said, was that he earned an A on his next examination and, his paper "was the top paper. . . ."

A day or two later, Lee came to school with a puppy and gave it Mrs. Livingston.

Along with the tendency to violence, Lee seemed to resent authority and resisted discipline. In high school, he tried out for the football team. After scrimmage, the coach ordered the boys to jog around the field briefly, a common practice during training. Lee refused. "This is a free country." he said, "and I don't have to do it." He was dropped from the squad.

Inevitably, he came into the hands of psychiatrists. They saw him heading for trouble, but they could not and did not predict that he would become a murderer.

By the summer of 1952, Lee alone was in his mother's care. Robert Oswald had joined the Marines. John Pic had married and was living in New York. In that year, Marguerite Oswald took Lee to the city. John Pic was genuinely glad to see his half-brother, took a week off from work, and showed him the sights in and around New York. Apparently, Marguerite intended to move in permanently with the Pics, but after the quarrel in which Lee pulled the pocket knife on Mrs. Pic and then struck his mother, the young couple asked them to leave. They moved to an apartment in the Bronx. Lee enrolled in a junior high school, P.S. 117.

In two months, however, he was absent from classes more than three-quarters of the time. He candidly told his mother that he was wandering around the city and not going to school. A truancy officer was assigned to the case. Lee called him "a damn Yankee" and refused to cooperate with him. As a result, he was remanded to Youth House, an institution for children who seemed to need psychiatric observation.

The Chief Psychiatrist, Dr. Renatus Hartog, and other members of his staff examined Lee. Dr. Hartog's report said:

> This 13 year old, well built boy has superior mental resources and functions only slightly below his capacity level. . . . No finding of neurological impairment or psychotic mental changes could be made. . . . Lee has to be seen as an emotionally quite disturbed youngster who suffers under the impact of a really existing emotional isolation and deprivation, lack of affection, absence of family life, and rejection by a self-involved and conflicted mother.

A social worker, Mrs. Evelyn Strickman Siegel, interviewed Lee and his mother. She wrote, "There are indications that he has suffered serious personality damage but if

113

he can receive help quickly this might be repaired." She observed in Lee "a rather pleasant, appealing quality about this emotionally starved, affectionless youngster which grows as one speaks to him."

Lee pleaded with his mother to get him out of Youth House. He said he disliked being forced to associate with other boys and, whatever significance it may have had, that he particularly disliked undressing in their presence asd taking showers with them.

John Carro, a probation officer, said Lee asserted with respect to his schoolmates, "They don't like me and I don't like them." And regarding his mother, "She's my mother. I guess I love her. I guess I do." (Marina Oswald was to state flatly that Lee did not love his mother, and his actions in later years appear to support this opinion.)

Carro said, "This kid was seeking acceptance, a sense of belonging, a feeling of identity that he didn't get here." He reported that after Lee returned to school in the autumn of 1953, he was a "disruptive influence." One of the manifestations of his resistance to authority was his refusal to salute the flag. He did little or no work in school and resisted the efforts to help him.

Whether the "serious personality damage" noted by Mrs. Siegel could have been repaired, and whether Lee Oswald might have been brought into an adjustment with the world around him, will never be known. Abruptly, in early 1954, his mother took him back to New Orleans. The educational authorities there were not told that psychiatric examination in New York had disclosed the boy's need for help.

A sad little relic of that period in New Orleans remains.

In Warren Easton High School, he was required to fill out a questionnaire regarding his personal history. Did he have any close friends in the school? "No," he wrote. The next line asked him to name two persons he considered as friends. Evidently, Lee wrote two names in the space but then erased them. In the space for "desired vocation," he wrote, "military service."

And this was to be his next move, the Marine Corps. How he thought he would be able to endure the iron discipline of the Corps is difficult to imagine, unless of course he was not aware of his congenital resistance to authority. In all probability, he was motivated by the knowledge that his brother Robert was enjoying his service in the Marines.

114

His mother found Lee poring over the Marine Corps manuals two years before he was old enough to enlist.

But before this, there came a radical turning point.

At 15, Lee somehow discovered Karl Marx and *Das Kapital*. It fascinated him as nothing he had ever encountered before. He read constantly. He never wholly absorbed Marx's philsosphy or the theories of books on socialism that he brought home from the public library. He was able to parrot the words, but discussion showed that he did not really understand what he had read. He lacked the intellectual depth and resources. His original interest undoubtedly came from his need to identify with something, to feel that he belonged, to have a Cause. It would be a rare 15-year-old who could discern the true differences between Communism and capitalism and make a choice based on experience and sound reasoning. Oswald harbored the illusion that the Soviet Union was the scene of an all-for-one and one-for-all crusade, a paradise where everybody was fulfilled and loved his neighbor. "Comrade Oswald." Lee Oswald had no comrades. There was not one boy he could call a friend. As for girls, if he ever felt the normal sex urges of adolescence, there was no evidence of it. Without realizing it, he had wrapped himself in an all but impenetrable cocoon, shutting our friends and lovers alike. Now he found a movement that meant to him that all men are brothers. In it, he envisioned a better world than the one he knew. Later, damning the capitalist system, and to give substance to his arguments in favor of Marxism, he described his mother's plight during the Great Depression. Such a phenomenon could not take place in Russia, where the State met the needs of the individual. Someday he would go to Russia and become "Comrade Oswald" and work for something he could believe in. Poor man. His experience there was to be one of the last of his failures, unadulterated wormwood.

A lesser disillusionment preceded it.

In 1956, a week after his seventeenth birthday, he enlisted in the Marine Corps. Now he was free of his mother, self-supporting, and within the bounds of regulations, free to do as he liked. In terms of the uniform, at least, he belonged to something.

He was first stationed in San Diego and then in Camp Pendleton, California. In aptitude tests, he fell two points below the average in the Marines. He listed as his preference for training Aircraft Maintenance and Repair and was recommended for this duty.

On the rifle range, at first, Oswald was a poor shot. But he improved until he scored 212 points in a test for the record, two points more than necessary to qualify for the grade of "sharpshooter," the middle rank in a scale of marksman-sharpshooter-expert. He also learned the use of riot guns and a .45-caliber pistol, but records were not kept showing his proficiency with these weapons.

In July, 1957, his unit was sent to Japan. The natural beauties of that country and the splendors of Japanese culture seem to have made no impression on him whatever. There is nothing to indicate that he noticed them. Japan could have opened his eyes. It could have taught him patience, humility, self-abnegation, and the lesson that to some things in life one can only say *"shikata ga nai,"* "It can't be helped." Japan could have remade Lee Oswald, but his perceptions were turned inward, and so he was blind to beauty and deaf to Japanese thought.

His hopes of finding—who knows what—in the Marine Corps had turned to ashes by that time. A barracks-mate said Oswald "always hated the outfit." He said the presence of American forces in Japan constituted "imperialism." He praised Nikita Khrushchev and said he would like to kill President Eisenhower. His fellow Marines found him an "oddball," they said, and called him "Ozzie Rabbit." In the Marines, as in his other worlds, he didn't belong.

Actually, his mates knew little about him. He was too withdrawn. He didn't have a buddy. He didn't carry a snapshot of a girl who couldn't wait for him to come home or brag about his prowess in bed. Obviously, he never received a "Dear John" letter. He may have acquired a Japanese girlfriend. Some of the Marines thought so. His manner changed, and he became belligerent and even pugnacious. He no longer was "Ozzie Rabbit." They attributed the change to the reassurance they supposed he had found in having a *koibito,* a sweetheart. One of his fellow Marines, Peter Conner, said, "When the fellows were heading out for a night on the town, Oswald would remain behind or leave before they did. Nobody ever knew what he did."

Others recalled that he devoted his off-duty time to studying the Russian alphabet and reading socialist theory. He developed a cheap little trick of trapping his superior

116

officers into discussions of Marxism and foreign policy. Obviously, since he had read a great deal in these fields, it was easy to expose their ignorance by contrast to his grasp of the subjects. Nelson Delgado, a Marine who had seen these performances, said, "Oswald tried to cut up anybody that was high ranking and make himself come out top dog." Here, as in his school days, was the congenital rebellion against authority.

Nevertheless, he won a good conduct medal and the stripe of a private first class.

However, he lost the stripe after being court-martialed twice. In the first, he was found guilty of unauthorized possession of a pistol, a derringer. It fell out of his locker, discharged when it hit the barracks floor, and the bullet struck Oswald in the elbow. Paul Murphy, a Marine who was in the barracks, heard the shot and rushed in to find Oswald staring at his elbow. His expression was blank, and all he said was, "I believe I shot myself." In another version of the incident, however, Oswald indicated that the shooting was not accidental. He led a barracks-mate to believe that owning a gun was "one way to get people to leave you alone." Next, he was court-martialed for assaulting a sergeant, abusive language, and challenging the man to a fist fight. The "assault" took the form of spilling a drink on the sergeant. Oswald testified that he wanted to transfer to another outfit, sat down with the sergeant in a Japanese bar to discuss it, and spilled the drink when the sergeant pushed him away. The court accepted his explanation but sentenced him to 28 days at hard labor and a $55 fine for cursing a superior.

Shortly after this, Oswald's outfit went out on sea duty. By an odd and unhappy coincidence, the ship to which they were assigned was named "Wexford County," the county of John F. Kennedy's forebears.

Toward the end of 1958, Oswald was shipped back to the United States and assigned to a Marine Air Control Squadron at El Toro, California. He served in a radar crew, the principal duty of which was aircraft surveillance. His commanders found him efficient, quick to learn, and cool in an emergency. There is some question as to whether this duty gave Oswald access to classified information on radar operations, and changes were made in certain operations after he defected to Russia.

In July, 1959, he received a letter from his mother telling him she had been injured in an accident and needed

117

money. A heavy box fell on her in the store where she worked. She was entitled to compensation, but the case had not been adjudicated, and she wrote that she had sold her furniture and was living on three dollars a week. Lee applied for and was granted a hardship discharge from the Marine Corps and joined her in Fort Worth in September.

He stayed with her only three days.

Then he said, "Mother, my mind is made up. I want to get a ship and travel. I think I could earn more money for both of us."

It developed that he had saved $1,000 during his hitch in the Marines. He gave his mother $100 and departed. He led her to believe that he intended to go into the import-export business and said he could make "big money." He must have been afraid to tell her the truth, which was that he was going to Russia. From Fort Worth, he went to New Orleans and booked passage on a ship bound for Le Havre, France. Before it sailed he wrote her.

> Dear Mother:
> Well, I have booked passage for Europe. I would have had to sooner or later and I think it's best I go now. Just remember above all else that my values are very different from Robert's or yours. It is difficult to tell you how I feel. Just remember this is what I must do. I did not tell you about my plans because you could harly be expected to understand.

(The reader is advised that in passages quoted from Oswald's letters and other writings, he will find what appear to be an extraordinary number of typographical errors, such as "harly." They are, in fact, his misspellings.)

Nearly a month passed before Marguerite Oswald learned anything further about her son's whereabouts. Then she read in a Fort Worth newspaper that he had defected to Russia.

He flew from England to Finland, obtained a short-term Soviet visa in Helsinki, and went from there by train to Moscow. On October 16, 1959, two days before his twentieth birthday, he found himself in his Promised Land.

Intourist, the official Soviet travel agency, assigned a woman guide and interpreter to him, one Rima Shirokova. He promptly told her he wanted to become a Soviet citizen, that he had been trained in the Marines as a radar specialist, and that he would turn over to Soviet authorities any information of value to them acquired during his military service. Her reaction was not quite what he expected. A diary that he began at that time descrbes her as being "flabbergassted . . . politly sympathetic but uneasy." No doubt, Miss Shirokova passed along this information to her superiors, who, Oswald soon discovered, were not at all impressed. She appears to have developed a certain degree of affection for him. On his birthday, she gave him a copy of Dostoevski's *The Idiot,* with an inscription, "Dear Lee. Great congratulations. May all your dreams come true. 18, 10, 1959." Curiously enough, although the psychiatrists in New York had diagnosed him as starved for affection, he did not take Miss Shirokova's gesture at face value. He wrote in his diary that she probably "felt sorry" for him. Soon afterward, she may have saved his life after he apparently attempted to commit suicide.

The cause of this was that the Soviet authorities in Moscow, far from clasping Oswald immediately to their collective bosoms, at first were utterly cool to his desire to become a Soviet citizen. On October 21, an official told him only that he would see if the visa could be extended—and shortly after this interview, Oswald received orders to leave Moscow within two hours. In what he was now calling his "Historic Diary," Oswald wrote that he intended to kill himself:

> I am shocked!! My dreams . . . I have waited for two years to be accepted. My fondes dreams are shattered because of a petty official. . . . I decided to end it. Soak rist in water to numb the pain. Then slash my left wrist. Then plaug wrist into bathtum of hot water. . . . Somewhere a violin plays as I wacth my life whirl away. I think to myself, 'How Easy to Die' and 'A Sweet Death' (to violins.)

Miss Shirokova found him unconscious in his hotel room and promptly got him to a hospital. She did more than that for him, and again her kindness went unrecognized. He wrote in his diary, "Poor Rimmea stays by my side as interrpator (my Russian is still very bad) far into the night. I tell her 'Go home' (my mood is bad) but she stays, she is 'my friend'." One wonders why he put "my friend" in quotation marks.

Russian psychiatrists in the hospital examined Oswald

and, like those in New York, concluded that he was not dangerous. They also concluded correctly that he had slashed his wrist "in order to postpone his departure" from the Soviet Union.

As soon as he was released from the hospital, Oswald went to the American embassy and said he wanted to renounce his citizenship. He was very vehement about it. He coupled this by sending a formal written statement declaring that he wanted his passport revoked. Fortunately for him, the embassy officers took no immediate action to comply. If they had, he might never have been able to return to the United States—or Texas.

American correspondents in Moscow, of course, soon learned about the incident at the embassy, and they tracked Oswald to his hotel, seeking interviews. The distinguished journalist A. I. Goldberg wrote:

> Oswald confirmed that . . . he had come to the Soviet Union hoping to live and work there.
> He was asked whether a woman was involved. He declined to say. He was asked what he intended to do and how he intended to live. He said he would get along. He declined to say whether the Soviet Union had promised him citizenship and refused to allow a photograph to be made.
> An Associated Press man advised Oswald that there had been a similar case recently of a Long Island man who thought he wanted to stay in the Soviet Union but found that the going was rough and reclaimed his passport, returning to the United States.
> Oswald answered, "Maybe he didn't have as good reasons as I have." He refused to say what they were.

In other interviews, one lasting five hours, American reporters attempted to discover his ideological opinions. They concluded that he had a poor understanding of Marxism and that his pretense to be an intellectual collapsed like a pricked balloon under close questioning.

Throughout his stay in the Soviet Union, Oswald remained somewhat fuzzy about his reasons for leaving the United States. It is almost as though he had to invent them. In discussions with Russian acquaintances, he did rail against the "American imperialism" he had seen in the Far East. He contrasted the luxury of Park Avenue in

New York with life in the slums, although it is doubtful that he ever saw a penthouse or a 20-room apartment. At some point, too, while in Russia, Oswald became aware of the plight of the Negroes in America and hotly condemned segregation. He had lived in Louisiana and Texas, but racial injustice seems not to have bothered him until after he left the South. Perhaps he was merely telling the Russians what he thought they wanted to hear.

The central fact is that in leaving the United States, Lee Oswald was trying to run away from himself. Life at home had been flinty and unrewarding, but he did not realize that his own maladjustments had made it so. He thought he could leave his emotional quirks behind, shedding them as a snake sheds its skin. He said as much in a letter to his brother Robert. "I am starting a new life and I do not wish to have anything to do with the old life," he wrote. And in another letter, he told his brother ". . . I'm afraid you would not be able to comprehend my reasons [for coming to Russia.]" He said he hated the United States, and if war came, he would kill Americans. It has been suggested that in his political myopia, he envisioned Communism as the wave of the future and people saying of him, a century hence, "That fellow knew what he was doing." Marina Oswald understood him, and she was to state the case very well. In discussing her husband's later desire to live in Cuba, she said, "I am sure that if he had gone there he would not have liked it there either. Only on the moon."

Marina, as has been said, was not his first love. She caught him on the rebound.

For reasons unknown, the Russian authorities decided to let him remain in the country. They gave him an Identity Document for Stateless Persons and assigned him to work in Minsk in a factory making radio and television parts.

There, he met a woman named Ella German and seems to have fallen in love with her at first sight. Her family invited him to spend New Year's Day with them. He told his "historic" diary that he had had a happy time. The following night, he took Ella German to a movie. Later, on the doorstep of her apartment, he asked her to marry him. She replied that she did not love him, but the shocker came when she said she was afraid to marry an American. She cited some fairly contemporary history to show why

121

she considered it dangerous to espouse a foreigner. Oswald wrote in his diary that he was "too stunned to think."

If he had possessed the smallest shred of humor, he would have seen the irony of his situation. Here was a man who resented authority from any quarter. Yet, he had taken himself to a land where omnipresent authority would order him to live in a specified place, do a particular kind of work, tell him where he would take his vacations, where he could and could not travel. Now, to cap it all, he had fallen in love with a woman who felt so unfree that she was afraid to marry him. What a sad little farce! The saving grace of humor, especially the ability to laugh at oneself, might have rescued Lee Oswald, but he was much too introverted to have a sense of humor.

The rejection by Ella German, partly due to his nationality, was not Oswald's first jolt in Russia. Signs in his diary indicate that he was beginning to perceive some cracks and seams in the socialist paradise. He wrote that he was becoming "increasingly conscious of just what sort of sociaty" he had found in Russia. He had money to spend but there was no place to spend it for entertainment. No bowling alleys! With respect to food, he wrote:

I have become habituatated to a small cafe which is where I dine in the evening. The food is generaly poor and alwas eactly the same, menue in any cafe, at any point in the city. The food is cheap and I don't really care about quiality after three years in the U.S.M.C."

He soon perceived that there was a privileged class in the Soviet Union. The differences in standards might not be as wide as those between Park Avenue and the slums of New York, but they existed. Oswald concluded that the members of the Communist party were mainly interested in their own welfare, not the condition of the masses.

His work began to bore him, and he was disappointed in his dream of being in a position to study in Russia. He had applied for admission to a university in Moscow, but the application was rejected on the ground that only students from underdeveloped countries of Asia, Africa, and Latin America were eligible to enroll.

On all counts, Oswald was beginning to find his life in Russia duplicating the pattern of frustration and disappointment he had known at home. His letters to his brother and his mother became more frequent. He inquired about his citizenship status in a letter to the American embassy. Toward the end of 1960, his eyes were turning homeward. He had not found Utopia, and he had not been able to run away from himself. The "new life" about which he had written Robert Oswald turned out to be no different from the one he had left.

He could not forget Ella German. On the contrary, his diary indicates that he determined to show her there were other fish in the Russian sea.

In March, 1961, at a dance, he saw a pretty blonde with delicate, vivacious features. He asked to be introduced. Her name was Marina Nikolaevna. She was living in Minsk with her aunt and uncle. She had been trained as a pharmacist. She was quick and intelligent. Oswald danced with her through most of the evening and then escorted her to her home. They arranged to meet again in the following week. A day or two later, however, he was hospitalized, and he asked her to visit him in the hospital, which she did. Wearing her pharmacist's uniform, Marina was able to come to the hospital whenever she pleased, and she visited him frequently, in and out of visiting hours. On Easter Sunday, she brought him a colored egg. She seems to have liked him from the beginning.

Soon after he left the hospital, they became engaged. Marina might have hesitated if she had known the reason for this romantic blitz.

Unlike Ella German, the prospect of marrying an American did not worry Marina or her aunt and uncle, possibly because of her uncle's privileged position in the Communist hierarchy. He was a party member and a colonel in the Ministry of Internal Affairs.

There is no reason to believe Marina consented to marry Oswald as a means of leaving the Soviet Union. She was pretty and popular, had numerous friends her own age (she was then nineteen), and had had one or two mild romances before she met Oswald. Apart from that, he indicated to her that he was not certain that he could return to the United States. After they were married, he told her he wanted to go home.

The wedding took place on April 30, 1961. The description of the wedding party in Oswald's diary is reminiscent of the nuptial scenes in Russian novels. Some twenty friends and "neboribos" attended, some of whom found his accent "disquiting" and, having seen few foreigners in Minsk, were curious about him. However, wine flowed,

123

and the gaiety mounted until Marina's uncle started a "fright" (Oswald must have meant "fight"), during which an overloaded fuse blew and all the lights went out. The bridal couple seized the opportunity to escape. Ah, the Russian soul!

The diary entry for the very next day, May 1, shows that romance was not the only factor, nor even the principal one, that motivated Oswald to take a wife. He wrote, "In spite of fact I married Marina to hurt Ella I found myself in love with Marina."

Another entry, written somewhat later, says:

The trassition of changing full love from Ella to Marina was very painfull esp. as I saw Ella almost every day at the factory but as the days & weeks went by I adjusted more and more to my wife mentaly. . . . she is madly in love with me from the start."

Here, it would seem, was Lee Harvey Oswald's golden opportunity to build a new world for himself and to climb to a higher plateau of fulfillment. The psychiatrists had diagnosed his mental and emotional maladjustments as stemming from having been starved for affection all his life. Now he found an attractive woman "madly in love" with him. Here, surely, was his chance for happiness, and for a time, he was happy. But in the long run, he reverted to type. Oswald was a taker, not a giver.

Before the end of May, he had made up his mind that he wanted to go home. He wrote the embassy in Moscow to that effect, said he had married a Russian woman, and would petition the Soviet authorities for an exit visa for his wife. To further his intentions, he also wrote Senator John Tower of Texas, "I beseech you, Senator Tower, to rise the question of holding by the Soviet Union of a citizen of the U.S. against his will and expressed desires." This was an overstatement. It was simply an effort by Oswald to speed up the wheels of bureaucracy, Russian and American.

Another letter went to John Connally, and it is significant on two counts, a different explanation of his reason for going to Russia and what appears to be an implied threat. When Oswald defected to Russia, the Marines changed the classification of his discharge from "honorable" to "undesirable." Oswald, who had said he "hated" the United States, now not only wanted to come home but

124

displayed a newfound pride in his status as a former Marine. Thinking Connally was still Secretary of the Navy, Oswald wrote him, "In November 1959 an event was well publicated in the Ft. Worth newspapers concerning a person who had gone to the Soviet Union to reside for a short time (much in the same way E. Hemingway resided in Paris.)"

He conveniently overlooked the fact that he had attempted to renounce his citizenship, and as for going to Russia at all, well, he had been just like another well-known expatriate. He then came to the point of his letter, demanding that Connally see to it that the Marines restore him to the status of one "honorably discharged." He said, "I shall employ all means to right this gross mistake or injustice to a bona-fide U.S. citizen and ex-serviceman."

This sentence was to cause speculation as to whether Oswald, whose Marine status remained "undesirable," was actually shooting at Connally on November 22, not the President. The physical circumstances would hardly support the theory. Connally was riding on the jump seat in front of Kennedy. Therefore, if the Governor had been Oswald's real target, Oswald would have had an unobstructed view of him as the limousine came toward the Book Building. Once the car turned the corner and began moving away from the Building, the position of the President in the rear seat would have pretty well obscured the view of Connally from the sixth-floor window.

In the summer of 1962, the Soviets granted Marina an exit visa. The State Department ruled that Oswald was an American citizen and entitled to return to his own country. The embassy in Moscow loaned him $435.71 for his passage, which he repaid later. With Marina and their four-month-old daughter, June Lee, he disembarked from the Holland-America liner "Maasdam" on June 13. An agent of the Traveler's Aid Society, Spas Raiken, helped them find hotel accommodations. "One thing that impressed me," Raiken said, "was that he was trying to avoid contact with anybody. It was like pulling teeth to try to get any information out of him." The patient Robert Oswald sent his brother $200 for the airplane tickets to Dallas.

So ended Oswald's Russian idyl, another failure, another defeat, another fruitless quest. He still hated the United States, but now he added Russia to his list of hatreds. Had he lived longer, he might have found himself hating all systems and ideologies. In his mind, however, he still had one left: Fidel Castro's Cuba.

From childhood, due to his mother's frequent moving, Oswald had never remained long in one place. Nor could he now when he attempted to settle down in Texas. Wandering seems to have become endemic in him. He first found employment in a sheet metal firm in Fort Worth. After about three months, he quit but lied about this to his wife. He told her he had been fired. They moved to Dallas. There, he got a job in commercial advertising, doing photographic work. He liked his work and began going to night school two or three times a week. He held the job for about six weeks, but his work was unsatisfactory, and he quarreled frequently with his co-workers, disputes that sometimes verged on fist fights. This time he really was fired. He thought he saw greener pastures in New Orleans and went there in April, 1963. He took a job greasing coffee-processing machines. Perhaps because he was ashamed of it, he wrote Marina that he was again working in photography. She had remained in Dallas in Ruth Paine's home.

This was not their first separation. On a number of previous occasions, when they were short of money, she lived with friends she had met in the Dallas-Fort Worth area.

Among them was a group of White Russians who liked Marina and felt sorry to see her living in what they considered poverty. Her standards were more modest than theirs, and she was to testify that she did not feel sorry for herself. She said she considered her husband's earnings "quite enough" to meet their needs. Nonetheless, her Russian friends undertook to help her. They gave her money and clothes. They bought food for her and the baby.

Lee Oswald bitterly resented her friends and their kindnesses. Perhaps it was natural; no man likes to feel that he is a poor provider. Here was a man who needed to feel superior, and did—and now he found others helping support his family with charity. His pride was cut to the quick. He was not too proud to accept welfare checks, but for Marina to accept gifts from individuals galled him. (Today's widespread welfare psychology?) Nor did he accept help from his mother with any better grace. When she bought some articles for the baby, he angrily told her not to do it again. She said, "He strongly put me in my place about buying things for his wife that he himself could not buy." Marina, despite her testimony that she

126

had not been dissatisfied, has been pictured as a nag who "threw it up to him" that Lee could not give her what her more affluent friends were providing. Two Russian acquaintances, George and Jeanne de Mohrenschildt, were to testify, "She was annoying him all the time—'Why don't you make some money?' Poor guy was going out of his mind." He made no effort to conceal his resentment. One evening when he came home, he found Marina with her friends. Ignoring them completely, he ordered her to prepare his dinner and ate it alone and in silence. Mrs. De Mohrenschildt said, "He was offensive with people and I can understand why. He could never give her what the people were showering on her . . . no matter how hard he worked—and he worked very hard." At one point, Oswald was taking as much overtime work as he could get.

They quarreled frequently, and not only about money. Oswald did not want his wife to smoke or use cosmetics. He wanted to improve his command of the Russian language and selfishly refused to permit her to learn English. Once she left him for two weeks, and he did not even know her whereabouts until one of the Russians told him. On another occasion, he blackened her eye. A letter from Marina to one of her ex-boyfriends in Russia accidentally fell into Lee's hands. She wrote that she was sorry she had not married the Russian. Lee read it and said he did not believe she meant what she wrote, but he insisted that these were her feelings. He hit her in the eye. Curiously enough, Marina seemed to consider that he might be within his rights in doing so.

As though all these strains were not enough, Marina was quoted by her friends as saying, openly and in her husband's presence, that he left her sexually unsatisfied. "Right in front of him," De Mohrenschildt testified, "She said, 'He sleeps with me just once a month and I never get any satisfaction out of it." Ruth Paine said Marina told her she found Oswald inadequate as a man.

He became increasingly nervous and irritable and tended to fly into rages over trivial things. Marina was to say that ". . . Lee changed. I did not know him as such a man in Russia."

No wonder. To his other failures, Lee Oswald could now add failure as the head of a family and failure as a male.

It is possible that by the spring of 1963, Oswald unconsciously had developed a death wish. His actions in an episode involving resigned Major General Edwin A. Walker suggest something of this nature.

At about nine o'clock on the night of April 10, 1963, a bullet went through the window of Walker's study, narrowly missing him. There were no witnesses. Oswald, Marina said, was away from home that night, and when he returned, "He was very pale. I don't remember the exact time but it was very late. And he told me not to ask any questions. He only told me he had shot at General Walker." Oswald did not know if he had hit the General but soon learned that he had missed.

Walker is a rightist. Marina said Oswald called him a "very bad man, a Fascist." She says she replied that this did not give anyone a right to try to kill him. To which she said her husband replied that if someone had killed Adolf Hitler, millions of lives would have been spared.

Evidently, he had been planning the attack for some time. He thoroughly familiarized himself with the bus schedules in Dallas (which may explain why he left the bus and took a taxi after the assassination of the President). More important, he wrote in Russian a list of instructions for Marina telling her what to do in case he should suddenly be taken from her. He wrote 11 numbered paragraphs. The second said, "Send the information *as to what has happened to me* to the [Soviet] Embassy and include newspaper clippings (should there be anything about me in the papers)". The italics have been supplied. The last paragraph contained the phrase, "If I am alive and taken prisoner. . . ."

Marina said she became very angry when he told her he had shot at Walker and made him promise never to take such action again. When he showed her the list of instructions, she said she took it away from him and threatened to use it against him if he ever did attempt some violent act.

If Oswald had been caught after he shot at Walker, his home would have been searched and the police would have found the incriminating document. They also would have found the photograph which showed him with the rifle and brandishing a copy of a Soviet magazine, as well as finding the rifle itself. The list of instructions, inferring that Marina might be left alone, and especially the eleventh paragraph, beginning "If I am alive . . . ," shows that Oswald had foreseen the possibility of being arrested and even killed. Naturally, too, being a man who craved

128

recognition, he pictured his name and photograph in the newspapers.

The whole episode raises the question: Had Lee Oswald reached the point where he wanted to die? Not peacefully in bed. Not by his own hand. He must go to his grave in a blaze of melodrama and a flurry of personal publicity that would fix his name in history. If this is so, it would explain the mysteries of his actions after he killed Kennedy. But then, why did he deny complicity in the assassination? Again, the pattern emerges, apparent irrationality concealing tangled reasoned behavior. Marina herself said, "I am guessing that perhaps he did it to appear to be a brave man in case he were arrested, but that is my supposition. . . ." He had baffled his wife, too.

The remainder of Lee Oswald's unhappy story is soon told.

In May, after he found a job, he sent for Marina and the baby. Ruth Paine drove them to New Orleans. They settled into a house, and for a time life seemed more serene than at any time since they left Russia. He took out a library card and came home at night carrying stacks of books. Some were devoted to anti-Communist subjects. Of possible significance is that another dealt with the assassination of Huey Long. At the same time, he showed a newfound interest in the father he had never known. During the time when he had been in New Orleans waiting to take the ship to Europe, he made no effort to find the grave of Robert E. L. Oswald. Now he did. He was at home every night with Marina and the infant daughter, whom he adored. He was less domineering toward his wife. In every respect, he gave the impression of being a normal family man.

Then the more familiar Oswald reappeared, the Mr. Hyde in his nature.

He became surly, and neighbors considered him arrogant. His landlady, Mrs. Lena Garner, recalled, "When he passed me or my husband in the yard, he just kept walking, head down." There are indications that he took to sitting in the dark on the screen porch at night, operating the bolt on his rifle. He was soon to lose his job.

At the same time, his pro-Castro activities began. One of his first moves was an offer to put his training in the Marines in the service of a group of *anti*-Castro Cubans, to train them as guerrillas. In all probability, his purpose was to try to infiltrate the organization, for only a day or two later he was plastering pro-Castro placards on the walls of his home. Mrs. Garner asked him to remove them. A singer in a bar, Connie Kay, said he upbraided her over a line in her act in which she referred to "Castro the Bastro." She said Oswald approached her and angrily asked, "Why are you mocking that man?" He became the Secretary—the only member—of the "New Orleans Chapter of the Fair Play For Cuba Committee." Its President was listed as "A. J. Hidell," the alias Oswald used to rent post office boxes. He knew a little Spanish and tried to brush up on the language. He talked of hijacking an airplane to get to Cuba. Was it all fantasy?

The weight of evidence indicates that he was sincere in wanting to go to Cuba. Henry Wade, the Dallas District Attorney, heard Oswald being questioned after the assassination and said he had the impression Oswald was "a sincere, dedicated believer in Fidel Castro." Had he succeeded in reaching Cuba, it would have been his last ploy in all probability, the final effort to identify himself with a Cause.

It may have been connected with an earlier move. Apparently reversing himself with respect to Russia, he talked of returning to the Soviet Union. He forced Marina to apply for a visa, and, although she said she was unhappy about it, she did so, mailing his application with hers. What she did not know was that he had enclosed a note to the Soviet embassy requesting the Russians to push through the visa for her as soon as possible but to consider his "separtably." It thus appears that Oswald had no intention of returning to Russia with Marina. He probably thought that having a Soviet visa would inprove his prospects for getting the Cuban visa. It all appears very devious.

In September, the Mexican consulate in New Orleans granted him a 15-day tourist card. He said he planned a photographic tour of Mexico, but his real aim, of course, was to contact the Cuban embassy in Mexico City.

Meanwhile, he had lost his job in the coffee warehouse. In his other jobs, although his work was not always satisfactory, he at least tried to be reliable in attendance. In New Orleans, it was different. His employer said, "He was never around when we needed him."

Ruth Paine passed through New Orleans in returning from a motor trip through the East. Marina was pregnant a second time, and it was decided that the Oswalds should go back to Texas. Mrs. Paine and Oswald loaded their belongings in her station wagon, and she drove them to Irving. Early on the mogrning of September 24, he left her home. He told her he was going to Houston to look for work.

Instead, he went to Nuevo Laredo, where he crossed the border into Mexico and rode the 750 miles to Mexico City on a bus.

Now came the last disappointment, the last failure.

On the morning after his arrival, he applied at the Cuban embassy for a transit visa. Oswald was well acquainted with red tape, but when he was advised that this would take time, he flew into a rage and stalked out of the embassy, slamming the door. From there, he went to see the officials in the Soviet embassy. They also told him that he might have to wait three months or more for the Cuban visa. Sick with frustration, Oswald railed against "petty officials."

His last dream exploded. He was finished.

He returned to Texas and the half-life began in terms of his marriage, with Marina in Irving and Oswald in Dallas. Night after night, he came from work to the rooming house and sat alone, reading or watching television. He himself was soon to appear again on the TV screen.

On the night of November 22, there was a riotous, shouting press conference in the Dallas jail. It may be asked why the law enforcement authorities of the city permitted it. The explanation has been advanced that they wanted to "lean over backward" to cooperate with the press in the hope of improving the now badly damaged image of Dallas. In any case, the bedlam of reporters and photographers and TV cameras took place. A man who was neither, but who had wormed his way into the jail by posing as a newspaperman, was present. He stood with his back against a wall, gravely watching the uproar. He wore dark glasses and held a pipe in his right hand.

His name was Jack Ruby.

12

"Air Force One" thundered on toward Washington, heavily freighted with grief and horror and memories and the aching sense of loss. In the rear of the airplane lay the body of the fallen Chief. His widow, still tearless, still wearing her bloodstained clothes, sat at a small desk. O'Brien, O'Donnell, Powers, and General McHugh stood beside her. Once, she pointed to an empty chair and indicated that someone should take it. None of the four men did so. They stood like an honor guard around Jacqueline Kennedy and the bronze casket on the floor. From time to time, she laid her hand on the cold metal.

In the forward compartment, the new President already was beginning to govern. He telephoned constantly. He called for the Cabinet to convene early Saturday morning. He told Washington he would like to have Robert S. McNamara, the Secretary of Defense, and McGeorge Bundy, the special adviser, at Andrews Air Force Base when he landed so that he could be briefed on any vital developments overseas or at home since the assassination. He telephoned Rose Kennedy. He telephoned Nellie Connally to ask about her husband's condition, and the airwaves brought his voice to her, saying, "We are praying for you, darling, and I know everything's going to be all right. Give him a hug and kiss for me." He dictated memoranda. He discussed legislative questions with the three Texas congressmen on the plane. He grasped the reins of power with a sure hand. There was no clashing of gears in the transition of the Presidency from John F. Kennedy to Lyndon Baines Johnson.

Power is a tangible thing. It breathes in the offices in Washington. It is an almost visible aura around a man wielding great authority. Before coming there, he may have been a businessman or a scholar with little influence outside his immediate circles. A new Administration takes over in Washington, and this man finds himself with a

132

large, thickly-carpeted office and just outside its doors an army of assistants and secretaries. He notices a pleasantly subtle change in the attitude toward him of men he has worked with and known well. He may press a button on his desk, and on the other side of the world, men will jump to do his bidding. His voice may very well be decisive in formulating a national policy of vast consequence. He would be less than human if he did not carry from the meeting a golden glow of pride and a sense of power. "O, it is fine to have the strength of a giant. . . ." The memoirs of former government officers—and especially the penciled annotations on the margins of their manuscript diaries—recall such triumphs and reflect the golden glow. Once having known great power, it is not easy to relinquish it. To paraphrase a well-known axiom; the *absence* of power may corrupt absolutely. And so, in the most ideal circumstances, the transition between Administrations is not always smooth and pleasant at all echelons.

The circumstances aboard "Air Force One" as it roared along its northeasterly course were anything but ideal.

Greatly differing versions circulate about the degree of tension between the Johnson and Kennedy people on the plane. Some noticed none. Others remember the atmosphere as having been heavy with tension. A passenger, who asked to remain unidentified, said he considered that Johnson displayed "impatience" when Mrs. Kennedy did not come forward immediately to witness the oath-taking. He added that the Kennedy men noticed and resented this. O'Brien does not recall it. Malcolm Kilduff was quoted as saying, "That was the sickest airplane I ever was on." He is said to have refused a "five-figure offer" to write his account of the flight. Another passenger said, "They refought the battles of 1960." True, the 1960 contest between Kennedy and Johnson had been a bitter one, and some of the opposing warriors were cooped up together now. However, it seems doubtful that any of those on either side would have had the stomach to rehash a political feud in the immediate aftermath of so great a tragedy. Jack Valenti and Homer Thornberry said they remembered no such discussion. There was, of course, the confrontation between Johnson and O'Donnell over when the plane should take off. O'Donnell wanted to leave immediately, thinking of Mrs. Kennedy and fearing that Dallas authorities might make another attempt to hold the President's body for an autopsy. Johnson wanted to be sworn in

133

on the ground, and his authority was paramount. But in general, the conflicting versions of the degree of friction on the plane seem to be the products of different interpretations of the same events and the choice of the adjectives used to describe them.

The accounts set down by two writers illustrate the point.

In his book, William Manchester wrote, "To those who loved John Kennedy, the transition of power seemed needlessly cruel. Consolidating the two groups on one airplane was to prove extremely unfortunate, and aspects of Johnson's behavior in a very understandable state of shock may have proven exacerbating, but the difficulty there was largely one of manners and mannerisms. Johnson was not himself that afternoon—no man was himself then." Manchester also pictured O'Donnell, during the swearing-in ceremony, as "pacing the corridor outside the bedroom like a caged tiger, his hands clapped over his ears as though to block the oath." * In fact, O'Donnell told the Warren Commission he was present at the ceremony, and a photograph published by the Boston *Globe* showed him standing at Mrs. Kennedy's elbow as Johnson took the oath.

Charles Roberts of *Newsweek Magazine* was aboard the plane as part of the press "pool" on the flight. He wrote:

As an unbiased witness to it [the transition], now that questions have been raised, I might add something more. It was careful, correct, considerate and compassionate. Considering that it occurred at a time when no one knew the full implications of Oswald's deed . . . it was a masterpiece of cool-headed improvisation.†

"Air Force One" hurtled toward Washington at 635 miles per hour. The setting sun filled the windows on the port side with rose-and-gold light. In the rear cabin, someone suggested a drink, a stiff drink. O'Donnell mixed a Scotch and water for Mrs. Kennedy. They all found that alcohol was a weak anesthetic for the kind of pain they

* William Manchester, *The Death of a President* (New York: Harper & Row, 1967), p. 325.

† Charles Roberts, *The Truth About the Assassination* (New York: Grosset & Dunlap, 1967), p. 106.

were feeling. So did countless Americans that Friday afternoon. The widow only sipped her drink. As O'Donnell phrased it later, "My recollection is that I had little success with that. She just wanted to reminisce."

She talked about their life together, recalling the experiences, big and small, pleasant and painful, that they had shared. It seemed to bring a measure of relief to retreat into the past, when she had her husband with her. Then, her thoughts began turning ahead. She said she wanted to conduct herself during the next three days, when she would be in the sight of so many Americans, in a manner that her husband would have approved. She would fight back the tears and hold her head high. Then she began speaking about funeral arrangements. Her husband had been looking forward with keen pleasure to attending the Army-Navy football game. Jacqueline Kennedy wondered whether cadets from all the Service academies could march in the funeral procession. And inasmuch as John Kennedy had been a Navy man, she wanted a Navy ambulance to take his body from Andrews, and the hospital, she said, would be the United States Naval Hospital at Bethesda, Maryland. A telephone call from the airplane to Washington set the wheels in motion for carrying out her wishes.

In the bedroom, Lyndon Johnson was writing the statement he would have to deliver at Andrews when he stepped down from the ramp. It was short, but he worked it over several times.

In the President's office in the White House, a sad task was going forward. They were removing some of his most prized mementos, the coconut shell in which he had sent the message for help after the *"Amagiri"* rammed and sank PT-109, the framed photographs of his wife and of Caroline and John-John at different ages, the silver calendar that marked the dates of the beginning and end of the Cuban missile crisis. His favorite rocking chair was taken away. Goodbye, Mr. President.

In front of the White House, the people stood, simply looking, although there was nothing to see except the gleaming white portico, and others milled aimlessly up and down Pennsylvania Avenue, back and forth, speaking in hushed tones. Policemen said, "Keep moving, please, keep moving." Their voices were gruff but not so peremptory as usual.

The White House announced in late afternoon that "Air

135

Force One" was expected to land at Andrews at 6:15. A crowd began gathering there, too. The blinding white television lights flooded the field, and the cameras picked up the figures of government officials and the stricken expressions everywhere. Unobserved, Robert Kennedy came to the field. He stood in the shadows, careful to avoid being recognized and then caught by the TV cameras.

At dusk, a pale sliver of a moon glowed in the sky. The plane came into sight, banked, and lined up with the runway. The TV crews shut off the floodlights so as not to interfere with the landing. They went up again as Jim Swindal brought the ship to a stop. They limned the identifications, "United States of America," blue on the white fuselage, and the flag painted on the tail assembly.

A gray Navy ambulance rolled across the apron to the side of the airplane, turned around, and backed into position to receive the casket. At the same time, a forklift truck, used to load and unload heavy freight, approached the ramp.

Robert Kennedy darted out of his hiding place, hurtling up the steps just as the door opened. He disappeared inside the plane. Eight uniformed pallbearers followed him, but they were not permitted to lift the casket to the forklift. O'Donnell, O'Brien, Powers, and McHugh insisted on rendering this last physical act of service to the man they cherished as friend and leader. They placed the heavy bronze on the lift. It lowered slowly until it stood level with the floor of the ambulance.

At that moment, Jacqueline Kennedy and Robert appeared in the door of the plane. He was gripping her right hand in his and his head was slightly bowed. The spectators, previously silent, gasped when they saw the blood on the front of her skirt. The millions of words pouring out of Dallas all afternoon had been shocking enough. Now, seeing the crimson stains, the full impact of the horror swept over them. Jacqueline Kennedy's dark eyes were wide, staring, as she watched the men below gently push the casket into the ambulance and close the folding door. Then she came down the steps with her brother-in-law. An officer started to guide her to a limousine, but she shook her head. Instead, she reached for the handle on the side door of the ambulance and stepped inside. Kennedy and McHugh followed her. There were no seats in the rear of the vehicle. They sat on the floor beside the casket, leaning

136

against it. The ambulance moved off the field. Five black limousines, like a funeral cortege, followed it.

Only then did Lyndon Johnson leave the airplane. He looked haggard and weary. He held his wife's elbow as they descended to the apron. All around him, he found familiar faces. He had asked that Bundy and McNamara be prepared to give him an immediate briefing, and so, not knowing where the President might wish to talk, they had come out to the airfield to meet him. In the floodlight, Johnson may have noticed that Senator Hubert Humphrey's eyes were red with weeping. Humphrey, like Johnson, had been crushed under the wheels of the Kennedy juggernaut in 1960 and had withdrawn early from the fight for the nomination. But whatever bitterness Humphrey felt at the time was washed away in his grief now. There were other senators, Everett McKinley Dirksen, the Republican leader, and his opposite number, Mike Mansfield. Kennedy's friends and lieutenants clustered together, Ted Sorensen, Arthur Schlesinger, Jr., and Ralph Dungan. George Ball, of the State Department, didn't know it then, but he was to be asked by Johnson to ride with him into Washington, along with McNamara and Bundy. Franklin Roosevelt, Jr., then in the Commerce Department, Postmaster John Grounouski, and Anthony Celebrezze, chief of Health, Education, and Welfare, waited near a bank of microphones. And there was Averell Harriman, tall, slightly stooped, gray-faced, a man who had served three Democratic Presidents and 11 years earlier had made his own bid for the White House. These were men who had made history and now appeared in one of its darkest chapters.

Johnson shook a few hands but said nothing. He approached the bank of microphones and put on his glasses and drew a slip of paper from his pocket, the message written during the flight from Dallas. He drew Mrs. Johnson closer to him and then began reading in a low, firm, voice:

This is a sad time for all people. We have suffered a loss that cannot be weighed. For it is a deep personal tragedy. I know the world shares the sorrow that Mrs. Kennedy and her family bear.

I will do my best. That is all I can do. I ask your help—and God's.

137

He turned away and stood for a moment talking with the Congressional leaders. McNamara and Bundy, in response to the message from him in flight, awaited him. Johnson then made his way toward a helicopter, shaking a hand here and there. He helped his wife into the aircraft. When the others were aboard, the helicopter rose in the air, heading for the White House.

Exactly 20 minutes after "Air Force One" touched down at Andrews, Johnson was on the White House lawn. He and his wife and Bundy and McNamara walked through the rose garden toward the Executive Office. They came to the French doors of the President's office. He entered alone. The others waited on the portico. The office was Johnson's now, and he intended to get to work immediately, but not in this room. Not yet. He remained there only a minute, looking around. Then he left and crossed the street to his own office on the second floor of the Executive Building. He continued the conference with McNamara and Bundy that had started on the helicopter flight. Congressional leaders and others appeared. They told him that in this hour, there were no Democrats nor Republicans, that regardless of party, they stood ready to help him. A new President always has a honeymoon with Congress, but Johnson's was set against the background of tragedy. The President called J. Edgar Hoover. By that time of course, Oswald had been in the hands of the Dallas police and under questioning for about four hours. They already felt more than reasonably sure that they had run to earth the President's assassin. Johnson ordered Hoover to throw all his resources into gathering evidence. A man described as a surly, twenty-four-year-old laborer was in custody, but the full implications of the assassination were not known; the nation and the new President needed to hear all the facts as soon as possible. He ate dinner at his desk with three friends, Bill Moyers, George Reedy, and Walter Jenkins. There would be a Cabinet meeting on Saturday, and Johnson set up other meetings for the coming day. He had taken over the Presidency.

Johnson went home at 9:24. He lived in Silver Spring, Maryland, in a large house built in the style of Norman architecture, "The Elms." In the front hall, he kept a silver-framed photograph of Sam Rayburn, "Mr. Sam," the stubby, bald, shrewd, immensely likable Texan who had been Speaker of the House for so many years. Johnson

138

paused beside the photograph and murmured, "Well, Mr. Speaker, I wish you were here tonight."

He meant it, deeply. Lyndon Johnson for years had known the workings of the machinery of government as well as or better than any man in Washington. He knew the complications, the intricate relationship between the White House and Congress, the subtleties in wheeling and dealing. Long before, it had been said of him, "He knows the deck." It meant that Johnson knew Capitol Hill like a pack of cards, the strengths and weaknesses and the human and political chords to touch to bring a desired response from a given senator or congressman. But the task confronting him now was a thousand times more awesome than steering legislation through Capitol Hill. Now he held the responsibility for decisions that might affect the very existence of the United States. He was conscious that he needed help. And so, invoking the shade of a man who would have given him invaluable help, he said, "Well, Mr. Speaker, I wish you were here tonight."

Lyndon Johnson was very human that night.

With friends, he watched television for a while. Every channel brought pictures of Dallas, Lee Harvey Oswald, press conferences, interviews with Texas law enforcement officers, scenes of the Kennedy Era in the White House, shots of Johnson. But when there came on the screen pictures of Kennedy at Love Field that very morning, less than 12 hours earlier, close-ups of Jacqueline Kennedy's radiance and the President grinning and grasping at a thicket of outstretched hands, Johnson abruptly snapped off the set. "I just can't take that," he said.

His thoughts turned from heavy responsibilities to simple matters, small acts of kindness that he might have set aside for the time being. He told James Rowley, Chief of the Secret Service, about Rufus Youngblood's swiftness and bravery when the first shot sounded on Elm Street and described the extraordinary precautions taken by the agent to protect him at the hospital and during the drive to Love Field. "I want you to do whatever you can, the best that can be done, for that boy," he said to Rowley.

Next, the President went to his study. He took two pieces of his stationery from an escritoire and began writing. His first letters as President were for Caroline and John-John. Some day, they would be old enough to understand his feelings for them and for their father and mother.

139

His day ended.

For Jacqueline Kennedy and those with her, the day was far from over. She waited on the 17th floor of the Naval Hospital. With her were members and in-laws of the Kennedy family, the White House aides who had been on the flight to Texas, and some friends. In the morgue below, three specialists were conducting the autopsy, Commander J. J. Humes, Commander Thornton Boswell and Lieutenant-Colonel Pierre A. Finck. It had been understood that the autopsy and embalming would be completed by midnight. The hour passed without word from the room below. As in Parkland Hospital, Jacqueline Kennedy would not leave until her husband's body was removed. Nobody left the 17th floor, although she urged the women who had been with her all day, the unbelievably long day, to go home and get some rest.

When it became evident that she was not going to follow her own advice, an overnight bag and makeup case marked with her initials, J.B.K., were brought to her in the hospital. She left both unopened. More friends came to the suite on the 17th floor. Robert McNamara came directly from the conference with Johnson to ask what he might do for Jacqueline Kennedy. And there were two friends, Charles and Martha Bartlett, who filled a special place in the story now ended. In 1951, they introduced Jacqueline Bouvier, a socialite then working as an inquiring photographer, to Representative Jack Kennedy of Massachusetts. Two years later, they attended the wedding. Bartlett is a widely-read columnist on political subjects.

Friends came to offer the consoling hand of friendship. The hour was late, and some of them were surprised to find Jacqueline Kennedy still awake, able to speak with them, and busy.

It was to be a sleepless night for her. She refused a sedative. With Robert Kennedy and Sargent Shriver, head of the Peace Corps and also a relative by marriage, she was thinking about plans for the funeral. Standard references were available. A copy of the manual *State, Official and Special Military Funeral Policies and Plans*, was taken to the White House that same night. Mrs. Kennedy herself had worked on the revision of the guidebook distributed by the White House Historical Association. It contains an engraving of Abraham Lincoln's body lying in state on a catafalque in the White House. A telephone call from the hospital to the artist, William Walton, asked him to find a

140

book in the White House with other sketches and photographs of Lincoln's funeral. John F. Kennedy's casket would rest on the Lincoln catafalque.

During the night, the White House drew up a schedule based on protocol for those who would come to view the body. The first hour, beginning at 10:00 A.M., Saturday, was reserved for the President's family. Thereafter, at specified times, Johnson, former Presidents Dwight D. Eisenhower and Harry S. Truman, and high-ranking officials of government would be together in the East Room of the White House. (Herbert Hoover, ailing and soon to go to his grave, sent word that he would not be present.) And after these groups, the senators and congressmen and members of the diplomatic corps would pay their respects. On the Sunday, the general public would file past the casket in the Great Rotunda in the Capitol.

After the funeral on Monday, the casket would be lowered into a grave in Arlington Cemetery on a particular site chosen by the Kennedys because they knew how much pleasure the President had found there. In March, he had gone for a stroll through Arlington with a friend. They walked part way up a hillside and stopped at a spot just below the white-columned Custis-Lee Mansion, the former home of General Robert E. Lee. Kennedy had stood there, admiring the view. He had looked across the Potomac, past the Lincoln Memorial and the Washington Monument and the buildings beyond. Apart from its beauty, the view stirred his strong sense of history. He had breathed deeply of the spring air and said, "I could stay here forever."

A line drawn from the flag in front of the mansion to the center of the Lincoln Memorial would pass directly over the spot where he had been standing. After Robert Kennedy suggested the site, McNamara sent a team of Army surveyors to position the gravesite on the exact spot, and the Secretary himself then went to inspect it.

It was Jacqueline Kennedy who wanted a flame to burn eternally beside the grave. Army Engineers installed the apparatus for it.

The long night wore on, still without word from the cold, brilliantly lighted morgue, outside which an honor guard had been standing for hours. The three specialists were conducting a thorough, painstaking autopsy. Their findings, particularly the points of entry, angle, and direction of the bullets that pierced the President's body, would

141

be of the greatest importance in the investigation of the assassination.

The entire body was X-rayed. Photographs in color and black-and-white were made showing the significant findings but were not developed.

Commander Humes telephoned Dr. Perry in Dallas to ascertain that he had enlarged the wound in the throat in performing the tracheotomy. Perry confirmed this. In Parkland, the surgeons had fought to save the President's life. They had not been primarily concerned as to whether the wound in the throat had been caused by a bullet entering or exiting at that point. They were concerned with the damage. But the wound, by entrance or exit, was to become a vital question after the Warren Report came under attack. An entrance wound tends to be well-defined, with clean, rounded edges. A bullet exiting from the body tends to tear the flesh, leaving a larger wound with jagged, stellate edges. If the bullet struck Kennedy in the throat and exited from the back of his neck, it meant that the assassin had fired from a point ahead of the limousine. Therefore, it meant that not all the shots had been fired from a point behind and above him. In short, it meant that Lee Oswald had accomplices, and together they caught the President in a cross fire. After the tracheotomy, it could not be determined with precision whether the hole in his throat was an exit or entrance wound.

Thus, the surgeons' autopsy report would say "the wound *presumably*" was an exit wound. The angle of the bullet's passage, downward from a point above the scapula, the shoulderblade, through the throat, tends to support this conclusion. In summarizing all the findings, the autopsy report went on to say, "Based on the above observations it is our opinion that the deceased died of two perforating gunshot wounds inflicted by high velocity projectiles. . . . The projectiles were fired from *a point behind and somewhat above the deceased.*" (All italics supplied.)

If these findings are correct, Kennedy was not hit by any shots fired from the railway overpass or the knoll on his right. The most likely point "above and behind" from which the bullets might have come was an upper floor of the Texas Book Depository Building, where the rifle and cartridge shells were found.

It was after 3:00 A.M. before the gruesome but essential procedures in the morgue were completed and the body could be clothed and taken to the White House. For the burial costume, they chose a blue suit, a white silk shirt, a blue tie with small dots, and black shoes. A white handkerchief with his JFK monogram was folded into the breast pocket of the coat. The handles of the red bronze casket had been damaged during the flight from Dallas. It was replaced by one of black mahogany.

At almost the last minute, O'Donnell told Mrs. Kennedy he thought her wedding ring should not go into the grave, that it was too precious a symbol for her to lose. He went downstairs and retrieved it.

They closed the casket and wheeled it outside to the ambulance. Police cars formed up ahead, and the rest of the group entered six limousines behind the gray Navy car. At 4:20, the knots of people still standing in front of the White House near the picket fence and in LaFayette Park across the street saw the blinking red lights of the police cars turn into Pennyslvania Avenue. No sirens sounded. The street was utterly still, silent, cold, and dark. Men took off their hats. Tears that had been stanched welled up again. Two lines of Marines snapped to attention. At a muffled command, they turned and escorted the ambulance as it moved slowly around the curving driveway to the North Portico. A triangle-shaped shroud of black crepe hung over the door. Yellow light gleamed softly in the windows of the family rooms on the second floor.

Soldiers, sailors, Marines, and airmen lifted the flag-draped casket and carried it inside. Jacqueline Kennedy, still wearing the soiled pink suit and supported by her relatives and friends, followed it to the East Room. The pallbearers placed it gently on the catafalque. The guard of honor, drawn from all branches of the Armed Services, stood at attention facing the sarcophagus. A priest sank to his knees before a prie-dieu. Another bowed his head over his prayer book, whispering. Soft light from the magnificent chandeliers, turned down to candleglow now, suffused the room and glinted on the bayonets of the servicemen. The silent mourners in the street and the park felt the first drops of a cold rain.

The President had returned to the White House.

Through the morning and into the late afternoon of Saturday, November 23, the black limousines inched up the driveway to the White House in an unbroken stream. They brought men of the Federal government and governors of states, representatives of the many-faceted American society and representatives of the world, men who had worked with the President and men who had fought him tooth and nail. In spite of the chilling rain, the crowd in front had grown. The spectators were able to identify only a few of the dignitaries, but the inevitable transistor radio told them who was entering and who was leaving. In the East Room, the mourners found a crucifix at the head of the sarcophagus and a spray of carnations and lilies at the foot. Crepe shrouded the white marble fireplaces. Some moved slowly past the bier, others walked with a quicker step and barely glanced at it. Some wept openly, others choked and swallowed hard to hold back the tears. They stood in the presence of the ancient mystery of death, and even those with faith that a Divine Providence ordains all things could not but picture John F. Kennedy beneath the shroud and ask themselves, "Why?" The belief that there is a meaning and purpose in life was outraged, or at least sorely tested, on that November weekend.

Harry Truman and his daughter, Mrs. Clifton Daniel, passed the catafalque. Sorrow was an expression seldom seen on the strong face of the little man from Missouri, but it was deeply etched there now.

Senator Clair Engle of California, bedridden after a brain operation, was brought to the East Room in a wheel chair.

A bitter political enemy, Governor George C. Wallace, of Alabama, came to pay his last respects. Wallace had bucked Kennedy's every move in the field of civil rights. He had dramatized his opposition by standing in the doorway of a building to block (only for a few hours) the enrollment of two Negroes in the University of Alabama. But Wallace, unlike those who actually rejoiced in Kennedy's death, now honored the armistice in political warfare. Unwittingly, the Governor may have come closer than anyone to pinpointing the motive for the assassination. When he heard the news, and before Oswald was captured, Wallace had gasped out, "Whoever did this must hate everything human."

Johnson caught sight of Dwight D. Eisenhower among the mourners and asked if they could have a talk before the former President returned to his farm in Gettysburg. They admired and liked each other. Johnson, as Senate Majority Leader, had been instrumental in securing passage of the civil rights bill Eisenhower sent to Congress, the first since Reconstruction. As amended, the bill was not wholly satisfactory to the President, but he considered it a start and had congratulated Johnson. Now President himself, Johnson simply wanted to talk with Eisenhower about the Presidency, to have the benefit of his experience. They talked more than two hours. Eisenhower then went to another office and began scribbling, filling sheet after sheet of yellow, legal-size paper. Edited and typewritten, the material then went to Johnson, and he said later he found it helpful. In those first hours in office, Johnson sought advice from every quarter.

Before the first mourners entered the East Room, Jacqueline Kennedy went there to attend a special family Mass in front of the casket. (In Rome, a few hours earlier, Pope Paul VI, offered Mass "for the peace of his soul, for the comfort of those who mourn his death, and that love and not hatred shall reign among humanity.") Only then, after the 24 terrible hours since she had appeared at the breakfast in Fort Worth, did she try to sleep. The curtains in her room were drawn to shut out all light, and for a little while she slipped into oblivion. When she wakened, she went to her desk to write a last letter to her husband. It was a long letter. She intended to leave it in the coffin along with one or two articles, his personal possessions that had given him pleasure. She told Caroline that she, too, must write a letter to "Daddy," and together they guided John-John's hand, scribbling his note to his father.

She rose early on Sunday morning and went unobserved to Arlington to see the gravesite. She dressed entirely in black. A black lace mantilla veiled her face. In the cemetery, she stood on the slope for a moment, gazing at the view beyond the Potomac, seeing it through her husband's eyes. Then she returned to the White House. She had told Robert Kennedy that she had wanted to see "Jack" for the last time and would leave the articles in the coffin. In the East Room, General McHugh folded back the flag and unlatched the lid of the coffin. The officer commanding the guard of honor assumed that Mrs. Kennedy and her brother-in-law would want to be alone. He ordered an "about face" and would have marched them out of the room. Jacqueline Kennedy whispered that she did not want them to leave, and Robert Kennedy countermanded the order. The men stood facing away from the coffin. She placed the letters in the coffin and then a pair of gold cuff links which she had given her husband for Christmas. Robert Kennedy left a gift to him from his wife, a silver rosary, and he slipped off his tieclasp, the PT-109 pin, and left that with the other articles. She took a lock of her husband's hair. The lid closed, and the flag covered the coffin again. They knelt beside it in prayer. In a short time, the coffin would be taken to the Capitol, carried up the 36 steps that Jack Kennedy had climbed so many times as a congressman, and placed in the Great Rotunda.

The procession already was forming. A detachment of sailors stood at parade rest on Pennsylvania Avenue. Three clergymen, a priest, rabbi, and minister, stood nearby. Behind them were the beribboned Joint Chiefs of Staff, and detachments of Army, Navy, Coast Guard, Marines, and Air Force men were in position on side streets, ready to fall into prescribed places in the procession as it passed.

A small group of men and women who would not march in the procession but who had been indirectly close to the President drifted out on the White House lawn. They were its chambermaids and laundresses, cooks and kitchen helpers.

At 12:20, the door of the North Portico opened. The guards carried the coffin to a caisson drawn by six matching grays. The three on the right were riderless. A signal was given. A muffled roll of drums sounded, cadencing the procession's pace, 100 steps a minute.

Jacqueline Kennedy and her children rode in a limousine between the silent walls of spectators. Stepping out in front of the steps to the Capitol, she put Caroline on her right and the little boy on her left, took them by the hands, and climbed the steps. Her expressions were to

146

vary in these two days, Sunday and Monday, a numbed look, a stony look, a slight frown, a brief moment of tears. But these were only slight variations on the expression of frozen, controlled grief. Now at the Capitol, behind the veil, her chin was slightly raised, and her expression seemed almost defiant, as though she could hear an inner voice intoning the lines of the Invictus.

As the casket went up the steps, singing broke the silence in the noble Capitol Plaza. A choir of midshipmen chanted one of Lieutenant Jack Kennedy's favorite songs, the "Navy Hymn."

She led her children to the velvet ropes separating the casket and honor guard from the groups gathered in the vaulted Rotunda.

In the dimness, the flag draped over the sarcophagus was the brightest splash of color. The story of America, captured in oil paintings, surrounded this latest chapter. The White House staff stood beneath DeSoto's Discovery. The Cabinet, Supreme Court, and the American delegates to the United Nations were placed near The Landing of Columbus and The Embarkation of the Pilgrims. The Baptism of Pocahontas looked down on the diplomatic corps.

The eulogies were mercifully short.

"He had the bravery and a sense of personal duty which made him willing to face up to the great task of being President in these trying times," said John McCormack, the tall, silver-haired Speaker of the House. "He had the warmth and the sense of humanity which made the burden of the task bearable for himself and his associates and which made all kinds of diverse peoples and races eager to be associated with him in his task."

From somewhere in the motionless throng came the sound of sobbing.

"If we really love this country," said Chief Justice Warren, "if we truly love justice and mercy, if we fervently want to make this nation better for those who are to follow us, we can at least abjure the hatred that consumes people, the false accusations that divide us, and the bitterness that begets violence."

And in that very hour, a man who had abjured mercy and taken justice into his own hands, Jack Ruby, walked up to Lee Harvey Oswald in the Dallas police station and shot him down at point-blank range.

Caroline Kennedy remained reasonably quiet for a child during the ceremonies. Her brother, however, soon grew restless. He liked to play soldier, and now he wanted to go inside the velvet ropes and stand closer to the uniforms there. A nurse took him into the Speaker's office, where he found a small American flag and began marching up and down with that, no doubt leading his legions.

The eulogies ended. Jacqueline Kennedy took Caroline's hand and led her to the sarcophagus. She whispered, "Kneel and kiss Daddy goodbye." They knelt together. The widow's lips touched the flag. The little girl lifted the edge of the flag and her white-gloved hand touched the mahogany as though to caress her father. Mother and daughter rose and returned to their places.

Then Lyndon Johnson moved toward the bier. Walking backward and carrying a wreath of red and white carnations, a soldier preceded him. The silk pennon said, "From President Johnson and the Nation." Johnson closed his eyes and bowed his head for a moment. Then he stepped back.

The ceremonies were ended. The Kennedys departed. The officials filed slowly past the casket, each with his own special memory of the man laid out beneath the flag.

Now, as had been announced, the general public could enter the Rotunda. The lines already were forming. Already they stretched back, eight abreast, more than 20 blocks. Throughout the night, there was the sound of shuffling feet, down the street, up the 36 steps, past the sarcophagus. Shuffling, shuffling, shuffling for hour after hour. In the planning, the heavy gold doors of the Rotunda were to have been closed at nine o'clock that night. The planners, however, had not reckoned with the rivers of emotion converging on Capitol Hill. From the cities and smaller communities on the Atlantic seaboard, groups of people chartered buses or crowded into automobiles with neighbors to come to Washington. In Jersey City, 36 nuns in a convent chartered a bus, and they told the beads of the rosaries and murmured prayers as they paused beside the bier. Joe Walcott, the former heavyweight boxing champion, stood in line more than eight hours, and finally, at 2:30 A.M., he entered the Rotunda. Hour after hour, guards and policemen urged the people to keep moving. Toward dawn, they told those still blocks away from the Capitol that it was doubtful they would get in before the doors closed. Few persons left. The line seemed endless, and perhaps it would have been if the exigencies of planning had not cut it off. It was not until midmorning on Sunday that the gold doors closed.

Jacqueline Kennedy could not seem to reconcile herself to the irrevocable fact of separation from her husband. With Robert Kennedy, she returned to the Rotunda during the night. She passed the red velvet ropes and knelt beside the coffin and kissed the flag. Then she rose and went outside with her brother-in-law. A limousine's door stood open for them. "Let's walk a little," she said. They walked down the hill, out of the glow of the brilliantly lighted Capitol dome, into the darkness.

Now came the most painful day, the day of the funeral and the long journey from St. Matthew's Cathedral to Arlington Cemetery and the moment, so inexpressibly final, when the casket would be lowered into the grave.

Mercifully, the day dawned fair and clear. The skies were a burnished blue, and the sun was warm.

Jacqueline Kennedy appeared on the steps of the White House with her children. For the moment, the veil was thrown back from her face. The expression of defiance was gone now. She looked tired and infinitely sad. The children were dressed in coats of identical color, sky blue. John-John stared with curiosity and pleasure at the pageantry, horses, uniforms, bayonets, and swords, the bandsmen's brass instruments gleaming in the sun.

The panoply was worthy of a crowned head. Kings and queens, presidents, prime ministers, princes, and the officials from 92 nations had gathered in Washington to attend the funeral. Not all could be called the representatives of governments friendly to the United States. Among them, for example, was Anastas Mikoyan, Deputy Premier of the Soviet Union. Nor was the political factor to be entirely discounted. In honoring John F. Kennedy, they were honoring the principles and the world position of the United States. At the same time, he had won the affection and admiration of those who had known him, and they had come to honor him as a man.

The widow had announced that she would walk from the White House to the cathedral. Many others, including some of the foreign dignitaries, also prepared to walk. The Secret Service, naturally, tried to persuade Lyndon Johnson to ride in a limousine. He refused in earthy Texas language.

Again, the muffled drums sounded. Church bells tolled as the caisson moved out behind the grays. A black horse followed it, riderless. A silver sword dangled from the saddle. Polished cavalry boots, pointed backward, were fixed in the stirrups. It is said that Genghis Khan's generals invented this symbol to mark a fallen leader when they interred his body in the Valley of Kilien.

Jacqueline Kennedy walked with her head high and shoulders as rigid as a soldier's. Robert Kennedy was on her right and Teddy Kennedy on her left. Sargent Shriver and Stephen Smith, husbands of the Kennedy sisters, and other relatives walked behind them. The Attorney General seemed to be staring into space. He held his sister-in-law's hand during most of the march.

The Secret Service agents surrounding Johnson continually looked upward, scanning the upper floor windows of the buildings he was passing.

The eerie skirling of bagpipes, like lost souls crying on the moors, sounded a funerary air. Kennedy had enjoyed the music of the Black Watch, and Jacqueline Kennedy had remembered and asked that bagpipes be a part of his last escort.

Richard Cardinal Cushing, robed and mitered, waited in the cathedral beneath its green dome. The gaunt, gray priest had married John Kennedy and Jacqueline Bouvier and baptized their children, and his throaty voice had besought God's help for the new President and the invocation at Kennedy's inaugural. And now, in death as in life, the Kennedys had called him again. When he saw the caisson draw up in front of the cathedral, he walked to the door to receive the body. There, he met the President's mother, veiled and wearing black. Her features were calm and composed. He embraced her and said, "Rose, my dear, my dear." Jacqueline Kennedy knelt to kiss his ring. The Cardinal bent down to kiss Caroline and pat her brother on the head. It was John-John's third birthday.

Then the mourners moved slowly up the steps, Charles de Gaulle in a simple brown French Army uniform without braid or ribbons, Haile Selassie, Emperor of Ethiopia, in full uniform glittering with medals and with a bottle-green sash across his chest. Queen Frederika of Greece was swathed in a heavy fur coat. The majority of the men wore cutaways or plain dark suits, Prince Philip of Britain, Prime Ministers Hayato Ikeda of Japan, Alec Douglas-Home of Britain, Eamon de Valera of Ireland, Lester Pearson of Canada, Chancellor Ludwig Erhard of West Germany, Presidents Diosdado Macapagal of the Philippines and Chung Hee Park of South Korea, and many others in many uniforms, 220 representatives of foreign governments.

When all was silent in the cathedral, the Cardinal intoned the opening prayer of the low Requiem Mass in Latin. The tenor, Luigi Vena, rose in the choir loft and sang the *"Ave Maria."* He had sung it for the Kennedys once before—at John Kennedy's wedding.

Ending the Mass, the Cardinal walked slowly around the coffin, holding a silver vessel filled with holy water. Now he spoke in English. "May the angels, dear Jack, lead you into Paradise. May the Martyrs receive you at your coming. May the spirit of God embrace you and mayest thou, with all those who made the supreme sacrifice for others, receive eternal rest and peace. Amen."

The rites closed with the eulogy delivered by the Most Reverend Philip M. Hanan, Auxiliary Bishop of Washington. He began with a passage that John F. Kennedy often quoted, a passage drawn from the third chapter of Ecclesiastes, "There is an appointed time for everything . . . a time to be born and a time to die." He closed with some ringing quotations from Kennedy's Inaugural Address, "But let us begin."

He had begun, and now he had come to his time to die.

The family and the Cardinal followed the coffin, and the pallbearers again placed it on the caisson. For the last time, the band struck up the lilting "Hail to the Chief." Mrs. Kennedy spoke to her son, "You can salute now." The little boy solemnly raised his right hand to his forehead, and across the land, Americans watching on television choked with tears.

In the slow funeral cadence, the procession passed the Lincoln Memorial and crossed the Memorial Bridge. At the turn, an Army fife-and-drum corps costumed in the scarlet uniforms and white cockades of the Revolutionary Army saluted the caisson, and along the entire route, the uniformed men lining it raised their hands to their visors as it passed. The clop-clop of the horses and the creaking of wooden wheels were the only sounds in the boulevards. It is three miles from the cathedral to the cemetery in Arlington. The cortege was so long that the first cars were passing through the gates before the last left the cathedral. Marching through the gates, an Air Force band played "The Mist Covered the Mountains." The cortege moved slowly past the white headstones marking the graves of

American fighting men, now to be joined by a Commander in Chief. At the slope, the Marines played "The Star Spangled Banner."

There were chairs for the President's widow and her relatives. The foreign chiefs of state and the American dignitaries surrounded them. The cemetery fell silent except for the sound of a soft wind rustling in the trees. Wreaths and bouquets of flowers were banked inside and outside the white picket fence around the gravesite. Again, Cardinal Cushing spoke. He commended to God's keeping "this wonderful man, Jack Kennedy." The rumble of jet aircraft sounded in the south. In another second or two, 50 jets swept over the gravesite. The plane that had taken Kennedy to Texas followed. As it passed his grave, the wings were dipped in salute. Three artillery pieces roared the 21-gun salute to a President. Then, there was a low-voiced command, and three riflemen fired across the grave. The plangent notes of a bugle rang out, echoing in the trees and across the graves of other fighting men, sounding "Taps." The bugler, probably under stress of emotion, hit a sour note. Finally, in that last sad but noble military rite, guardsmen withdrew the flag from the casket, folded it, and handed it to Jacqueline Kennedy. She held it in her left hand and stepped forward to light the eternal flame. It flickered brightly in the sunshine and against the flowers of many colors. The Lord's Prayer was spoken. The family moved away from the grave.

Tears glistened beneath Jacqueline Kennedy's veil. She seemed uncertain of what to do next. Robert Kennedy took her hand and guided her down the slope.

At 3:34, the casket was lowered, and all those present and the American nation and the world said goodbye to John Fitzgerald Kennedy.

To the widow, a final task remained. She no longer was the First Lady, but she had not yet departed the White House, and to that degree it was still, in her words, "our house." The foreign chiefs of state and other dignitaries were gathering there. She considered it her duty to receive them. This she did. The reception and her last official responsibility ended at five o'clock.

That night, with Robert Kennedy, she returned to the grave, bringing a sprig of lilies of the valley. In the stillness, they could hear the hum of traffic on the bridge and the highways leading to Washington. A Secret Service agent unlatched the gate and walked away, joining the two military policemen on guard at the site. The flame, blue-white, was like a beacon in the darkness, a touch of warmth in the cold. The sorrowing woman and man knelt in prayer. Then, they rose, and she placed her flowers on the cold earth. From across the river came the deep-throated bell tolling the hour.

She would visit the grave many times, and time would heal the wounds and ease the pain.

14

Jack Ruby couldn't keep his hands off the telephone that day, and he couldn't seem to stop crying, long distance. From Dallas, he phoned relatives in various cities around the country. He called boyhood friends at opposite ends of the continent. He dialed the numbers of the Dallas *Morning News* to cancel the weekend advertising for his two nightclubs, and of radio stations, with the important news that his places would be dark for the time being. He telephoned a former girlfriend who, not having heard from him in several years, was understandably puzzled. During most of these calls, he was crying.

It was the afternoon of November 22, the day of the assassination.

At the moment when the President's motorcade was approaching the Book Depository Building, Ruby was in the advertising department of the *Morning News* on the second floor. He usually wrote the ads himself for his nightclubs, Carousel and Vegas, which featured as much nudity as the law allowed, and now he was composing the come-ons for weekend visitors to Dallas. If he had gone downstairs and walked a block or so, he would have seen Kennedy pass within a few feet of him. Or, he could have stood in a window in the advertising department and had a relatively unobstructed view of the President on Houston Street. But he paid no attention. He continued to concentrate on writing his ads, undisturbed by the thunder of applause and excitement only a short distance away.

It is difficult to reconcile Ruby's apparent disinterest in the President at about 12:28 and the crying jag that began soon after he heard about the assassination. But then, Jack Ruby frequently was a hard man to figure. His actions, like those of Lee Harvey Oswald, were not always susceptible to rational explanation. Like Oswald, he had a history of emotional instability dating back to his childhood. In fact, a somewhat striking parallel appears in an examination of the lives of these two strange figures in history. It is almost as though they were foreordained to meet in violence and blood.

Ruby grew up in a tough ghetto world.

He was the sixth of nine children and his parents were both Polish immigrants. His father, Joseph Rubenstein, was a carpenter. While he was in the Russian Army, a professional matchmaker arranged his marriage to Fannie Turek Rutkowski. Rubenstein settled in Chicago in 1903, and it appears that his wife followed him a year or so later.

The exact date of Jack's birth is uncertain, but it was either in March or April of 1911. He grew up in a district known as the Maxwell Street ghetto. There were pushcarts in the streets, and the smell of chicken soup and kosher cooking came from the kitchen windows in the flats. The early environment, however, does not explain Jack Ruby. It was a poor neighborhood, but there were good people there, hard-working men and women, children determined to get an education, people who used their brains and ran while others walked. Ruby, like Oswald, was a dropout, without so much as a high school education.

Unlike Oswald, Ruby's parents required him and all their children to attend a religious school after regular school hours. The discipline there was strict. Jack's brother Earl recalled, "I don't know how many times Sparky took a hit on the head. We used to get such a hit with a ruler." For Orthodox Jews, age thirteen is the year of confirmation, and it is celebrated by their sons' participating for the first time in the synagogue service—a *bar mitzvah*, the traditionally vital ceremony in Jewish life. Ruby did not have one.

His sister Eva nicknamed him "Sparky." The way he walked reminded her of Sparkplug, the horse in a comic strip.

In the first five years of Jack's life, his parents moved

154

four times, and the family was constantly uprooted thereafter. (Marguerite Oswald also moved frequently.)

Joseph and Fannie Rubenstein separated, temporarily, in 1921. It appears that they fought continually, and Jack's mother filed assault and battery charges against his father. (Ekdahl's suit for divorce accused Lee Oswald's mother of throwing things at him.) During this separation, Jack and three other children were placed in foster homes. (So, for a time, were Mrs. Oswald's children.)

The district adjacent to Maxwell Street was populated largely by Italians, and they fought frequently with the Jewish boys. Jack learned to use his fists at an early age. He was easily provoked into fights, and, like Oswald, never backed away from one. He outfought older and bigger boys, and that made his father proud of him and thus indirectly encouraged him to go on being a brawler.

When Jack was eleven years old, the Jewish Social Service Bureau referred him to the Institute for Juvenile Research. The psychiatric findings were remarkably similar to those recorded of Lee Harvey Oswald, "truancy . . . incorrigible at home . . . delinquencies." Jack's mother was no more able to control him than Marguerite Oswald could control Lee. Jack considered his mother inferior. He told an interviewer in the institute that he ran away from home because she beat him and lied to him. In the report of his findings, the interviewer wrote:

> He is egocentric and expects much attention but is unable to get it as there are many children at home. His behavior is further colored by his early sex experiences . . . and the gang situation in the street. From a superficial examination of his mother who was here with him, it is apparent that she has no insight into his problem, and she is thoroughly inadequate in the further training of this boy.

Records show that Jack completed grade school, but whether he entered high school is uncertain. If he did, it was for a brief time. He was on the streets, full time, when he was sixteen.

He liked to hang around a pool room on Roosevelt Road and in gymnasiums where boxers worked out. His first hero was Barney Ross, later the lightweight and welterweight champion of the world. Ross recalled, "When I was in the amateurs, Sparky was with me. He'd come

around to carry my bags and go in free at the club fights."
They became lifelong friends, and Ross testified for Ruby
in his trial for murdering Oswald.

The boy did not like steady work. He preferred to
peddle almost anything that swam into his craw, novelties,
cigars, janitor supplies, automobile accessories, razor
blades, watches, plaques and gewgaws, punchboards for
candy, and pizza crusts to restaurants. What he liked best
was to scalp tickets to athletic events. He managed to
crash the celebrated championship fight between Gene
Tunney and Jack Dempsey in Chicago in 1927. A policeman, trying to catch Ruby and eject him, threw his night-
stick at the boy. It missed, but out of this episode came
the legend that Ruby carried a silver plate in his head.

In 1933, he went to California and lived for a time in
Los Angeles, selling handicappers' tip-sheets at the Santa
Anita racetrack. At a Jewish community center dance in
San Francisco, he met Virginia Belasco, granddaughter of
the actor and playwright David Belasco. Ruby dated her
several times. During this period, he seems to have been
well-mannered and presentable, something of a lady's
man. He may have wished to marry Miss Belasco. "She
was a very high-class, refined girl," he said later. Class had
come to be an important word in Ruby's lexicon. He never
married, although he dated one woman for 11 years.

In 1937, he was back in Chicago, hustling anything he
could find to buy and sell and scalping tickets to theaters
and sports events. Then, he went into the trade-union
movement. In Local 20467 of the Scrap Iron and Junk
Handlers Union, he worked as an organizer and did some
negotiating with employers.

The only evidence of any political interest on Ruby's
part was more ethnical than political. With some friends,
he brawled with members of the German-American Bund,
which was pro-Nazi and anti-Semitic. Throughout Ruby's
life, an anti-Semitic remark would bring him to his feet,
ready to fight.

After Pearl Harbor, his brothers immediately went into
the Armed Forces. Earl enlisted in the Navy, Sam was in
Army Air Force Intelligence, and Hyman served in the
field artillery. But Jack asked to be classified 3-A, a category applying to men who are needed at home for economic reasons. In 1943, he was reclassified 1-A. He ap-
pealed to his draft board without success and was inducted

into the Army Air Force on May 21, 1943. He received an honorable discharge on February 21, 1946.

He moved to Dallas in 1947, legally changed his name to Ruby, and went into some businesses that failed. The reverse caused him to have what he called a "mental breakdown," and he said he was so depressed that he "hibernated" in a hotel for several months, refusing to see anyone.

Not long afterward, he found himself operating nightclubs. He was making more money than ever before in his life and was in a position to consider himself what he desperately needed to become, a big shot. He never smoked cigars, but otherwise he was a two-bit imitation of Edward G. Robinson in the old Warner Brothers pictures. "Stick with me, Baby, and you'll be wearing diamonds."

He was not an easy man to work for. He hit one employee with a blackjack, beat a musician with brass knuckles, badly cutting his face, and knocked a guitarist to the floor and then kicked him in the groin. The Warren Report said:

> There is considerable evidence that Ruby tended to dominate his employees, frequently resorted to violence in dealing with them, publicly embarrassed them, sometimes attempted to cheat them of their pay, and delayed paying their salaries. Other employees reported Ruby continually harassed his help, and used obscene language in their presence. However, he frequently aplogized, sought to atone for his many temper tantrums, and completely forgot others.

It was not only Ruby's employees who ran afoul of such behavior. Witnesses in his trial said in more or less the same words, "Jack would fly into a rage over something, any old thing. He might even take a swing at you. And then a couple minutes later he acted as though he had forgotten all about it. You never could figure him."

Like Lee Oswald, Ruby craved recognition. Oswald dreamed of becoming an important man in politics. Recognition to Ruby meant knowing and being known to persons he considered important. He was a name-dropper, especially the names of policemen and newspapermen.

Around every police station in every community in America, there are hangers-on, men who would rather be on a first-name basis with the cops than with the president of a bank. They seem to feel that in some way they share a policeman's authority, a vicarious feeling of power, and from the police they pick up morsels of information that never appear in the papers. They are on the inside. That seems to give them a sense of importance. Ruby was one of these.

He boasted that he knew every policeman in Dallas, all 1,200 of them. This was a typical exaggeration, but he did know quite a number. They came to his nightclubs, and it was understood that they paid no cover charge nor received a check for anything they drank. At the same time, there was no evidence that Ruby ever tried to bribe a policeman or sought any special favors from them.

Still, for a man of Jack Ruby's stamp, it might come in handy to have friends on the force, for Ruby had numerous brushes with the law. Over a period of years, he was charged with disturbing the peace, carrying a concealed weapon, violating a peace bond, permitting dancing after hours, simple assault, and ignoring some 20 traffic tickets. Once, he was suspended for five days when a striptease act slipped beyond the bounds of what might be called normal nightclub prurience into outright obscenity. He was acquitted of some of the charges and paid fines or posted bonds for others. Some complaints were dismissed, and there were occasions when no charges were filed after he was arrested. So, perhaps it paid to be "in" with the boys who handled such matters.

Ruby habitually carried a gun, a nickel-plated .38-caliber pistol, sometimes in his clothing, sometimes in the trunk rack of his car. He went armed, he said, because he often brought several thousand dollars in cash to his apartment at night after closing the nightclubs.

In spite of his often erratic behavior, he had a number of men friends. He might bloody a man's nose in the morning and lend him $300 without asking for an I.O.U. in the afternoon. While he showed little interest in women, there was no evidence that he was a homosexual. He shared an apartment with a friend, George Senator, who occasionally worked for him. Ruby liked dogs, and he kept three dachshunds in the apartment, referring to them as "my children." One, named Sheba, he called "my wife."

He was an eccentric, to say the least.

"The action," wherever it might be, drew Ruby like a magnet. Therefore, it seems strange that he was not among the crowds lining the streets in Dallas to see Ken-

nedy. But, true to form, Ruby showed up on the third floor of the Police Department at about 11:15 after Oswald's arrest. He wormed his way in by posing as a reporter. He walked from the elevator toward the Homicide Bureau between two reporters. They both wore identification cards, "Kennedy Press," on the lapels of their coats. Ruby hunched over as he walked, talking rapidly to them and scribbling on a pad of paper. Toward midnight, Henry Wade and Chief Curry told reporters they would hold a press conference in the basement and would have Oswald there. By this time, the police already were convinced that Oswald was their man. Captain Fritz said the case against him was "cinched," and Chief Curry added on Saturday, "we are sure of our case." After these and other statements by Dallas authorities, it is difficult to imagine how an unbiased jury could have been assembled to try Oswald, as the American Bar Association was to observe.

Ruby made it to the press conference, too. He had found a role for himself, he said, as "translator for the Israeli press." Oswald was brought in. He raised a clenched fist, handcuffs and all, in a simulated Communist salute. "I didn't kill anybody," he said. The fight with the police in the Texas Theater left a purple-black bruise under his eyes. A kind of sneer or smirk twisted the corners of his mouth. To Jack Ruby, Oswald seemed cocky, "proud of what he had done." Ruby could easily have killed Oswald then. He was only a few feet away from Oswald. Perhaps this was one of the instances when he left his gun locked in his car.

Ruby seemed to have recovered fully from the near-hysteria of the afternoon, when he was sobbing, "Those poor kids, those poor kids." After the press conference, he passed out guest-cards for the Carousel Club to the out-of-town newspapermen. A line drawing on the cards showed a nude woman in black net stockings and black gloves holding a glass of champagne. The cards said, "Your host, Jack Ruby." It paid to be "in" with the reporters, too, even if they were not from Dallas.

At the press conference, Wade said Oswald probably would be moved to the county jail in the Criminal Courts Building early in the next week. The buildings were about 13 blocks apart. In fact, plans were being drawn to make the transfer on Sunday morning. Ruby made a number of attempts on Saturday to ascertain the time of the move.

He called several radio stations and was overheard to say on the telephone, "You know I'll be there." On Saturday night, when the reporters asked Chief Curry when Oswald would be moved, he said, "If you fellows are here by 10:00 A.M., you'll be early enough."

There were grounds for believing that an attempt might be made to kill Oswald. Threats had been telephoned both to the police and the Dallas office of the FBI. The transfer plan, as finally worked out, entailed using an armored car and an unmarked police car. Oswald would ride in the police car, the other vehicle serving as a decoy and taking a different route to the Criminal Courts Building. A would-be killer waiting there would assume that the prisoner would come out of the armored car. Confronted with the same problem after James A. Garfield was assassinated, the police solved it with an even more ingenious ruse. They dressed the assassin in a policeman's uniform. But that was before the days of television, and the Dallas police, bent on cooperating with the news media, were to permit television cameras to be near when Oswald emerged from the jail.

Ruby left his apartment a little before eleven o'clock on the morning of Sunday, November 24. Remember that Chief Curry had indicated that the transfer would take place some time after ten o'clock. Ruby slipped his gun in his pocket. He put Sheba in his car. He was carrying more than $2,000 in cash. Driving downtown, he passed the site of the assassination, which he had visited numerous times on Friday and Saturday. He noticed the wreaths already placed on the slope of the knoll. He also saw a crowd gathered around the police and courts building. He parked his car and entered a Western Union office, where he sent a money order for $25 to one of his strippers in Fort Worth. She had called him the night before and told him she needed money to pay the rent.

The receipt for the money order was time-stamped 11:17 A.M.

When he went outside, Ruby looked at the crowd near the police station. "The action" was there, and there he must go. He started walking, and in about three minutes, he was at the head of the ramp leading to the basement of the Police Department.

Manwhile, the gears in the machinery for the transfer of Oswald were anything but meshed. Without advising Captain Fritz, someone decreed that the prisoner should

160

ride in the armored car. The captain countermanded this when he heard about it, shortly after eleven o'clock. A few minutes later, he was advised that everything was in readiness below. Some reporters went down in the elevator with him.

On the fourth floor cell block, a detective, James R. Leavelle, handcuffed Oswald's right wrist to his own left wrist. Another officer, L. C. Graves, manacled the other. Leavelle said to Oswald, "If anybody shoots at you, I hope they are as good a shot as you are."

A ghost of a smile crossed Oswald's face. "Nobody is going to shoot at me," he said.

On the ramp, police checked credentials of the reporters and cameramen. They knew by sight the FBI men gathered on the scene. About 50 persons were there. Across the ramp, television cameras trained their red eyes on the door where Oswald would emerge. NBC was televising the scene "live." It would only briefly interrupt the pictures of the rites taking place in Washington.

The word sent up to Captain Fritz that the arrangements to start the transfer were complete had been premature. The police car was not yet backed into position in front of the door.

Oswald appeared. He wore a black sweater and slacks. His eyes narrowed, squinting in the television lights. He looked calm. There was a small smirk on his face.

Suddenly, a burly figure lunged out of the crowd, hunched over. He had a gun in his hand. It was Jack Ruby. A policeman, B. H. Combest, recognized him and saw what he was about to do. "Jack, you son-of-a-bitch," Combest yelled, but he was not close enough to stop Ruby. The gun roared. The bullet ripped into Oswald's abdomen.

His face contorted with agony, mouth open, eyes closed, left arm pressing hard against the place where the bullet hit him. Innumerable viewers saw it on television. But the classic picture, snapped just as Ruby fired, was made by Robert Jackson, of the Dallas *Times-Herald*.

First, the assassination. And then, less than 48 hours later, a manacled man surrounded by policemen shot down in cold blood. "My God, my God, what are we coming to?" Americans gasped. In the eyes of the world, America must have been seen as a nation of savages.

In hindsight, the weekend of November 22-24 seems covered with a sheen of paranoia.

The police jumped Ruby, wrestled him to the floor of

the ramp, and disarmed him. Ruby was shouting, "Hey, you guys. What are you doing? You know me. I'm Jack Ruby." He began babbling, and the words attributed to him by the police were to weigh heavily against him when he went on trial for murder.

By Jack Ruby's standards, he had finally made it. He had been seen, if only for an instant, on nationwide television, and in a matter of minutes his name and photograph would appear in newspapers all over the world. He was notorious beyond his wildest fantasies. Ruby and Lee Oswald both had achieved what they desired so intensely—recognition.

The drama now formed into a pattern of classic unity.

An ambulance carrying the dying Oswald raced to Parkland Hospital across the same route taken by the limousine carrying the dying President. Some of the same surgeons, including Dr. Malcolm Perry, were called to Trauma Two to try to save Oswald's life.

They almost did. "We were very close to saving him," Dr. Perry said later.

Oswald was unconscious on arrival. The death pallor showed in his face. In spasms, he gasped for breath. The bullet had pierced his spleen, pancreas, liver, and one kidney and had nicked the aorta, the great artery of the heart. Massive hemorrhaging filled the abdominal cavity with quarts of blood. Even so, Oswald's chances for survival when the surgeons went to work appeared better than Kennedy's when they first saw his wounds. They managed to stop the bleeding. But about ten minutes later, his heart stopped. Perry opened his chest and began massaging the heart muscle. There was a feeble response, but it did not continue. They drew the sheet over Lee Oswald's face at the same hour, almost to the minute, that they had pronounced the President dead.

For her own protection, Marina Oswald had been taken with her children to the home of the Chief of Police in Irving, C. J. Wirasnik. She had been watching television and saw the shooting. In the commotion in the ramp, however, the cameras had been jostled, and exactly what had happened was not clear. Marguerite Oswald heard the news on the radio of a police patrol car in which she was sitting. She rushed into the house. Marina broke down, sobbing, "I want to see him. I want to see him." The police car took the two women to Parkland. They were too late.

On Monday, November 25, the last rites were performed for three of the four principals in the tragedy of Dallas, for the President in Washington, for Officer Tippit in Dallas, and for Lee Harvey Oswald in Forth Worth.

The Beckley Hills Baptist Church was too small to accommodate the numbers of mourners who came to attend Tippit's funeral. More than 1,000 persons stood outside. They heard the Reverend C. D. Tipps deliver the eulogy, saying, "He was doing his duty when he was taken from us by a poor, confused, misguided assassin, as was the President of the United States."

"He was doing his duty. . . ." This is what the President and the Attorney General had said when they telephoned Tippit's widow, offering condolences.

Oswald's funeral, like his life, was pitiful and lacking in grace.

The Federal government paid for the arrangements, some $500, and attempted to keep them a secret. The grave diggers were told the grave was for a man named William Bobo. They barely had time to finish their work. The clergyman who had been asked to perform the service did not appear. There were no pallbearers. Only two floral offerings, sprays of red carnations and white carnations, lay beside the grave. The only mourners were Marina, Marguerite, and Robert Oswald.

The reporters in Dallas, of course, got wind of the time and place of the funeral. They trooped out to the Rose Hill Cemetery and persuaded the police and Federal authorities to admit them—all of which attracted the attention of other spectators, who soon learned what was taking place. In the absence of appointed pallbearers, seven newsmen volunteered to carry the coffin from the chapel to the grave. At the last minute, the Reverend Louis Saunders, Executive Secretary of the Fort Worth Council of Churches, volunteered to perform the rites. "Someone had to help the family," he said.

Two police cars brought the Oswalds to the cemetery. During the service, Marina and Marguerite held the two children on their laps.

Reverend Saunders did not mention Oswald by name. "God of the open sky and of the infinite universe," he prayed, "we pray and petition for this family who are heartbroken. Those who suffer and have tears in their hearts will pray for them. Their need is great.

"We are not here to judge. We are here to lay him away before an understanding God."

Marina understood only a part of the prayer and the Twenty-Third Psalm read by the minister, but she wept. She said to her daughter June in broken English, "Look, Daddy sleeps." She bent over to kiss the cold face and slipped two rings on her husband's fingers.

So Lee Harvey Oswald went to his grave. He took with him the monumental secret: Why did he assassinate John Fitzgerald Kennedy?

15

Jack Ruby went to trial in Dallas on February 17, 1964, accused of murder with malice. This was the legal wording of the charge. In bringing it against him, the State of Texas alleged that the crime was premeditated, that he had a motive for killing Lee Harvey Oswald. What was it? Had he known Oswald? Had they both known Officer Tippitt? Had they been seen together in the Carousel Club in the company of a mysterious third person?

Anticipating that Ruby's trial might provide the answers to these questions and bring to the surface aspects of the assassination not then known, a large press corps assembled in Dallas. An unusually large number represented the communications media of Europe, where the belief that the President had been the victim of a conspiracy already was unshakably fixed. Convinced of this from the start, European newsmen had been busy digging up half-truths and fragments of facts, building hypotheses on other hypotheses to lend credence to the conspiracy theory. Europeans, unaccustomed to apolitical assassination, simply could never accept the proposition that all three Dallas murders were the products of two deranged minds and a set of almost unbelievable improbablities. The waters had been muddied. The trial, it was hoped, might serve to clear them.

"It promises to be an American classic," one writer prophesied, and in a way it was, but not in the way he anticipated.

The presiding judge, Joe B. Brown, was not what might be called a lawyer's lawyer. He is a big man, tall and barrel-bodied. A shock of iron-gray hair makes him look taller than he is. He has a square, craggy face, a slow drawl, and a friendly, easygoing manner. His qualifications for the bench were not impressive. He had studied law at a commercial school in Dallas, the Jefferson University School of Law. One of his instructors there had been a young woman named Sarah T. Hughes, who 32 years later was to swear in Lyndon Johnson as President of the United States. A college degree was not required for entering Jefferson. A high school diploma alone would do, and that was what Joe Brown had. There are attorneys who love the law as a man loves his mistress, but Joe Brown was not one of these. After graduating from Jefferson, he debated whether to practice law or go into politics. In effect, he did both. He ran for Justice of the Peace and was elected. In his courtroom, he liked the atmosphere to be relaxed and informal. He permitted smoking, and he did not ride herd too tightly on the attorneys. Of his profession, he said, "The law is based on common sense," and "there is nothing mystic about a trial." Custom and common sense change, however, and so does common law; and perhaps for this reason, the judge sometimes seemed a little shaky on technical points of law that arose in Ruby's trial.

The size of the press corps covering the proceedings seemed also to impress Brown greatly. Looking out over the crowded courtroom one day, he said to a bailiff, "Just think, we've got newsmen from all over the world here and Pulitzer Prize winners and famous columnists and TV commentators right here in my courtroom." He sounded like an agent who had organized a book-and-authors luncheon and was highly gratified to find so many "names" attending. It was reported that he would have liked the whole trial to be televised. A member of the power structure in Dallas said, "We had a terrible time talking him out of that." The judge did permit cameras in the courtroom when the jury returned with the verdict. And when an attack of influenza forced him to take himself off the bench for one day, he let the TV cameras enter his sickroom and show him on his bed of pain.

The courthouse is diagonally across the street from the

Texas Book Depository Building and the spot where the bullets struck down the President. This fact in itself may have impaired the machinery for giving Ruby a fair trial. It was a constant reminder to witnesses and candidates for the jury, and for everyone who came and went, that the man on trial had foreclosed forever the definitive inquiry into Oswald's motive and had caused to be buried in Oswald's grave the answers to a thousand dreadful questions. Yet, Dallas was an overmaligned city at that time, and it is doubtful that the degree of resentment against Ruby there was greater than elsewhere in Texas. A visitor from San Antonio who had seen Kennedy there said in Dallas, "Hell, the boys down our way would've got that son-of-a-bitch if they had to wait until he came into the courtroom."

In any case, well before the trial began, Ruby's chief defense counsel, Melvin Belli, was trumpeting his contention that his client could not get a fair trial in Dallas. He charged that there was a "high-level conspiracy" to cheat Ruby of justice, that he had to be convicted in the interests of rescuing the city's battered reputation, that he was, in short, the blood offering on the altar of civic pride. Belli formally moved for a change of venue. After a hearing, Judge Brown ruled that the case must be tried in Dallas. Belli later wrote:

> I recognized the Ruby case as another fight for an unpopular cause, another trial of the underdog. I knew that when I went to Dallas if I couldn't get a change of venue from Dallas to another city in Texas, the Ruby case would be lost *in the trial court.* [His italics.]
> But another trial, of another unpopular cause of another underdog, made Jack Ruby, whom the Dallas District Attorney immediately characterized as "a Jew boy," kith and kin to those many, many poor plaintiffs I've* been trying to help for going on to 30 years. . . .*

Melvin Belli is a portly, handsome man with luxuriant white hair, worn long like an actor's. He has a sonorous voice, and in court, when he chooses, he can be as cour-

* Melvin Belli, *Ready for the Plaintiff* (New York: Popular Library, Inc., 1965), p. 7.

teous as a Southern gentleman dancing the minuet. Indeed, he showed considerable acting ability in the Ruby trial. After a witness described Ruby's expression when he heard about the assassination, Belli rose to his feet. "Did he look like this?" he asked. He stood for a long moment, rigid, transfixed, staring out the window as though in a trance. "Why, yes," said the witness, "he did look pretty much like that." Belli bowed. "Thank you," he said. An actor taking a curtain call could not have looked more pleased. Belli's reputation preceded him from his office in San Francisco to Dallas. He said a national magazine had dubbed him "King of Torts." (A tort is a civil, as opposed to a criminal, wrong.) He was best known for winning huge damages in lawsuits resulting from personal injury. He can be scathingly funny about the ethics of what he calls the "Holy Grail Insurance Company." However, he said he always considered himself a criminal trial lawyer. His tactics as an attorney had caused him to be described as "flamboyant," an adjective he dislikes. He said he is simply "colorful." It was reported that he kept a brass cannon on the roof of his office building in San Francisco and that whenever it roared, the citizens knew that "Mel" had won another damage suit. At the Ruby trial, Belli did not bring his papers into court in an ordinary attaché case. Nobody would have noticed that. He carried them in a bulging carpetbag, beautifully flowered in blood red and black embroidery.

As his Texas associate he chose Joe Tonahill, who stands some six-feet-four and speaks in a deep drawl. Tonahill shrewdly combined Texas corn with a solid knowledge of Texas law in the defense of Ruby. Once, in a fit of real or simulated exasperation with Brown, Tonahill threw his pencil, and it rattled loudly against the judge's bench. Brown had put up patiently with the wrangling between attorneys and some rather unorthodox courtroom behavior, but this was too much. He cited Tonahill for contempt of court and fined him $25. The attorney said he was carrying nothing smaller than a $100 bill, which was probably true, and the judge calmly told him to get it changed during the noon recess. It was amusing, if you could overlook the fact that the man in the dock was on trial for his life.

If Belli came into the case with a formidable reputation as an attorney, so did the Dallas County District Attorney, Henry Wade. He is medium-sized with curly gray hair, a cigar-chewer who affects a deceptively sleepy manner.

167

"Hank is all grin and granite," someone said of Wade. During the Second World War, as an FBI agent Wade cracked a spy case of such dimensions that it became the basis for a motion picture. Before he prosecuted Ruby, Wade had convicted 24 of 25 persons accused of murder. He said he would ask the death penalty for Ruby.

The duel between Wade and Belli promised to be dramatic—and it was.

An unusual rite took place outside the courtroom. For security purposes, the bailiffs were ordered to frisk everyone entering the room, no matter how many times in a day. Two pretty lady bailiffs patted the women in places where a gun might be concealed, and they examined handbags and any other parcels. They did find a pistol in one woman's handbag. Why she was carrying it was not explained. Several men were apprehended in the corridors near the courtroom carrying arms.

So, the stage was set for the trial of Jack Ruby.

It became apparent at once that selecting the jury was going to be a difficult process. Some candidates immediately disqualified themselves when they said they were opposed to capital punishment. The defense attorneys' problem was complicated by those TV pictures showing Ruby gunning down his victim. The majority of those examined for jury duty admitted they had seen the pictures. The defense question then was, "Did that cause you to have an opinion about this case? Did it affect your feelings with respect to Jack Ruby?" Some said it had, and the judge promptly excused them. Others, however, denied having been affected. In order to conserve their allotment of peremptory challenges when they did not like the looks of a prospective juror, Belli and Tonahill tried to get him to admit that seeing a real murder on television had caused him, perhaps unconsciously, to prejudge the case against Ruby. (A peremptory challenge permits the attorneys on either side to disqualify a candidate for the jury without stating a reason.)

In one such instance, Tonahill was questioning a man readily accepted for the jury by the prosecution. Obviously, the defense did not want him on the panel. The attorney deftly led up to the matter of the murder pictures. Yes, he had seen the shooting. Yep, saw it several times again in the reruns. "I suppose that made a deep impression on your mind," Tonahill said. Nope. Rephrasing his question in a half-dozen different ways, Tonahill tried to make the man change his testimony. He stubbornly insisted that the scene had meant nothing to him. "Nah," he said, "it looked to me like just another shootin'." He seemed as disinterested as if the murder of Oswald had been a scene in a Western movie. Tonahill had to use a challenge from the dwindling allotment of peremptories to keep him off the jury. Eventually, the defense allotment was exhausted. Brown, trying to be fair, granted the defense some additional ones. But before the jury was completed, these too were gone, and Belli and Tonahill had to accept as jurors those already accepted by the prosecution, unless they could find the means to induce them to disqualify themselves. The defense attorneys looked distinctly unhappy when one woman was seated on the panel after they had used up all their peremptories. Wade asked her the usual question as to whether she had any objections, on religious or other grounds, to capital punishment. "None," she said. Continuing, he advised her, as he did all the other candidates, that if the jury found Ruby guilty as charged, she would be required to sign the verdict, "death in the electric chair." Wade asked her if she believed she could do this. "I certainly could," she replied, firmly.

Ruby followed the proceedings with what seemed to be close attention. His face was expressionless. Guarded by deputies, he entered and left the courtroom with a brisk, businesslike step. He huddled with Belli and Tonahill before they accepted someone for the jury. In their testimony about him, some witnesses were harsh and some were kind. He seemed impassive to both.

In all, nearly two weeks passed before the twelfth juror was seated. The number of candidates questioned totaled 162, a very high figure, nearly 14 called for every one chosen. All seemed intelligent, well-spoken, and well-educated, some in technical fields. All were white, Protestant, and married.

Belli did not use the acronym WASP when reporters asked him what he thought of the jury, but he professed to be unhappy. "I'd feel better," he said, "if there were Jews and Catholics on that jury." The remark, of course, was consistent with his implacable contention that Ruby could not get a fair trial in Dallas. WASP, if it is necessary to explain, means "white Anglo-Saxon Protestant."

The heart of Belli's defense was that Ruby's mind had been affected by a rare disease, psychomotor epilepsy. A characteristic of the disease, he said, was that a severe emotional shock could trigger the victim into an act of extreme violence without his being at all aware of it. The defense introduced testimony to show that Ruby idolized Kennedy and his family, which he was said to have described as "the ideal family of America." The assassination, then, was depicted as the emotional trigger that caused Ruby to kill Oswald while he was blacked out. Belli showed the jurors charts of the electrical activity of Ruby's brain, encephalographs, in support of his statement that Ruby was afflicted with psychomotor epilepsy. Standing beside the jury box, he pointed to what he said were wave-lines indicating variations from the norm. Belli said two specialists, who studied all the objective and subjective evidence independently of each other, arrived at the same conclusion. He called as witnesses specialists with formidable reputations in their field, and they testified that in their opinion, Ruby was not sane when he killed Oswald. Thus, in the classic legal definition, referred to earlier, Ruby was not guilty.

The prosecution, of course, countered this testimony with a time-tested courtroom maneuver: Wade summoned to the witness stand other specialists, also with formidable reputations, who expressed the opinion that Ruby was sane when he shot down Oswald.

Where did the diametrically opposed opinions of the two sets of specialists leave the jury? Evidently, the testimony did not cause them to feel even "reasonable doubt," which would have precluded a verdict of guilty as charged.

The heart of the prosecution's case rested on testimony given by the police officers who disarmed Ruby, knocked him down, and heard him say, allegedly, in the next few minutes:

You didn't think I was going to let him get away with it, did you?

Somebody had to do it. You guys couldn't, and somebody had to do it.

I intended to shoot the son-of-a-bitch three times, but you guys moved in on me too fast.

I did it to show the world that Jews do have guts.

The policemen also testified that Ruby said he could not endure the thought of Jacqueline Kennedy being subjected

170

to questioning when Oswald stood trial for killing the President.

Ruby's attorneys did not put him on the witness stand. Perhaps they were afraid of what he might say or what Wade, with his steel-trap mind, would do to him on cross-examination. So, the officers' statements stood. Later, in a lie detector test for the Warren Commission, Ruby denied having said anything of this nature. He confirmed, however, that he shot Oswald "in order to save Mrs. Kennedy the ordeal of a trial."

The statements attributed to him by the officers were highly self-incriminating. They went into the record under the rule of *res gestae*, which permits self-damaging statements to be used against an accused man during his trial. The basic principle underlying *res gestae* is spontaneity, words blurted out in the immediate aftermath of the action that brought the prisoner to book, presumably before he had time to compose himself and think what he should say. For example, a motorist accidentally hits and kills a pedestrian. In his shock and horror, he blurts out to a policeman, "I dropped a lighted cigarette on the cushion, and I was trying to pick it up, and I just didn't see him." A judge might rule this admissible on the ground that it was a truthful statement induced by the motorist's mental and emotional state at the time.

But how elastic is the rule? How long after the event can a prisoner's words be called "spontaneous"? It seems that some of the remarks attributed by policemen to Ruby were uttered as long as 25 minutes after he shot Oswald.

Nonetheless, they went into the record against him. Here, the prosecution said, was his composite motive, showing that he knew what he was doing and premeditated it.

Wade and his associates demolished the defense picture of Ruby as a man who idolized the President. In final summations, they reminded the jury that Ruby had not so much as walked to the window in the Dallas Morning-News Building, let alone go downstairs and stand on the street to see his idol pass. The prosecution pointed out that the sight of Oswald at the Friday-night press conference had not touched off Ruby's alleged emotional fuse, which, the defense contended, exploded on Sunday, nearly 48 hours later. On the contrary, business-as-usual Ruby had passed out the nude-girl cards to the reporters then. The prosecution argued that Ruby had killed in cold blood, en-

171

visioning himself emerging as a hero to millions of Americans. They said he was carrying $2,000 in cash when he was arrested and suggested that he intended to use it to make bail. He could not have been taking the money to the bank on Sunday.

The defense hammered what should have been a telling point in disputing any premeditation—the time factor in his movements Sunday morning, the fateful four minutes. Remember that Chief Curry had told the reporters "by 10:00 A.M., you'll be early enough" for the transfer of Oswald. Ruby did not even go to the Western Union office until after 11:00 A.M. His receipt for the money order was time-stamped 11:17. He walked a block to the police station, went down the ramp, saw Oswald being led to the car, and shot him at 11:21. He could not have known the exact moment when he would confront Oswald, because the police had fixed no exact moment. Fritz did not start downstairs with Oswald until the erroneous word came to him that the arrangements for the transfer were complete. It might have come earlier, say at 11:15, in which case Ruby would still have been in the Western Union office. Or it might have come later, in which case the chances are that the police would have spotted him waiting on the ramp and ordered him back to the street. Instead, he came down the ramp at the exact split second to confront Oswald. Even in that instant, he was recognized by one officer, Combest, who could not reach him in time. The odds would seem to be 1,000-to-1 against Ruby's deliberately timing his move so exactly. The confrontation appears, rather, to have been the result of an unbelievable coincidence, another of the wild improbabilities of that weekend, improbabilities which nevertheless did take place.

This also bears on the theory that Ruby and Oswald were together in a conspiracy and that Ruby's role, after Oswald was caught, was to execute him to prevent him from talking. A conspirator would not have cut his timing so close.

Later, Ruby said that if he had not made an illegal turn on Main Street on the way to the telegraph office, he would have been too late to confront Oswald. He said it was a matter of 30 seconds.

After his death, Capitol Records, Inc., disclosed that he had been interviewed in the hospital for a program, "Controversy," the firm was preparing. In the tape-recording, Ruby said he noted the crowd outside the jail. He said:

> And the curiosity had aroused me. So I walked toward the ramp, and I noticed a police squad car on the head of the ramp and an officer leaning over talking to him [Ruby probably meant to the driver] with his back to me. All I did was walk down there, down to the bottom of the ramp, and that's when the incident happened. It happened in such a blur that before I knew it, I was down on the ground.
> The ironic part of this is that if I hadn't made an illegal turn behind the bus to the parking lot, had I gone the way I was supposed to go—straight down Main Street—I would never have met this fate. Because the difference in meeting this fate was 30 seconds.

Almost a month after the trial began, the jury brought in a verdict of guilty and decreed the death penalty for Ruby. On television, viewers witnessed Belli's volcanic explosion and heard him shout, "a victory for Dallas bigotry."

Whatever the facts, Ruby's trial did not shed any significant new light on the circumstances of the assassination. Some months later, Ruby demanded that the Warren Commission give him a lie-detector test. The Warren Report quoted him as saying:

> I would like to be able to get a lie detector test or truth serum of what motivated me to do what I did at that particular time, and it seems as you get further into something, even though you know what you did, it operates against you somehow, brain washes you. . . .

In the polygraph test, there were these questions and answers:

> Q. Did you know Oswald before November 22, 1963?
> A. No.
> Q. Did you assist Oswald in the assassination?
> A. No.
> Q. Did you shoot Oswald in order to silence him?

173

A. No.

Q. Did you first decide to shoot Oswald on Sunday morning?

A. Yes.

Q. Did you do business with Castro-Cuba?

A. No.

Q. Was your trip to Cuba solely for pleasure?

A. Yes.

Q. Did any foreign influence cause you to shoot Oswald?

A. No.

Q. Did you shoot Oswald because of any influence of the underworld?

A. No.

Q. Did you shoot Oswald in order to save Mrs. Kennedy the ordeal of a trial?

A. Yes.

Q. Did you ever meet with Oswald and Officer Tippit at your club?

A. No.

Ruby answered many other questions. These are the most germane to the question of his motivation and some of the other allegations made later. How valid was the test? The Commission noted:

> An accurate evaluation of Ruby's polygraph examination depends on whether he was psychotic. Since a psychotic is divorced from reality, the polygraph tracings could not be logically interpreted on such an individual. A psychotic person might believe a false answer was true, so he would not register an emotional response characteristic of deception as a normal person would.

However, the Report went on to say that Dr. William R. Beavers, who had examined Ruby, observed his behavior during the test. It quoted him as saying:

> In the greater proportion of the time that he answered the questions, I felt that he was aware of the questions and that he understood them, and that he was giving answers based on an appreciation of reality.

On October 10, 1966, the Court of Criminal Appeals of Texas reversed the verdict against Ruby and ordered a new trial for him. The court found, among other things, that the statements attributed to him by the Dallas police officers could not be considered spontaneous and therefore were not admissible as part of the *res gestae*.

But the retrial of Ruby was not to be.

For the third time, Parkland Hospital became the center stage in the Dallas tragedy. Ruby was taken there for examination, and on December 10, the hospital announced that he was suffering from cancer. He died 24 days later. He went to his grave insisting that he had not been part of a conspiracy to assassinate the President or murder Oswald.

Tonahill wrote in the *Trial Lawyers Forum*, "There may be cases on record where patients have died 24 days after a diagnosis of malignancy, but it would seem that Jack Ruby went awfully fast."

This sounded like an innuendo, but Tonahill predicted that it would occur to others, and therefore, he urged that a team of cancer specialists should examine the records of Ruby's treatment at Parkland. He added, "Only by following such a forthright and open procedure will the irresponsible elements be defeated in their effort to conjure up sinister and evil motives where no basis in fact exists. Otherwise, we may expect the whispering and wailing to grow into painful and incessant shouting."

The autopsy appeared to be so conclusive that no further examination was necessary, and none was made. It showed that a blood clot extended from Ruby's ankle to his pelvis. This broke free and lodged in his lungs, causing death. As for the drugs used in treating Ruby, Dr. Eugene Frenkel said they had noted "a decrease in the size of the tumors" a few days before Ruby died. "It looked as if we were beginning to get some decrease at last. But he had lung embarrassment to start with, so any small straw such as a blood clot would have thrown him off balance," Dr. Frenkel said. The doctors said Ruby had been "jovial" and had eaten a sizable breakfast on the morning of his death.

Meanwhile, the "whispering and wailing" already was rising to gale strength. The Warren Report had been issued more than two years earlier, and a great many persons were, in effect, studying it under a microscope, looking for flaws and loose ends, and raising questions. Some of them suggested that Jack Ruby had been cast in the role of the executioner in a superplot.

16

John Wilkes Booth assassinated Abraham Lincoln in full view of hundreds of horrified men and women. A conspiracy was uncovered, and he was shown to be its mainspring. His motive? Perhaps, like Oswald and Ruby, Booth was seeking public recognition and a sense of importance. More probably, he acted from some psychotic idea that in killing Lincoln he avenged the defeat of the Confederacy. The high-minded leaders of the South were in no way linked with Booth and his sleazy gang of plotters. Most of the conspirators were convicted and executed. The case seemed closed.

Nonetheless, it was not long before the more-to-this-than-meets-the-eye school began muttering darkly. Questions arose. Lincoln had wanted Thomas T. Eckert, a strong-arm, to guard him when he went to Ford's Theater with Mrs. Lincoln. Why did Secretary of War Edwin Stanton not grant the request? Why were there no detectives in the audience or near the Presidential box? Why was the regular guard there replaced by a drunken policeman, who was not at his post when Booth entered the box? Why were there no roadblocks on the Chain Bridge to prevent Booth from fleeing Washington? Was it really he who was shot and killed in the barn? Exotic theories were invented to explain the improbabilities which, nevertheless, did happen that night. There *had* to be a superplot, much bigger than an actor and his accomplices.

Today, it all sounds dreadfully familiar.

A century after Lincoln, the tragedy was recreated in the assassination of John F. Kennedy, but with some important differences. Oswald, unlike Booth, was not actually seen pulling the trigger. He denied he had killed anybody. The evidence against him was circumstantial. It was not difficult, since the sound of the shots echoed and reechoed, to find scores of persons who were firmly convinced that the shots were fired from the grassy knoll or the railroad overpass, not the Book Depository Building. The X-rays and photographs taken during the autopsy went, unseen by the Warren Commission, into the National Archives. They may not be studied by nonofficial persons for at least five years. And finally, Jack Ruby forever silenced Oswald.

All of which left ample room for the assertion that Oswald had accomplices and that Kennedy was the victim of a conspiracy. Again, bizarre theories were invented—for example, to account for Oswald's movements when he left his rooming house after the assassination and why he entered the Texas Theater. Again, there *had* to be a superplot.

In Lincoln's day, nobody made much money out of whispering of sinister things. In Kennedy's day, people did make money—lots of it.

Without Oswald, it is impossible to prove that a conspiracy never existed. All the Warren Commission could say was:

> The Commission has found no evidence that Oswald was involved with any person or group in a conspiracy. . . . If there is any such evidence, it has been beyond the reach of all the investigative agencies and resources of the United States and has not come to the attention of the Commission.

The investigative resources of the United States are very great, and they were lavished on the inquiry into the three deaths in Dallas. Never in history was a crime probed so intensely, and never in history was the inquiry itself subjected to such intense scrutiny.

The Warren Commission worked for ten months, beginning in January, 1964. It took the testimony of 552 witnesses, most of it orally, some in the form of sworn statements. The FBI and the Secret Service interviewed and reinterviewed 26,550 persons and submitted reports running to 30,000 pages. Along with these agencies, the Commission called on the Central Intelligence Agency, the State Department, and the Treasury for information. The Attorney General of Texas conducted a separate investigation and furnished the Commission with a mass of details. Innumerable tests were conducted. How long would it have taken Patrolman Baker to rush into the Book Building and up to the second floor, where he found Oswald beside the vending machine? How long would it have taken Oswald to run downstairs from the sixth floor? Stopwatches were held on the men simulating the movements of Oswald and Baker, not once but several times. How long would it have taken William Whaley, the cabbie, to drive from the bus station to the Beckley Street address Oswald gave him? The route was retraced several times and timed to the second. They repeatedly time-checked the distance from the Western Union office, which Jack Ruby left at approximately 11:17 A.M., walking from there to the basement of the police station. Ballistics tests and the studies of fingerprints and handwriting came into play. They proved that the bullets came from Oswald's rifle. They fired bullets from it through the carcasses of animals and through blocks of gelatine, examining the configuration of entrance and exit holes and measuring the grains of metal left in passage. Members of the Commission themselves went to the window on the sixth floor of the Book Building and peered through the telescopic sight at a limousine traveling at about 12 miles an hour down Elm Street toward the railroad overpass. They saw exactly what Oswald saw through the cross hairs of his scope; only the men in the car were different. Through a mass of subjective and objective evidence, the investigators and the Commissioners examined a thousand-and-one minute details.

It seems certain that if Oswald had accomplices, their footprints would have been found under such a microscopic examination.

The Warren Report and the testimony of witnesses, millions of words, filled 27 volumes. The foreword says, "The Commission has functioned neither as a court presiding over an adversary proceeding nor as a prosecutor determined to prove a case, but as a fact-finding agency committed to the ascertainment of the truth."

The chairman, Chief Justice Earl Warren, several times assured witnesses that the Commission was not trying to convict anyone, that it was probing for facts alone.

The critics, who quickly appeared, were soon having a field day challenging the Commission's findings.

The ink was scarcely dry on the Report before they began attacking it like sharks attacking a whale. They questioned both the findings and the methods used in reaching them. In general, their thesis was that the Report was not meant to be objective, that the Commission *was* trying to prove something with it. They pictured it as a giant tranquilizer designed to assure the nation that Lee Harvey Oswald alone assassinated the President, to dispel rumors of a conspiracy, and to remove fears that persons involved in it were still at large somewhere. Therefore, they asserted, the Commission accepted facts substantiating this premise and ignored or minimized information that conflicted with it.

More than that, there were assertions that someone tampered with the Zapruder film of the assassination. Critical writers said investigators chivvied witnesses, trying to persuade them to change their testimony, and that some witnesses gave the critics, making independent inquiries, information at variance with what appeared in the Warren Report.

Suppose the Commission had unearthed evidence of a conspiracy. Why conceal it? Somehow, the theory developed that the American people are so prone to panic, so morally fragile, that they had to be tranquilized with a finding that one man, who was dead, had perpetrated the crime.

The French radio, which is government-controlled, took this line in a critique of the Warren Report broadcast in November, 1966. It said the truth about the assassination would probably never be known unless someone were to come forward and confess. "Do the American people want this?" the commentator asked. He quoted an unnamed coed at George Washington University as saying, "I would not want to see it as a political plot. That would really give me fear."

"There," said the commentator, "the big word is out. Fear. Fear again such as three years ago struck the American people with the assassination of President Kennedy." His prepared text contained a phrase saying, "Fear of uncovering a whole world seething with intrigues and lies. . . ." This was deleted from the script as broadcast.

So, the critics inferred, the Commission had not even told the half-naked truth. Nobody wanted to worry that unnamed college girl, they said.

The very thoroughness of the Warren investigation aided them. They could read the testimony given by a witness on a given facet of the events in Dallas. Good. Now to find someone who also was there and who would say it wasn't that way at all. Or it was possible to quote a witness' testimony, but not in full, omitting the parts that conflicted with the case they were trying to prove. It was soon to be pointed out that the writers of these books were doing what they claimed the Commission had done, namely, selecting some facts and ignoring others in order to prove a case. They were accused of weaving tissues of inference and innuendo, asking but not answering questions, implying something sinister.

To some of them, this proved highly lucrative. Books and magazine articles rolled off the presses. The critics signed up for lecture tours at home and abroad and often played to packed houses. Films were produced and sold. The professional skeptics appeared on radio and television panels. Mark Lane's book, *Rush to Judgement*, made the best-seller lists. Of the many who challenged the Warren Report, he made the biggest splash.

Lane is a New York lawyer, a former member of the New York legislature, a former officer in Army intelligence, an espouser of liberal causes, and an unsuccessful candidate for nomination to Congress. Lecturing in London, he said the Warren Commission "will never get the facts." In Budapest, he said Kennedy's killers are still at large and suggested an international commission be appointed to investigate.

Lane testified before the Commission. Warren told him that without corroboration, he had "every reason to doubt the truthfulness" of some of his testimony.

He says he came into the inquiry as the result of a phone call from Marguerite Oswald in December, 1963. She asked him to represent her son's interests before the Warren Commission. "I accepted and thus began an investigation that has continued for more than two and a half years," Lane wrote.

Leon Jaworski, special counsel in the Texas Attorney General's investigation of the assassination, said Lane's book "deserves to be a best-seller in the fiction category." Governor Connally called Lane a "scavenger." He said in a press conference, "It is shocking to me that in the backlash of tragedy, journalistic scavengers such as Mark Lane attempt to impugn the motives of these members of the Warren Commission, cast doubts upon the Commission as a whole, and question the credibility of the government itself."

Lane retorted, "It is to be regretted that Governor Connally has sought to terminate the search for truth—an effort that has begun in this country so recently. It is even more astonishing that he has sought to bring back the days of McCarthyism by questioning the loyalty and motives of those who will not accept a false governmental edict."

Wesley J. Liebeler, an assistant counsel for the Commission, challenged Lane to his face to sue him for libel. "His book is a tissue of distortion," Liebeler said. "At a press conference at the University of California at Los Angeles, Mr. Lane's response was to threaten to sue me for libel, and I've been waiting anxiously for those papers. If you have them here this morning, I'll be glad to accept service of process, Mr. Lane, because you know very well as soon as you do that, you're going to have to submit yourself to deposition under oath, and go through discovery proceedings, and that day I'll wait for, sir."

Such exchanges, along with the rising wave of interest in the Warren Report and the comments, pro and con, fanned the interest in it to a white heat. It became clearly apparent that here was a market. Out came more critical books: *Inquest,* by Edward Jay Epstein, *The Oswald Affair,* by Leo Sauvage, *Whitewash,* by Harold Weisberg, *The Second Oswald,* by Richard H. Popkin, *The Unanswered Questions About President Kennedy's Assassination,* etc., etc.

As against these, CBS produced a four-part series of telecasts examining some of the principal questions that had been raised. Conclusion: The network agreed with the findings of the Commission. Judge Arnold L. Fein of the Civil Court of the City of New York wrote in a magazine article, "It was obvious from the outset that there were so many conflicting clues and reports it would be impossible to reconcile them all. . . . Seizing these gaps or contradictions, some of which were inevitable and many of which the Commission could have avoided or explained, each of these critics has launched an attack on the motives of the Commission. . . ." Bernard Gavzer and Sid Moody of The Associated Press conducted a point-by-point study of the Warren Report vis-a-vis what the critics wrote. They concluded, "But while, as of this date, there may be doubters, books and speculation, the critics have yet to produce that one essential of proof—evidence."

William Manchester, who was supposed to write the authorized history of the assassination, did not disagree with the central finding of the Warren Report. However, he was critical of the Commission itself. He wrote in a maga-

181

zine article, "The prestigious names on Earl Warren's panel did little except glitter; the long hours were put in by junior staff men."

Manchester's book, *The Death of a President*, stirred one of the noisiest repercussions to the tragedy. His battle with the Kennedy family, raging publicly for weeks, temporarily overshadowed the controversy over the Warren Report.

Within a month after the President's death, the Kennedys said they were being deluged with requests from authors for their cooperation in writing a history of the tragedy. In order to have a single, authorized record, the Kennedys decided to choose one writer and cooperate only with him. Pierre Salinger, while still White House Press Secretary, recommended Manchester. The Kennedys and Manchester then signed a "Memorandum of Understanding" which stipulated that the proposed book would not be published without their approval.

Manchester delivered his manuscript on February 15, 1966.

Robert Kennedy asked a number of his former associates in government to read it for him and for Mrs. Kennedy. They disapproved many parts of it, recommending some 150 changes or deletions. Next, Mrs. Kennedy was described as "horrified" when she learned that Manchester had contracted to serialize the book for $650,000. In the inception, the Kennedys had told Manchester they did not visualize the book as "an ordinary commercial venture."

The upshot was that Mrs. Kennedy filed a suit to block publication of the book based on the Memorandum that said it could not be published without her approval. She called it "tasteless and distorted." Manchester retorted that the book was being censored for "political" reasons related to Robert Kennedy's political future. He characterized the Kennedys' behavior as "sheer insanity." The changes having been made in the manuscript, Mrs. Kennedy withdrew her suit. She and her brother-in-law disavowed the book when it appeared.

Another bizarre literary outgrowth of the assassination was the book *A Mother in History,* by Jean Stafford, based on her tape-recorded conversations with Marguerite Oswald. One passage quotes Oswald's mother:

"Now maybe Lee Harvey Oswald was the assassin," she pursued, stirring her coffee. "But does that make him a louse? No, no! Killing does not necessarily mean badness. You find killing in some very fine homes for one reason or another. And as we all know, President Kennedy was a dying man. So I say it is possible that my son was chosen to shoot him in a mercy killing for the security of the country. And if this is true, it was a fine thing to do and my son is a hero."

Miss Stafford wrote that she was "staggered by this cluster of fictions stated as irrefutable fact."

If that is "staggering," consider the case of Penn Jones, Jr., editor of the weekly Midlothian, Texas, *Mirror*. Jones picked up an angle that the others missed. Or perhaps they concluded that to preserve the aspect of serious inquiry into the assassination, this was too far out. He listed the deaths of 14 persons who were involved, to whatever degree, in the investigation of the assassination and the theory of a conspiracy. That was as of November 1966. Since another year has elapsed, probably others have died, and no matter what the manner of their passing may have been, Jones probably found the means to link them with the alleged conspiracy. *Ramparts Magazine* reprinted some of Jones' weird reports. To cite three juicy examples:

That Oswald's landlady, Earlene Roberts, was subjected to "intensive police harassment," and after her death, "no autopsy was performed." Inference: Somebody did away with her for reasons unknown.

That William Whaley, the cab driver, was killed in a head-on collision with another car, although he had never had an accident before, and further, that he was the first Dallas cabbie killed on duty since 1937. The inference here is hard to perceive, and the reader is left to supply his own.

That Jim Koethe, a reporter on the Dallas *Times-Herald*, was "killed by a karate chop" in his apartment. Koethe was one of several men who met in Ruby's apartment on the Sunday night after Ruby shot Oswald. Inference: Koethe discovered information linking Ruby and Oswald.

Time Magazine reported, however:

That an autopsy was performed on Mrs. Roberts' body at Parkland Hospital, and the cause of death was attributed to "acute myocardial infarction," in short, a heart attack.

That a car traveling north careened across the highway center line into the path of Whaley's cab, traveling south. The other driver, an eighty-three-year-old man, had died at the wheel, apparently of a heart attack.

That Koethe was strangled, not karate-chopped to death. *Time* said, "Police suggested that homosexuality may have been a motive."

Having paraded all the skeletons in his closet, Jones summed up, "We repeat our prediction that more killings are going to be necessary to keep this crime quiet." He referred to the murder of Oswald.

To this and other extraordinary statements must be added one that appears in Professor Popkin's, *The Second Oswald*. It reads, "The Western European critics can only see Kennedy's assassination as part of a subtle conspiracy, involving perhaps some of the Dallas police, the FBI, the right-wing lunatic fringe in Dallas, or perhaps even (*in rumors I have often heard*) Kennedy's successor." The italics are supplied because the phrase was so typical of so much that was written to support the theory of conspiracy. Would a serious student of the case simply repeat a staggering rumor without examining it or stating the source of it?

"Rumors I have often heard." The mind boggles at the thought of the countless rumors that came into being and were circulated, for money, for creating cocktail party sensations, or for other unexplained motives and the uncritical gullibility with which they were swallowed.

The Warren Commission anticipated some of them, but no one could have foreseen all the myths that were to arise. In their Report, the writers included a long section captioned "Speculations and Rumors," grouped under ten subheadings. For example:

Speculation—The police had been withdrawn from the area in which Tippit found Oswald.
Commission Finding—Other police cars were operating in the Oak Cliff area at the same time as Tippit. They participated in the search for and apprehension of Tippit's slayer.
Speculation—Tippit violated a procedure governing radio cars when he failed to notify headquarters that he was stopping to question a subject.
Commission Finding—The Dallas Police Department had no requirement or regulation for police officers to

184

notify headquarters when stopping to question a subject.

In these two instances, as can be seen, these are questions of fact. Either Tippit's was the only police car in Oak Cliff or it wasn't. Either there was such a regulation or there wasn't. It was easy to dispel the rumor with the demonstrable fact.

But some were less amenable to instant refutation. In a single TV panel discussion, it was stated or suggested (1) that there was more than one assassin, (2) that Oswald was a decoy, (3) that the rifle never was shown to be in Oswald's possession, (4) that Marina was unable to identify the rifle, (5) that the rifle was wrongly identified by the police, (6) that the ammunition used by Oswald was defective, (7) that the rifle was unreliable, (8) that the photograph showing Oswald holding the rifle was a composite, (9) that those who identified Oswald as the man they saw in the window on the sixth floor of the Book Building could not possibly have seen him because the afternoon sun made a "mirror" of the windowpane, blotting him from view from below, (10) that a man who closely resembled Oswald practiced frequently at a rifle range so that he would be "well noticed" by other marksmen there.

Most of this was speculation, misstatement, or an individual's personal interpretation of the evidence. But one was perfectly true—Number 5. Seymour Weitzman, a Dallas deputy constable, did originally identify the rifle found on the sixth floor as a Mauser. The sinister inference here is that someone, for reasons unknown, substituted Oswald's Mannlicher-Carcano for the Mauser, forgetting that the bullets were traced to Oswald's rifle. Joseph A. Ball, an assistant counsel to the Warren Commission, provided an explanation in another panel discussion, in which Mark Lane participated. Ball said:

Seymour Weitzman is an expert on guns, and that's just the reason he made the mistake he made, because —what Mr. Lane doesn't tell you, but what he knows as well as I do and Seymour Weitzman knows—this is a bolt action rifle.

The basic patent on bolt action rifles is Mauser. This is an Italian rifle built on the Mauser patent, and because he is an expert, Weitzman made the mistake of calling it a Mauser.

185

As a result of such discussions and the books, magazine articles, and lectures, an army of Warren Report "buffs" came into existence. Innumerable people paid the $76 to the Government Printing Office for the full transcript of the testimony. The Report itself became a best seller. People became so fascinated with it that they studied it to a point where they could quote chapter and verse on any given facet. Some compiled their own indexes of the thousands of names. Some dug into the mass of material in the National Archives. People traded clues, or what they regarded as shreds of new evidence, much as boys trade stamps and marbles. Fascination with the Report grew, and it probably will continue to do so for many years.

Part of the fascination, of course, lay in delving into the question of the direction of the shots that killed Kennedy, the single-bullet theory, the location of Kennedy's wounds, and the disparity between the FBI reports of the autopsy findings and the final report of the specialists who performed the autopsy. These are the principal pillars on which the conspiracy theory was erected. To briefly examine them:

As has been said, some eyewitnesses in Dealey Plaza were and are convinced that the sound of the shots came from the grassy knoll on the right of the President's limousine and from the railroad overpass which it was approaching. Others, of course, thought the sounds came from the Book Building or in the vicinity of it. A few thought they saw a puff of smoke, although a rifle does not emit a puff of smoke. Immediately after the shooting, officers ran to the knoll and searched around the fence and grounds behind. They found no weapons, no expended cartridges, nor any other physical evidence around the knoll or the overpass. The conflicting impression probably arose from the fact that a bullet traveling at high velocity sets up shock waves at right angles to its course. The sound of the explosion bounces off solid objects and reechoes. And so, earshot testimony is likely to be highly unreliable.

Those who propounded the conspiracy theory could point to a statement by Dr. Malcolm Perry in a press conference not long after the President died. The last sentence of a news report said, "When asked to specify, Perry said the entrance wound was in the front of the head." Perry testified, however, that the press conference was a "bedlam" in which reporters interrupted him before he completed an answer and broke in on each other, shouting questions. He said he found numerous errors and misstatements of his replies in the published reports. Moreover, Perry's attention had been focused primarily on Kennedy's breathing and circulatory system, not on the wound in his head.

Lane made another point. He asserted that fragments of the President's skull hurtled backward from the car. He argued that fragments of an object torn off by a bullet follow the trajectory of the bullet. Therefore, he continued, the assassin—or one of several assassins—must have fired from a point in front of, not behind, the President.

The Commission's single-bullet finding holds that one shot pierced Kennedy's throat, traveled about four feet, and inflicted wounds in Connally's chest, wrist, and thigh. Evidence indicates the two men were both wounded within a span of 1.6 seconds. Oswald's rifle, however, could not be fired faster than once every 2.3 seconds. Thus, unless one bullet struck both men, the conclusion would have to be that more than one rifle was fired and that there was more than one rifleman.

Connally himself did not question the overall findings of the Commission. But he firmly believes he was hit by the second shot, not the first. "I heard a shot," he told me. "A bullet travels faster than the speed of sound, so I would have felt it hit me before I heard the explosion." Mrs. Connally is doubtful of this. She said she heard her husband cry out "Oh, no, no, no" before she heard the sound of the second shot. If so, the Comission's single-bullet theory stands, but if not, a serious question remains as to the time when the two men were hit.

Meanwhile, the attacks on the Report developed in another sector—the precise location of Kennedy's wounds. A discrepancy appeared between two FBI reports on the findings from the autopsy and those of the pathologists in their official report. The agents, of course, were laymen taking notes of what the surgeons said while they worked. The FBI reports stated that Commander Humes, chief autopsy surgeon, located what appeared to be a bullet hole in Kennedy's back, below the shoulder, and probed it to the end with his finger. The doctors were unable to explain at that time why they could not find a bullet or point of exit. Later, they traced the bullet and found where it exited, but the FBI agents did not know this. Further, a sketch made by one of the pathologists indicated the wound in the back was too low for the bullet to have emerged through the President's throat. He explained, however, that it was only a rough working sketch designed to refresh his memory and not meant to be an accurate representation. In their final report, the pathologists located the wound at 14 centimeters, or 5.5 inches, below the right mastoid process, or bony tip behind the right ear, at the base of the neck.

Here again, the critics could claim to have found proof that the Commission tampered with the evidence, disregarding FBI reports on the autopsy and adopting another which supported its predetermined premise that the only bullets that struck the President came from above and behind him.

As the furor escalated, J. Edgar Hoover released information about evidence found in the clothes Kennedy was wearing when he was assassinated. The examination, Hoover said, "revealed a small hole in the back of his coat and shirt and a slit characteristic of the exit hole below the collar button. A bullet hole on the left side of the tie knot, possibly caused by the same projectile which passed through the shirt, also was noted."

The fabric in the back of the President's coat also furnished an important detail. It was bent inward.

The clothing eventually was turned over to the National Archives. The Archives also received, on November 1, 1966, 65 X-rays and photographic negatives, plus some prints, all taken while the autopsy was being performed.

They had been in the possession of the Kennedy family for nearly three years. In placing them in the Archives, the family laid down stringent terms with respect to when they could be seen and by whom. For five years, it was to be all but impossible for anyone other than government investigators to study the X-rays and photographs. After that period, it was stipulated that forensic pathologists and specialists might examine them, but only after obtaining the permission of the family.

This struck many persons as a strange development. Why were the Kennedys in possession of the evidence for nearly three years? How was it that they could set the conditions in which it could be studied? It would seem that the X-rays and photographic material would be the property of the American peoople, with the Federal government as the custodian.

No doubt, the photographs are unsightly, and the Kennedys would not want them examined by any Tom, Dick,

188

or Harry. But X-rays are not unsightly. A trained forensic pathologist, examining them, probably could determine exactly the path of the bullets through Kennedy's body and the direction from which they came. This would have effectively answered the assertions that bullets may have struck the President from a point, or points, other than from above and behind him. Along with many others, I requested permission to retain two distinguished forensic pathologists to examine the X-rays. I would then have published thier findings. The request was refused. Nothing of that nature could be done for at least five years.

In sequestering this material as they did, the Kennedys furnished professional skeptics with more ammunition with which to attack the Warren Report. Indeed, in another of the innumerable panel debates, Edward J. Epstein leaped at the opportunity. He said:

> They were not entered into evidence before the Commission or examined by the Commission's staff or analyzed by any group of experts in forensic pathology. In fact, the absence of the autopsy photographs from the Commission's evidence left a very important missing link in the Warren Report. The fact that these photographs had to be produced at this late date is, I think, indicative of how embarrassing this gap was for the Commission.

Now Epstein reraised the question of those two FBI reports on the autopsy. "The Autopsy photographs were the only evidence that could clear up the contradictions in the Commission's evidence," he said. "The contradiction I am referring to is the contradiction between the FBI's report of the autopsy findings and the doctors' report of the findings."

The members of the Commission did not examine the X-rays or photographs when the pathologists testified before them. One Commissioner, John J. McCloy, said later he feels the Commission should have studied them. He added, however, that the Commission "had the best evidence—the pathology in respect to the President's wounds."

Why didn't the Commission see the photographic material? "We were perhaps a little oversensitive to what we understood were the sensitivities of the Kennedy family," McCloy said.

A late entrant in the conspiracy derby was Jim Garrison, the District Attorney of New Orleans. In all apparent seriousness, he advanced the claim that the conspirators arranged matters in such a way that the Dallas police would kill Oswald after he shot the President. When that didn't work out as planned, Garrison said, Jack Ruby had to act as executioner. Garrison said:

> They had what I think was a rather clever plan. It's well known that police officers react violently to the murder of a police officer.
> All they did was arrange for an officer to be sent out to Tenth Street, and when Officer Tippit arrived there, he was murdered. Oswald was pointed to, sitting in the back of the Texas Theater where he had been told to wait. The Dallas police—at least the arresting officers—had more humanity than the planners had in mind, and this was the first point at which the plan did not work completely.
> So Oswald was not killed. He was arrested. It was necessary for one of the people involved to kill him.

To use one of Governor Connally's favorite expressions, "How does that grip you?"

Garrison did not explain how the planners could arrange things so that Oswald would be sure to encounter Tippit or the other officers patrolling in Oak Cliff. Moreover, when Oswald was spotted by Tippit, he was hurrying along Tenth Street on a course taking him *away* from the Texas Theater.

At the same time, responsible men expressed lingering dissatisfaction with the Warren Report. One was a member of the Commission, Senator Richard B. Russell of Georgia. He said in an interview with a reporter from the Atlanta *Journal,* "I'm the only one that bucked the Report. I told them, 'I'm not going to sign it as long as it's this way.'"

Russell said he objected to the wording that stated categorically there had been no conspiracy behind the assassination. He insisted the Report should go no further than a finding that Oswald fired the shots that killed Kennedy and wounded Connally.

"Warren was determined he was going to have a unanimous report," Russell said. "I said it wouldn't be any trouble just to put a little asterisk up here [in the text] and